Household Medicine in Seventeenth-Century England

Household Medicine in Seventeenth-Century England

Anne Stobart

Bloomsbury Academic
An imprint of Bloomsbury Publishing Plc

B L O O M S B U R Y
LONDON · OXFORD · NEW YORK · NEW DELHI · SYDNEY

Bloomsbury Academic

An imprint of Bloomsbury Publishing Plc

50 Bedford Square	1385 Broadway
London	New York
WC1B 3DP	NY 10018
UK	USA

www.bloomsbury.com

BLOOMSBURY and the Diana logo are trademarks of Bloomsbury Publishing Plc

First published 2016

© Anne Stobart, 2016

Anne Stobart has asserted her right under the Copyright, Designs and Patents Act, 1988, to be identified as Author of this work.

British Library Cataloguing-in-Publication Data
A catalogue record for this book is available from the British Library.

ISBN:	HB:	978-1-4725-8035-1
	PB:	978-1-4725-8034-4
	ePDF:	978-1-4725-8036-8
	ePub:	978-1-4725-8037-5

Library of Congress Cataloging-in-Publication Data
A catalog record for this book is available from the Library of Congress.

Cover design: Catherine Wood
Cover image © Wellcome Library, London, UK

Typeset by RefineCatch Limited, Bungay, Suffolk
Printed and bound in India

This book is dedicated to my parents, Margaret and Raymond.

Michelle Dimeo, Todd Gray, Chris Lewin, Ian Mortimer, Margaret Pelling, Lisa Smith, Sarah Toulalan and many others. I am especially grateful to Elaine Hobby, Elaine Leong, Sally Osborn, Frances Watkins, Jane Whittle and Alun Withey for their advice on drafts, and to the anonymous reviewers for helpful suggestions. My thanks to readers of the manuscript, Jill Baines, Julia Jervis and Linda Lever. My appreciation is also due to the editors and staff at Bloomsbury Academic for their understanding. Finally, I could not have done without the affectionate support of Kay throughout the ups and downs of preparing the text for publication.

ABBREVIATIONS

BIWLD British and Irish Women's Letters and Diaries, 1500–1950

CFA Clifford Family Archive

DHC Devon Heritage Centre

ODNB *Oxford Dictionary of National Biography*

OED *Oxford English Dictionary*

SHC Somerset Heritage Centre

Introduction:
Household Healthcare Matters

How did early modern households provide their own care in efforts to maintain health and treat illness? Although it is widely assumed that there was much self-help, there has been little research on household healthcare activities. This book draws on extensive family papers to reveal the complexity and detail of how health and disease were managed on a day-to-day basis in seventeenth-century England. The extent to which households made their own favourite medicines is considered alongside their expenditure on prepared medicines and medical services, and these activities are related to the context of commercial expansion of medicine. This book shows the involvement of both lay women and men in household healthcare, and how they liaised with medical practitioners and other advisers, often drawing on their self-help experience, to determine therapeutic approaches and medicines used.

There are a number of reasons why such a study of household medicine in the seventeenth century is needed. First, it is vital to obtain a fuller picture of what actually happened in the household in order to understand the nature of self-help more accurately. As Peregrine Horden says, 'self-help and domestic care constitute the great submerged ice sheets of the history of health'.[1] We need to understand what information about health and illness was sought and shared by households, and we need to know what resources were available for carrying out healthcare, including medicines. Historical writers often refer to the wide use of homemade remedies by early modern families when faced with illness, but general statements like 'home remedies were the most common way of handling illness' are rarely quantified in detail.[2] Contrasting views on the extent of self-sufficiency in medicines can be found; for example, Lucinda Beier notes that 'lay-people were often required by healers to make or apply their own remedies',[3] whereas Patrick Wallis suggests 'a picture of the sick often buying pre-made medicines for commonplace purposes'.[4] A study of Elizabeth Freke's extensive medicine cupboard by Elaine Leong shows that medicines were both made and purchased,[5] but we do not know how typical this was of most households. As we will see in this book, there was variation in the ways that different households obtained and used medicines: some were more self-reliant than others, although none of them were completely self-sufficient.

Second, study of household medicine is needed for a better understanding of the involvement of women in healthcare. Part of the frontispiece in the popular advice book *The Accomplished Ladies Rich Closet of Rarities*, first published in 1687 (see cover image), shows a woman hard at work at distillation, just one of numerous household activities.[6] This image suggests an active role for early modern women in preparing household medicines, and studies of early modern diaries do provide examples of some women of high status active in providing healthcare.[7] Such activities of gentry and aristocratic women are described as demonstrating an interest in science, and as 'chymical housewifery'.[8] Thus, these households are identified as sites for the development of early modern science and technology.[9] Women of lesser status are also identified as providers of healthcare, acting 'in the capacity of nurse and physician if a neighbour were in need'.[10] Indeed, Patricia Crawford and Laura Gowing argue that annotations on medicinal recipes show that women transcended class differences in the context of healthcare, so that 'a wealthier woman might find assistance from a poorer woman' and this contributed to female networks.[11] More recently, Amanda Herbert notes the importance of women's alliances in a patriarchal world, and how these were developed and maintained through a range of tasks including distilling.[12] Since most healthcare took place in the home, and associated domestic tasks helped to define gender roles,[13] further understanding is needed of how household healthcare and women's roles evolved in the early modern period. Men were also active in family healthcare and Lisa Smith shows that men had a contribution to make in terms of health concerns and roles.[14] Gender roles in self-help healthcare are explored in this book to help our understanding of the domestic identity which emerged from further separation of private and public spheres or spaces.[15]

Third, the study of seventeenth-century household medicine is needed to provide a window on changing lay beliefs about health and disease. People expressed their views in many ways, from medical advice in letters to the selection of medicinal recipes and purchase of items related to healthcare. Some historians of medicine, such as Doreen Nagy, argue that there was little change in either healthcare beliefs or practices in the early modern period, whether in professional or lay hands.[16] However, Andrew Wear shows that there were substantial shifts in medical knowledge and understanding by 1680, despite persisting similarities in medical practice.[17] This background of change in the seventeenth century contributed to contrasting kinds of advice and treatment, including those deriving from the works of Paracelsus (1493–1541) and Van Helmont (1579–1644),[18] as well as the widespread use of chemical medicines. Long-standing beliefs based on the works of Galen were increasingly challenged in the seventeenth century, giving rise to new and more detailed observations of the body and disease.[19] Changing views of the body undermined humoral understandings of health that saw corrupted matter as the cause of illness, leading towards ontologically-based views of each disease as a specific entity.[20] The professional structure of medicine was also evolving as boundaries between apothecaries, physicians and surgeons were becoming less clear-cut, and 'irregulars' and 'empirics' threatened the previous order.[21] This was not an uncontested process and there were many and varied medical claims in the early modern period, some leading to the promotion of individual cults.[22] In this book, the close examination of self-help healthcare in a number of households illuminates how lay beliefs and concerns varied alongside changes in medical theories and practice. Although healthcare involved a wide range of activities, the following chapters show how medicines became highly significant in negotiations between lay and medical people.

Fourth, it is necessary to understand how household medicine related to developments in commercial medicine.[23] The extent to which prepared medicines were purchased by households in the seventeenth century is considered here alongside spending on medical services, and how this related to self-help in healthcare. Although consumption studies have burgeoned in recent years, especially in identifying the importance of gender identity and women's roles in consumption,[24] limited attention has been paid to medicines. Imported medicines and Paracelsian preparations were included early on in the *London Pharmacopoeia* and powerful or imported remedies such as antimony, mercury and sarsaparilla were available to purchase from the first decades of the seventeenth century.[25] A study of the household accounts of Alice Le Strange in Norfolk shows that various prepared medicines were purchased in the early seventeenth century.[26] Illness involved further expenditure than usual, according to Mary Dobson who highlights this in the accounts of the wealthy, 'Extra food was purchased, additional supplies of fuel were brought in, fresh linen was needed, the quantities of soap increased and the list of household bills lengthened'.[27] Further research on drug consumption through study of port books and customs records indicates a substantial increase in consumption of imported drugs that took place during the seventeenth century.[28] Expenditure on medical services was also rising during this period, as found in Ian Mortimer's study of probate records and medical and nursing assistance for the dying.[29] Further understanding of seventeenth-century household medicine in relation to this growing 'medical marketplace' is needed.[30] As this book shows, there were a variety of reasons for greater expenditure on medicines during this period, which can be understood through studying self-help healthcare.

Defining household medicine and self-help

In this book I use the term 'household' to refer to a group of people living together as a unit, rather than simply a physical space. Thus a household included family members, resident visitors and servants, and could vary considerably in terms of the number and relationship of occupants, their status and wealth as well as size, location and the available physical resources.[31] Wealthier households might have operated from several bases since there was frequent – often seasonal – movement as individuals or families travelled for business, health or other reasons to London, Bath and elsewhere.[32] Households considered in this book are largely determined by the sources available, and so are mainly aristocratic or gentry in nature.[33] Some households were extensively involved with medicine as a business, such as those of the surgeon or apothecary and wife, although these are not the focus of this book and are considered elsewhere.[34]

A plethora of terms have been used by historical researchers in studies of lay healthcare, ranging from family medicine to domestic medicine, household medicine, lay medicine, popular medicine and vernacular medicine. The meaning of these terms can vary[35] and some carry particular connotations such as the involvement of women, or are more readily associated with unlicensed practitioners or folklore.[36] This is further complicated since the term 'medicine' has multiple meanings, ranging from a complete programme of therapeutic treatment to a specific medicament or drug.[37] Thus, 'household medicine' might be understood in a number of ways from making medicines at home to the provision of all healthcare in the household. In this book, I use the term 'household medicine' in the narrowest sense to refer to a specific medicament which could be prepared in the home or purchased for use in a self-help context. I use the broader term 'household healthcare' to refer to a wider range of medical activity and treatment initiated or carried out by household members and related to health and wellbeing. This range of activity includes the provision and seeking of advice, preventative care, nursing and administering medical treatment, obtaining and making medicines, and steps to promote recovery.[38] Some studies have recognized, as I do, additional aspects of healthcare such as the advice given in regimens on food and lifestyle, and these are further discussed in Chapter 5.[39]

Some further clarification of the reasons for self-help is needed. In 1989, Dorothy Porter and Roy Porter suggested that 'necessity, traditions of sturdy independence and the dictates of Protestant, and then Enlightenment, individualism all conspired to create, and to continue to breathe life into, a self-help medical culture'.[40] Although much of early modern household healthcare has been described as self-help in nature, little attempt has been made to further define self-help: sometimes it is used to indicate home-produced remedies while at other times is used to indicate independence from learned medical practitioners. Most early modern healthcare in England took place in the home, whether supported by a medical practitioner or not, as there was limited institutional care for those who were ill, and few hospitals were established until the early eighteenth century,[41] while charitable care consisted of various elements, drawing on church and parish sources, as well as the family and neighbourhood.[42] Self-help has been portrayed as essential in rural settings when medical practitioners were difficult to find.[43] Yet, as Ian Mortimer shows, medical services were much more accessible in the seventeenth century than previously thought since most people were within two hours walk of a town

Bridget and Hugh Fortescue of Filleigh, Devon

Bridget Fortescue (1666–1708) was the daughter and heir of Hugh Boscawen (d. 1701) and Margaret (d. 1688) of Tregothnan in Cornwall. Bridget's father, Hugh Boscawen, was 'one of the leading magnates in Cornwall', seated at Tregothnan. A Member of Parliament and staunch Puritan, he was vociferous in 1680 in support of the Exclusion Bill.[77] Bridget's mother, Margaret Boscawen, was one of three daughters and co-heirs of Theophilus Clinton, Baron Lincoln (1600–67). Margaret had at least nine other children between 1651 and 1664 before Bridget but none survived childhood.[78] In 1692, Bridget married Hugh Fortescue (1665–1719) who was heir to Arthur Fortescue of Penwarne. They lived at Castle Hill, Filleigh in North Devon and had nine children.[79]

Anne Strode of Parnham, Dorset

Anne Strode (1652–1727) was a wealthy spinster in Dorset. She was the daughter of Sir John Strode of Parnham by his first wife, Ann Hewett. Sir John married again in 1665 and wrote a will in 1679 which included a bequest of £1,500 to Anne.[80] She outlived several of her brothers and was their executrix.[81]

The variety of archival sources has necessitated some structure to consider them in a methodical way and, following this introduction, the book is divided into sections based on the three themes of information, resources and practice. Section One explores healthcare information, with Chapters 1 and 2 providing analysis of family letters and household medicinal recipes respectively. Section Two explores the theme of resources for healthcare and Chapters 3, 4 and 5 focus on household expenditure, recipe ingredients and kitchen resources, respectively. Section Three addresses the theme of practice and Chapter 6 considers household patients and children's complaints while Chapter 7 considers chronic complaints and relations between patients and practitioners. The conclusion provides an overview of household healthcare in the seventeenth century. There are two appendices, Appendix 1 providing examples of household expenditure on medicinal supplies, and Appendix 2 giving average costs of purchased medicinal items where units of quantity are known.

SECTION ONE

Information

Healthcare-related information is explored in this section in the form of family letters and recipes. Chapter 1 considers family letters which reveal many activities including self-help medical treatments, nursing care and steps toward recovery. The news carried in letters was not only based on reports of the sick, but also contained concerns and opinions about health, alongside further suggestions such as dietary and lifestyle advice. It is striking how often the letter-writers, both men and women, took particular care in selecting and presenting news relating to health matters. Family letters, as well as diaries, reveal that self-help healthcare advice and activities were broad-ranging in nature, from expressing fears and sharing recipes to bloodletting and using remedies. Writing about illness also provided opportunities for advancement and networking, and those who entered into correspondence on the subject can be seen to manage information to promote health (or at least reduce ill health) and to seek advantage. Information in household recipe collections is explored in Chapter 2, which provides a focus on remedies which were medicines in the seventeenth century. Individual recipes were organized into family recipe collections, and named contributors are considered alongside printed book sources. Factors affecting choice of recipes included the nature of the ailments indicated, and I show other reasons for selection of recipes which varied in different households. Recipes could convey medical knowledge, whether this was based on long-standing approaches to healthcare or new additions in practice. A large proportion of medicinal recipes required ingredients which needed to be purchased but, like letters, medicinal recipes could have other uses, particularly in building networks and seeking advantage. The value of recipes meant that they were not always readily shared, either by men or women. Overall this section shows the range of self-help activities in healthcare and ways in which information about health and illness could be managed.

SECTION ONE

Information

FIGURE 1.1 *Seventeenth-century posset cup made in London in 1651 (credit: Wellcome Library, London).*

water and bitt of brown paper will cure it agen'.[29] Hungary water was a popular distilled water based on rosemary, according to the physician John Quincy (d. 1772).[30] Mary also described using Hungary water for herself, alongside other items. She wrote to Edward, 'this morning by the use of Hungrey water and the rest I find the redness is now quite gone and the swelling much abated'.[31] No recipes for Hungary water were found in the Clarke household recipe collection, although rosemary was a frequent ingredient in other distilled waters in the recipe book. John Pechey's (1655–1716) *Compleat Herbal* provides an example of how this preparation could be made:

> The Queen of Hungary's Water is made in the following manner: Fill a Glass or Earthen Cucurbite half full with Rosemary-flowers, gather'd when they are at best, pour upon them a sufficient quantity of Spirit of Wine to infuse them; set the Cucurbite in a Bath, and joyning its Head and Receiver, lute close the Junctures, and give it a digesting Fire for three Days; after which, unlute them, and pour into the Cucurbite that which may have been distill'd; re-fit your Limbeck, and increase the Fire so as to make the Liquor to distil Drop by Drop; when you have drawn about two Thirds of it, put out the Fire, let the Vessels cool, and unlute them, and put the Water so distill'd into a Vial well stop'd. 'Tis good in a Palsie, Lethargy, Apoplexy, and for Hysterical Diseases. The Dose is, from one Dram to two. 'Tis likewise used outwardly, for Burns, Tumours, Cold Pains, Contusions, Palsie, and in all other Cases wherein it is requisite to revive the Spirits. Ladies use to mix half an Ounce of it with six Ounces of Lilly-water, or Bean-flower-water, and wash their Faces with it.[32]

It seems likely that the Hungary water, a readily available prepared item, was not necessarily made by Mary Clarke but rather purchased.[33] Other prepared remedies which were widely favoured were syrups, and sometimes these too were purchased (examples can be seen in Chapter 3) although they could also be made in a household. For instance, Elizabeth Isham added a note in her Book of Rememberance [*sic*] that she 'had a coffe which my parents feared to be the coffe of the lungs; I tooke som easey things for it which did me some good' including 'sirupt of fulfoot [foalfoot] and the reut of elepampan [elecampane] in serop which since I have made for my selfe use'.[34] Thus, Elizabeth specified in her note that she later made her own syrups.

Sending to the medical practitioner

Within the correspondence of the Clarke family there are examples of seeking advice from a range of learned medical practitioners, both locally and further afield. For instance, Edward Clarke wrote to his father in 1676 with the aim of persuading him to allow a local doctor to send details of his condition, so that the 'best Physitions' might advise, saying:

> I doe most earnestly desire you to permitt Doctor Jarvis to write the state of your condition fully, and to order the sending of it to mee (especially if there bee noe amendment) by the next post Both that I may thereupon

take the advice of the best Physitions of this place and imediately wait on you with their prescriptions.[35]

Spouses, especially men, seemed to be particularly instrumental in seeking advice from physicians. Jane Strachey (1643–1727), in a letter to Mary, wrote of her son's insistence that his wife should take advice in London: 'She hath taken advice there for her brest It hath A Knob which pains her at times ever since it hath bin whole and he being in London would not be sattisfied but she must come'.[36] The insistence of these men on medical practitioner advice is forcefully expressed in the phrases 'earnestly desire' and 'would not be sattisfied'.

There were numerous requests in the correspondence of Edward Clarke to John Locke (1632–1704) for suggestions of treatment for his wife, for the children, and for servants of the household. Locke's involvement in the Clarke's family health was extensive, links between them having been established from 1682 onwards.[37] Locke often obliged with medical advice, although he is more widely known for his advice on the education of the Clarke children;[38] for example, at various times he suggested that Edward should drink spa water,[39] he advised Mary to take Peruvian bark,[40] and he also sent instructions for a diet drink for a servant.[41] Mary benefited from Locke's medical advice directly although his recommendations were frequently mediated through her husband Edward whilst he was in London. In one letter Edward explained how he visited Locke and provided an account of Mary's condition: 'I went to Mr Lock and luckily enough found Him at home, where all the time then togather was spent in his inquierying into All the circumstances of your Case and your present state of Health'.[42] Recommendations might also be sought from other learned friends in the metropolis. Some years later, Mary wrote to Edward to ask him to obtain advice from friends in London when she had loose teeth:

> I have had such a violent paine in my teeth of late as I never had since I breed my children . . . the pains has bin so severe that it has made all my teeth loose and I am in doupt those few I have left will come out therefor if among your acquaintance you could larne what was good to fassen ones teeth it might do me a kindness.[43]

However, not all medical help was so readily accessible, and some letters reveal the considerable difficulties experienced when sending for a medical practitioner. Ursula Venner made frequent efforts to obtain the personal presence of a physician to attend to her father, Edward Clarke Senior. In June 1676, she wrote to her brother, Edward, that their father continued 'still weake, we have sent to Doctor Dyke but he was ill in the gout and could not come'.[44] Later that year their father was sick again and Dr Dyke 'directed a vomit for my father which he sayth is the only way to help him'.[45] On this occasion their father recovered but he sickened again just over a year later in April 1678. Ursula had further problems in obtaining medical advice:

> I sent a munday to Dr Dykes and yesterday to Sir William Wyndhams where I found he and Mr Smith were gone, and desired the doctors advice and that he would come to my father if possibly he could, and likewise I writ to Mr Smith to desire him to come to him but neither of them came, nor directed any thing for him, which very much troubles mee but I will use the best meanes for him that I can my selfe and pray God blesse it and comfort him.[46]

Ursula was left to her own devices since the physicians were not readily persuaded to attend her father. When the physician was again sought in May 1678, Ursula wrote of success through arranging a coach for him: 'Doctor Dyke was by your assistance of our good friend Mr Blewetts coach home and saw my father yesterday'.[47] Ursula subsequently sought something from the apothecary for her father, remarking: 'he hath been somewhat troubled with the toothake these two or three days; and I am now sending to Mr Smith for something to give him ease therein'.[48] Ursula's experiences suggest that even wealth and status could not always guarantee a doctor's availability to attend a household although, for some complaints, the apothecary could readily be relied on to provide a preparation which might provide 'ease'.

Nursing care

Anne Summers defines nursing as attending to all the needs of a permanently or temporarily disabled patient. This includes administering food, drink and medicines; maintaining temperature with suitable clothing, bedding and ventilation; keeping the patient and surroundings clean, dealing with bodily evacuations, washing clothes, keeping the patient quiet and cheerful, observing the patient and their reactions to food and therapy.[49] Of particular interest in the Clarke family correspondence is the range of nursing activity which Ursula Venner mentioned when caring for her father, Edward Clarke Senior, during his long illness – staying up all night with him, giving reports on patient progress, administering medications including enemas, supporting him to walk across the room, letter-writing on his behalf, making cordials and other activities.[50] Although she would have had the aid of servants in these activities, Ursula's letters suggest much direct involvement in this care, and once she wrote to her brother, Edward, that 'I have not been in my bedd this sennight'.[51] Indeed her 'care and kindness' were recognized by her father when he made his will in 1677.[52]

Obtaining compliance, that is, successful administration of medicines to a patient, was sometimes an issue reported in letters. Ursula wrote that 'my father is altogether averse to the takeing of it all which mightily troubles me ensure that her proposed journey to London to seek advice about her illness should not be common knowledge:

> I desiar you want [won't] let anybody know it before I come and I donte intend to let it be knowen hear ... I desire to give net hear to cover my preparrasions that will take annebel to visit my frends for 3 wekes or a months time and not say wh[at] way till I am just going away.[83]

Bridget's letters to her husband in London on business were sometimes alarming to him when she mentioned her illness. Whilst she assured him that she was keeping him informed, it is also evident that she did not always wish to tell the full extent of her condition. In her letter of 29 February 1707/8, she explained what changes there had been in her condition, and expressed concern about his likely reaction to her news. She did not want to trouble him, 'but becas of your temper and your busnes I wold never tell the greatnes of the degree of my weknes'.[84] She suggested that her local medical advisers should communicate directly with Hugh to provide reassurance. She would 'depend on the sattesfakshon that I thost [thought] you might have from Mr Baller and Mr Jenkinson'.[85] Bridget's view was that these medical practitioners, the apothecary and surgeon, could authenticate her reassurances about her illness, an example of drawing support from her medical advisers further discussed in Chapter 7.

Taking advantage of illness

A sympathetic enquiry about health or illness could reap benefits, as it provided a very acceptable basis for raising other matters. When Bridget Fortescue's uncle Edward Boscawen (b. 1628–85) died, his widow Jael Boscawen sought to ensure her children did not lose out on further inheritances. After Bridget's father, Hugh Boscawen (1625–1701) died, Jael wrote to Bridget during the settling of affairs, saying: 'I did not intend dear Madam to have troubled you soe soon with my insignificant letters but hearing from my sister Northcote you have been soe very ill since I heard from yourself I cant forbear enquiring after your health in hopes to a better account of it then she gives me'.[86] A few months later, she explained that her illness prevented travel and she sought to ensure that family business was being settled, and she was: 'very glad to hear you are better in your health and I hope my cosen Fortescue is before this time returned to you and that he found the trustees in a good disposition, to proceed regularly in the dispatch of the business before them'.[87] Jael used her concern for Bridget's health as a reason for writing so that she could put her point of view about the likely outcome of the trustees' deliberations on the will. Bridget drafted a polite response – 'sorry to find that you want the waters this time of year besides your complaint of something heavie upon you' – adding that 'all I can say at present I will advise and if I can be satisfied that it will be no hindrance to the performance of the will and for the true intrests of the family which I shall ever respect you shall not find me wanting on my part'.[88] Bridget's response sympathized about Jael's health, but emphasized that she was dealing with matters in a timely and appropriate way.

Medical practitioners also took the opportunity arising from illness to help develop their relationship with a possible patron, allowing further requests to be made in their letters. The surgeon, Mr Jenkinson, hoped to profit by his association with the Fortescue family through treating Bridget, and he wrote of 'admiralty promises', presumably of a position going to sea, which could be 'effectually secured' by Hugh Fortescue, 'a kind freind and my best Benefactor'.[89] In a further letter, several days later, he cautiously affirmed his success in treating Bridget, saying that 'the sore of her Ladyships neck continues as I writt you to heal every day'.[90] The surgeon's expectations of a position were dependent on showing that he could provide effective medical care, and he took pains to provide updates about improvements in Bridget's condition.

Other individuals might also take the opportunity to promote their services on hearing of poor health. George Short, whose wife provided wet nursing in Ditton, wrote to Mary Clarke in December 1686, on hearing of Ward's improvement following his illness, and offered help:

> Madam, I am most hartily glad to heare that master Edward is able to go downe stairs I pray god increase his strength more and more to him madam if you please to send him to Ditton for the air hee shall bee very wellcome and all the care taken of him that possible can bee as for his lodgeing.[91]

Thus, a service could be proffered in response to news about illness, in this case the offer of lodging which could accommodate nursing care.

Other healthcare prevention and self-help

Some other aspects of preventative care were mentioned in family correspondence and diaries. For instance, bloodletting was often mentioned, suggesting the widespread use of such procedures both as preventative measures and treatments. Bloodletting before and after the cold months was thought to help avoid accumulation of corrupt and waste matter,[92] and it was often carried out in the home. Adam Eyre (1614–61) recorded on 26 May 1647 that 'after dinner, I blooded my wife in her sore foot, which bled very well'.[93] The involvement of other family members in providing bloodletting was not uncommon, as Mary Woodforde recorded in 1686, 'I was let blood by my Cousin, Jethro Longworth. God grant it may do me good' and again noted bloodletting with his help in 1687.[94] Other families used the services of a medical practitioner, or a servant. Lady Rachel Russell (1636–1723) wrote a letter in 1685 saying 'I had carried a surgeon on the day before to let my niece blood, by Dr Loure's direction'.[95]

Views of the necessity of bloodletting varied somewhat and Hannah Newton points out that it was advised against for small children.[96] However, letters show that even children could be bled on occasion if it was deemed appropriate. One of the Clarke children was staying with John Locke during March 1691 when Edward Clarke wrote to Locke saying, 'I am concerned to hear the childe's cough continues . . . I am verie glad to understand that you intended to have him bleeded'; the reply came several days later, 'Master was let bloud on Friday, since which he finds his cough better'.[97] It seems that older children might be considered strong enough to undergo bloodletting as a treatment. However, there was some reluctance on the part of medical practitioners to use or recommend bloodletting in every circumstance. In the casebook of the surgeon Joseph Binns (d. 1664), based in London in the seventeenth century, no prophylactic bleeding was recorded, only bleeding in specific cases of injury, such as those affecting the head.[98] And Edward, Lord Herbert of Cherbury, thought that bloodletting was 'only necessary for those who abound in blood'.[99] Thus, even those less inclined to bloodletting saw it as appropriate on occasion, a view based on humoral beliefs regarding the dangers of an excess of certain fluids in the body, whether blood or undesirable humours. Some individuals were very firmly convinced of the need to let blood; Alice Thornton insisted on being bled when heavily pregnant and against her physician's advice.[100] There was opposition to bloodletting expressed by some physicians who pointed to the views of Galen and Hippocrates regarding the inadvisability of bloodletting during the crisis of diseases,[101] while Helmontian physicians argued that bloodletting diverted the body from expelling feverish matter,[102] but bloodletting was maintained by many practitioners as it continued to be demanded by patients.[103]

Conclusion

As we have seen above, writers identified many health matters in letters, communicating concerns and activities involved in the management of household health through prevention, treatment and recovery. Prevention of illness and health maintenance incorporated prayer, hopes and fears, preventative advice and warnings, the control of ill news, collection of advice, and use of prophylactics intended to avoid illness. Treatment and care began with efforts to identify complaints, followed by arranging of visits of practitioners, preparation of remedies, administration of medicines, maintaining control of news, and reporting of the effects of treatment. Lastly, recovery involved continuing nursing care, feeding and washing, close observation, restorative diet, physical encouragement, coming downstairs, providing further reports and emotional support, and the acceptance of providence.

The older widowed carer for the elderly sick relative, the mother concerned with her young children, and the spouse seeking suitable medical advice all became more visible in these letters. Ill health brought both potential danger and great opportunities. Information was managed by both women and men. Patients carefully pitched their written news to spouses and others about their complaints, while spouses and relatives expressed their care and concern. For lay people, ill health brought the chance to take responsibility or to raise other matters, while for a medical practitioner there were opportunities to gain further recognition or to advance oneself. Women, as carers and household practitioners, could assume significant roles in place of a sick person, and some women made key decisions about information and treatment. Both men and women could gain medical information through their contacts, although they might also withhold information about their own illnesses and concerns in order to avoid creating conditions for further upset. The role of husbands in encouraging access to further learned advice becomes more apparent in letters. It must be noted, however, that it was not only men who were in contact with physicians, since elite women could also access such information in their own right; for example, Anne Conway's help was sought by Henry More in order to obtain medical advice for his niece from Francis Mercury Van Helmont (1614–98).[104] And we have seen that Ursula's father, Edward Clarke Senior, despite having status as a wealthy landowner, was unable to gain the attendance of medical practitioners on every desired occasion. Thus gender roles were not always sharply defined in relation to healthcare and, although access to medical advice and treatment could be determined more readily by wealth and status, these were not the only factors that determined treatment. For these households, self-help healthcare appeared to be interspersed with medical practitioner services, rather than expressed clearly as an alternative form of medical treatment. Family letters provide an indication of the range of self-help activities in household healthcare, including efforts to control and manage information, but we still lack detail about the day-to-day use of medicines in a household. In Chapter 2, there is a closer look at a different form of information which was widely sought and shared by households: medicinal recipes.

2

Medicines or Remedies: Recipes for Health and Illness

Medicinal recipes were widely collected and could have provided a basis for much self-help in early modern household healthcare. This chapter provides an overview of medicinal recipes in both household collections and printed books of the seventeenth century. Selected household recipe collections are analysed alongside printed sources to help answer a number of questions. Who provided these recipes? How were recipes chosen to add to household collections? What kinds of ingredients did these recipes require? Although many household recipe collections appear similar in the range of medical complaints that they covered, closer examination shows that households could differ somewhat in their selection of recipes. In several examples we will see that some types of recipes were particularly favoured, and consider why. The first example is the household recipe collection started by Bridget Fortescue's mother, Margaret Boscawen, in the latter half of the seventeenth century. Margaret gathered many recipes from family and friends, and included some lists of recipe titles from printed books. We will see that her choice of medicinal recipes from printed sources was not only determined by therapeutic purpose in treating particular complaints, but was also based on ease of preparation and safety of use. The second example is that of the recipe collection of the Clifford household which included recipe volumes compiled by several different generations, and some recipes were copied numerous times. These 'favourite' recipes suggest other factors affecting choice of recipes in the Clifford household including potential use of the preparations as cure-alls.

Recipes were often called 'receipts' in the seventeenth century, both terms denoting information communicated about making a variety of preparations from foods and medicines to cosmetics and household aids. The recipe format is still readily recognizable today, with a number of key components usually including purpose or indication as well as ingredients and processes. Early modern recipes might also include further information about ingredient quantities, dosage recommendations, claims about effectiveness or other advice. In the seventeenth century, medicinal recipes could be described both as medicines and remedies. They were a means to ensure health, according to the writer of the epistle in *Most Excellent and Approved Medicines and Remedies*, a book full of recipes attributed to Alexander Read (1586?–1641) and published in 1651. The epistle writer claimed that disease and sickness were sent by God who 'hath appointed severall Medicines or Remedies to encounter them', and added furthermore that these could be had 'at a cheap and easie rate'.[1] The seventeenth century saw a large increase in printed medical advice with recipes, much deriving from sources previously described as secrets.[2] These medicinal recipes focused almost exclusively on the making of medicinal preparations rather than providing explanations of mechanisms of action and medical theory. Yet the information in recipes often suggested an underlying understanding of health and illness, and this was often based on classically derived humoral approaches. In this chapter we will see that medicinal recipes were valued, although the use of recipes might not have been solely focused on making up preparations. Some recipes were clearly sought and exchanged for medicinal purposes but other uses of making links with possible patrons, and gaining status, were also reasons for sharing recipes, reminding us of the way that some letters similarly sought advantage in connection with health matters in Chapter 1. A further issue of the nature of recipe ingredients is also introduced in this chapter since detailed analysis shows that the great majority of recipes required at least one or more purchased ingredient. Many recipe ingredients are mentioned in this chapter and the reader can consult the Glossary for further detail on specific named ingredients.

Sources for a household recipe collection

Sharing recipes was a great interest in the seventeenth century and many recipes were passed round in manuscript form via social networks; sometimes complete copies of recipe collections were made as gifts.[3] Much of this handwritten information was further copied and circulated widely even while printed material began to increase rapidly at this time, and these two formats were not necessarily different in content.[4] Many loose individual household recipes were re-organized and copied into household recipe collections, and Elaine Leong has extensively described the processes involved in such compilations.[5] Other individual recipes can often be found scribbled in a variety of contexts, such as in the front and back of books of household accounts.[6] At the time of writing this book, I have identified a handlist of 275 seventeenth-century manuscript recipe collections of English origin containing largely medicinal items.[7] My handlist, according to inspection of the catalogue entries, consists of about two-thirds of collections attributed to women while the remainder are attributed to men or unspecified.[8] Household medicinal recipes are thought to reflect actual practice, or at least potential practice, in making medicines.[9] However, manuscript recipe collections present a number of problems to modern researchers seeking to analyse their content, since authorial attribution to recipes is rarely possible, even where individual recipes are associated with named sources.[10] Nevertheless, dedications in printed medicinal recipe books can reveal both the involvement of women, from aristocratic patrons to gentlewomen and aspiring servants, and the involvement of men who were engaged with the circulation of recipes.[11] Furthermore, whilst some marginalia added in to manuscripts and printed books are highly suggestive of actual use, there is evidence that many phrases about use, such as '*probatum est* [it is proved]' were simply copied.[12]

Medicinal recipes in household archives from the seventeenth century were sometimes organized in collections but can also be readily found on scraps of paper. Here I use the term 'household collection' to refer to all of the manuscript recipes relating to one household, whether compiled in a volume, written on loose papers, or included in letters. All of the household recipe collections selected for further analysis in this study were primarily medicinal in purpose although some also contained culinary, household, cosmetic and veterinary recipes.[13] Altogether 8,209 entries in recipe collections from households and printed books were identified. Of this total, 6,513 (79.3 per cent) recipes had primarily medicinal purpose, 1,232 (15 per cent) were culinary, 153 (1.9 per cent) were cosmetic, 125 (1.5 per cent) were household-related, 90 (1.1 per cent) were veterinary and 96 (1.2 per cent) were miscellaneous items of advice.[14]

Attribution of a recipe to an individual contributor could provide credibility for the recipe's efficacy as well as clarifying the relationship of the recipe compiler to its contributor.[15] In addition to printed sources, there were four types of named contributor seen in the analysis of household recipes: medical practitioner; family, including servants; household supplier; social or other acquaintance. Overall 881 household recipes, just under 14 per cent, were individually associated with named contributors.[16] The likely sex of named contributors could be identified in 829 recipes and of these, 44 per cent came from women and 56 per cent from men (some fifty-two recipes were associated with initials only or indeterminate names). In the recipes of the aristocratic Clifford family, of the females named as contributors, most were recorded as 'lady' or 'mistress/mrs'. Other recipes came from a 'doctor', and less frequent contributors were identified as 'lord', 'mr', 'captain', 'countess' or had unspecified status. The Fortescue family recipes included a number of female contributors for twenty-seven recipes but most of these named individuals were not given any description of status. Letters in the Fortescue family papers suggest that these recipes were contributed by individuals of varied status, from family members to the local apothecary and wives of clergy and merchants. Most of the recipes that were attributed to kin (8.1 per cent) were from women, including an aunt, niece or sister (only cousins were unverifiable as to gender). Compared to the Clifford family, Bridget Fortescue, and her mother Margaret Boscawen before her, recorded medicinal recipes from a wider range of sources, both lay and professional, family and friend, merchant and servant. However, since the majority of recipes were not associated with named contributors, it is not possible to be sure that those who were named were typical contributors of recipes.

We cannot assume that every recipe that was contributed to a household was written down. As seen in Chapter 1, some sources referred to 'possets' even though detailed instructions were not given for making these preparations. It is possible that some recipes for commonly used preparations were not recorded, but were passed on verbally from generation to generation.[17] This might have been the case for commonplace items which were frequently made or did not need reminders of step-by-step instructions that were originally conveyed orally. Oral sources are particularly difficult to evidence, although Elizabeth Tebeaux notes a residue of orality in books where recipes lack quantities, suggesting that the spoken word was originally used.[18] Not only recipe ingredients may have been passed on this way but also techniques of preparation. Such knowledge has been termed 'tacit' knowledge and has become more widely recognized in recent scholarship.[19] Occasionally the household recipes included written instructions which convey an impression of being spoken and written down by a person as they were recounted. For instance, Bridget Fortescue recorded on a note of a remedy for a pain in the side that the recipe was 'The Licker mrs Harvey used to make for my mother', given here both in the original form and in a modernized form (see Figure 2.1).

A Litel cammel flowars Litel pelatory of the wall the Leaves a Litel marsh mallow a Littel Angellecow a Litel bame a Litel tamaru a Litel winter savery and a sprick of rosmary a Litel vilat Leves and Lickrus and Anesead and sweat feanel sead boyel it in spring water till the rawnes of the earbes be gon about a cavarter of an hower the arbes must be as near as posebel not over mastur one another but the most of marshas malas and tamaras.

[A little chamomile flowers, little pellitory of the wall the leaves, a little marshmallow, a little angelica, a little balm, a little tamarisk, a little winter savoury and a sprig of rosemary, a little violet leaves and liquorice and aniseed and sweet fennel seed, boil it in spring water till the rawness of the herbs be gone, about a quarter of an hour, the herbs must as near as possible not over master one another but the most of marshmallow and tamarisk.][20]

Mrs Harvey, the housekeeper in the Boscawen household in Cornwall, was probably related to the family steward, Thomas Harvey. In the 'large book' of recipes that she received from her mother, Bridget had other remedies which were acquired through Mrs Harvey, such as the recipe, 'For the colleck', which was accompanied by a note that 'cousen Barres commended it to Harvey'.[21] Thus, Mrs Harvey acted as a conduit for medical advice and

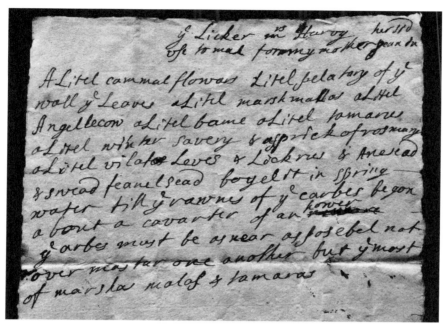

FIGURE 2.1 *'The Licker mrs Harvey use[d] to mak[e] for my mother' recipe,
Fortescue of Castle Hill papers, 1262M/FC/8, Devon Heritage Centre (courtesy of
the Countess of Arran).*

recipes in the Boscawen household, and occasionally the form of some
recipes suggested a 'retelling', based on oral transmission of essential content,
which was then set down on paper by her employer. In the recipe for the
'Liquor', the purpose of the medicinal preparation has been omitted since it
was likely known to the family. Although it is not possible here, with few
examples of this kind, to fully explore whether orally transmitted recipes
were retold from a tradition with different medical knowledge and
understanding, further linguistic studies could assist in determining whether
some of these recipes were unique to an oral tradition.[22] As we shall see in
the next section, there was also considerable interplay between printed and
household recipe collections.

Medicinal recipes from printed sources

Printed medical advice books were much in demand in the seventeenth
century, and the numbers of new vernacular books of household and
husbandry advice dramatically increased after 1650, many publications
containing recipes.[23] The origins of these books with medicinal advice can
be seen both from books of secrets and other sources containing craft

knowledge and skill relevant to household needs.[24] Other books were published which gave regimens instructing on diet and lifestyle, often drawn from classical medical sources, and these are further considered in Chapter 5. Some of the earlier printed books were expensive, and illustrated herbals were particularly costly, such as those of John Gerard (1545–1612) and William Turner (d. 1568).[25] Many country houses had medical advice books on hand: for example, the library of the Duke and Duchess of Hamilton in the later seventeenth century contained *The Country Physician*, 'Mr Boyle's Book of Physick', 'Dr Willis's treatise on scurvy' and *The Treatise on Gout*.[26] The location of books in houses of the seventeenth century could vary from a closet to rooms that were more public and allowed display to a wider audience, providing an indication of wealth and status.[27] Such books were also highly valued to the extent that they could be mentioned in wills, for example, the 'Gerards Herball' and other medical material bequeathed to his son by William Oldisworth (d. 1680).[28] Books of physic were not only bequeathed to sons and, as Nagy records, the will of Sarah Gater of London in 1654 gave Gerard's *Herball* and other 'Physick and Chirurgerie books' to her sister, and the will of Alice Thornton in 1705 gave all her 'medicall books and recepts, together with my stock of salves and oyntments' to a daughter.[29] Despite being expensive printed texts, herbals were accessed by women, and Rebecca Laroche provides a detailed analysis of significant herbals and their use alongside, or instead of, medical practitioners.[30] A number of more affordable early modern advice books, published from the sixteenth century onward, linked women to the provision of healthcare as part of housewifery. In the preface of John Partridge's (1644–1715) *The Treasurie of Commodious Conceits* (1591), a poem was addressed 'to all women, that covet the practise of good Huswiferie' enabling them 'to remedie each griefe' since 'Amongst the rest of Phisicks helps, the huswifes help is chiefe'.[31] The *Treasurie* included 'Conserves and Sirops sweet to comfort heart and braine' and also 'good medicines' used 'for present health'.[32] At 4d this book claimed to be good value, containing 135 recipes with instructions for cosmetic, garden, household and medicinal use. Another popular early modern publication was *The English House-Wife* by Gervase Markham (1568?–1637), first printed in 1615. Markham wrote that a housewife should have a 'phisicall kind of knowledge' in order to 'administer many wholsome recipes or medicines for the good of their healths, as well to prevent the first occasion of sickness as to take away the effects and evil of the same when it hath made seizure on the body'.[33] Markham provided detailed advice on the preparation of many medicinal items, including the distillation of waters, although he also opined that the 'Art of Physicke is farre beyond the capacity of the most skilful woman'.[34]

Some medical books containing recipes were credited to individual women of high status, or at least dedicated to them. *A Choice Manuall of Rare Conceits* by Elizabeth Grey (1582–1651) was first published in 1653;

The Queens Closet Opened, published in 1655, was attributed to Queen Henrietta Maria (1609–69); and, in the same year, *Natura Exenterata* was published, attributed to Alethea Talbot (d. 1654) who married Philip Howard, Earl of Surrey and Arundel.[35] There has been debate as to whether the printed books supplied recipes for household collections or vice versa.[36] In reality, there must have been considerable interplay between both and, although many recipe collections were compiled by women, others were compiled by men or jointly compiled by families.[37] Leong shows that there were varied reading practices in selecting recipes from printed sources,[38] and medicinal recipes not only appeared in popular advice books, but also in more learned publications: for example, some of the recipes of Katherine Jones, Lady Ranelagh (1615–91), were incorporated into Thomas Willis's (1621–75) *Pharmacopoeia Rationalis*.[39] Later in the seventeenth century, the audience for print was further expanding, drawing in women from a wider range of society, and Elaine Hobby draws attention to the publications of Hannah Wolley (fl. 1670, d. 1674?) which were aimed at the 'upwardly-aspirant woman', with advice on practical household matters and social behaviour as well as cookery and medicinal recipes, books so popular that some editions after 1673 were pirated versions of earlier books.[40] The cover picture of this book is extracted from *The Accomplished Ladies Rich Closet of Rarities*, by John Shirley (fl. 1680–1702), a book that was aimed at both gentlewomen and maid-servants.[41] Such a purchase could enable a lady to instruct a servant as to how preparations should be made. Later seventeenth-century publications also incorporated the use of medical names which could bolster the standing of the recipe collection, such as books associated with Dr Lower, likely the physician Richard Lower (1631–91), and Robert Boyle (1627–91).[42] A selection of these printed books, spanning a period from the late sixteenth century to the early eighteenth century, is considered here for comparison with the household recipe collections incorporated into the database.[43] The choice of texts is somewhat pragmatic, including a range of books aimed at housewives, some books attributed to women, and some popular editions of medical advice books containing recipes from eminent or learned sources.

What made a good recipe?

Household recipe collections have been described as 'textual medicine chests',[44] implying that households gathered recipes so that they might find a remedy which could be prepared for almost every ailment. A key element of a medicinal recipe was the indication, or ailment for which it was intended, and so every recipe in the database was examined for ailments expressed in both the recipe title and text. To aid the analysis, the individual ailments are grouped and placed in ailment categories (Table 2.1). These thirteen ailment categories are primarily based on early modern understandings of health and disease, and do not entirely correspond to present day understandings of these. In particular, external symptoms in the past were not necessarily seen as related to specific internal causes: thus a number of conditions are listed as 'dermatological' here because they presented with skin-related signs or symptoms; scurvy is one such example. An early modern humoral understanding linked together the heart and liver, as both were regarded as directly involved in the circulation and production of blood, and thus liver complaints are included in the 'circulatory' category. General humoral complaints are placed in a 'miscellaneous' category along with prophylactic and purging recipes. Whilst there might still be debate about the placing of ailments in respective categories, the main concern is to enable consistency for purposes of analysis.[45]

TABLE 2.1 *Ailment categories in medicinal recipes*

Ailment category	Ailments included in category
Circulatory	Heart, dropsy, jaundice, blood complaints
Dermatological	Boils, tetters, impostumes, swellings, cancer, kings evil, scurvy
Digestive	Mouth and teeth, stomach, spleen, surfeit, worms, flux
Infectious	Plague, smallpox, measles, fever, pestilence, French pox
Miscellaneous	Prophylactics, purges, humours, poison, physic, weakness, corruption
Musculo-skeletal	Aches, ague, pains, gout, arthritis, sciatica, lameness, cramp, rickets
Neurological	Headache, migraine, fits, palsy, vertigo, apoplexy, convulsions
Psychological	Melancholy, misery, sleeplessness
Reproductive	Breasts, uterine, pregnancy, childbirth, breastfeeding, fertility
Respiratory	Colds, lung complaints, consumption, chest ailments, throat
Sensory	Eye, ear, deafness, pin and web
Surgical	Burns, wounds and other injuries, bruise, sore, ulcer, fistula
Urinary	Running of the reins, stone, urinary problems

Source: Stobart, Recipes and Expenditure Database.

We saw above that some of the household recipes were associated with named contributors, and analysis shows that the range of ailments differed according to whether a contributor was named. A comparison of the ailment categories of recipes which came from named and un-named contributors (Figure 2.2(a) shows that digestive ailments were frequent in both groups (16.4 per cent and 15.8 per cent respectively)). Named contributor recipes were rather more likely than un-named contributor recipes to relate to ailment categories of miscellaneous (10.9 per cent and 8.6 per cent), neurological (8.6 per cent and 5.5 per cent) and urinary (7.0 per cent and 4.8 per cent) ailments. Named contributor recipes were less likely than those from un-named contributors to relate to dermatological (7.6 per cent and 10.4 per cent) or surgical (6.6 per cent and 11.4 per cent) complaints. If the named contributors are split into male and female sources, then these differences become more marked (Figure 2.2(b)), and it can be seen that male contributors were more likely to be associated with digestive, miscellaneous, respiratory and urinary ailments. In contrast female contributors were more likely to be associated with dermatological, musculoskeletal, neurological, reproductive and surgical recipes. This analysis can only be indicative, however, because it is entirely possible that male recipe contributors were more readily recorded by name, whereas female recipe contributors were not.

A comparison of the range of ailments can also be made for the recipes from household manuscript and printed book sources. This shows an overall similar distribution of categories in both manuscript and printed collections, with the largest group of recipes relating to digestive complaints, and this was especially pronounced in the printed books (Figure 2.2(c)). The high level of recipes relating to digestive complaints likely reflects the close links between food and health in the early modern period and this link is further explored in Chapter 5.

Choosing recipes from books

Apart from the choice of particular ailment indications when selecting a recipe, other considerations appeared to matter to early modern individuals. In the case of Margaret Boscawen, her selections of recipes followed a number of interests. Several lists of recipe titles were made by Margaret which she selected directly from printed book sources. Her 'large book' of recipes included three pages of lengthy listings of recipes by title alone.[46] Altogether she listed 111 recipe titles from four printed books; these were Elizabeth Grey's *Choice Manuall* (61), the *Queens Closet Opened* (24), Alexander Read's *Most Excellent and Approved Remedies* (17), and the *London Dispensatory* (9), in the 1654 edition from Nicholas Culpeper (1616–54).[47] Margaret annotated some of the recipe titles with comments such as 'very good', 'very pretty' and 'easy to be made', suggesting that she made a choice to record these recipe titles as of special interest. A particular interest was in distillation, since one-third of the items, thirty-seven of the

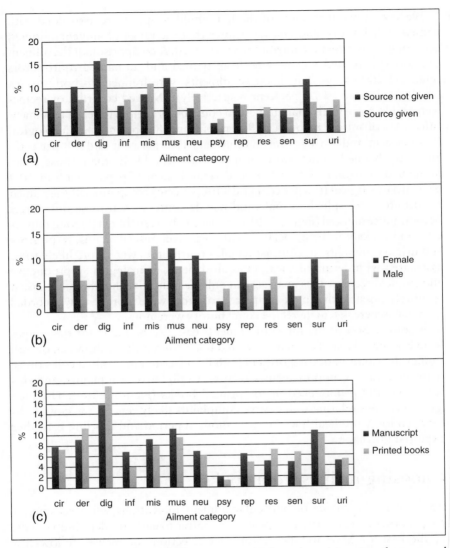

FIGURE 2.2 *Proportions of ailment categories in recipes: (a) recipes from named sources (876 recipes); (b) recipes from male and female named sources (821 recipes as 55 of named sources could not be clearly identified as to sex); (c) recipes from manuscript and printed book recipes.*

Abbreviations: cir: circulatory; der: dermatological; dig: digestive; inf: infectious; mis: miscellaneous; mus: musculo-skeletal; neu: neurological; psy: psychological; rep: reproductive; res: respiratory; sen: sensory; sur: surgical; uri: urinary.

Source: Stobart, Recipes and Expenditure Database.

recipe titles, were for distilled waters. Although the range of preparations selected did vary from internal drinks to external plasters and ointments, one of Margaret's pages focused exclusively on distilled waters. This list of thirty waters drew from all four printed sources. Each recipe title was accompanied by a page number, and it appears that she methodically worked through copies of each printed text and wrote the recipe titles in succession. As Margaret listed the distilled waters, she recorded some additional thoughts. For example, next to the entry for 'Aqua composita for the collick and stone' she added 'for which I must remember to have some strong Ale', next to 'synamon [cinnamon] water' she noted that there were '3 or 4 severall ways' to make it.[48] Her concerns in relation to these waters were focused on the processes and ingredients needed for making these preparations. She wrote of 'an approved water for to breake the stonne in the kidneys' that 'in May it must be done', and of another water for the stone she noted that it was to be made 'in a limbacke [limbeck]'.[49] Margaret added a further note following a recipe for making gentian water, 'Severall other things very easy to be maide',[50] her comments suggesting that ease of preparation was a prime concern.

    In addition to practical aspects of making these preparations, Margaret's attention also focused on the safety and effectiveness of the medicines; she observed, for instance, that a recipe 'For the stonne in the kidneys' was 'a very safe madison'.[51] In the original text this recipe was attributed to Sir John [sic] Digby, although Margaret did not list the source name in her note and perhaps the name of the recipe source was of less interest to her.[52] This medicine consisted of honey, water and cloves, and so the statement made by Margaret about a 'safe madison' may have been connected to the known and digestible nature of the ingredients and, although these were not inexpensive ingredients, these items might have been readily available in a substantial household. Another of the lists of recipe titles compiled by Margaret had a particular focus on children, as she identified a number of recipes from the *Queens Closet Opened* for teething, purging, worms and rickets (see Chapter 6 for more on treating children). The remaining list of recipes included many titles drawn from 'Lady Kent's' book, the *Choice Manuall*. Overall, the largest group of recipe titles, twenty-three recipes, related to digestive complaints including wind, surfeit or excessive consumption and stomach troubles, and a further nine recipes concerned purging humours such as phlegm and rheum. Apart from seven recipes for the stone, she also listed twelve for sores and wounds, ten for the eyes, eight for coughs and respiratory complaints, five for melancholy conditions and four to assist in conception and childbirth. Few of Margaret's recipe selections could be regarded as polychrests or cure-alls, and altogether the 111 recipes in her lists referred to 123 ailments. Although she listed few other cure-alls, Margaret's interest appeared to be sparked by the 'Drink for all kind of Surfets' which she described as 'A very pretty drinke', this being a water made from aqua vitae with cowslips, sage, rosemary, sweet marjoram, pellitory of the wall, betony, balm, cinnamon, nutmeg, fennel, aniseed, coriander seed, caraway seed, gromel [gromwell] seed, juniper berries, all mixed with sugar in May and allowed to stand for nine days in the sun, and somewhat atypical in not requiring distillation. She also described a recipe for 'Aqua mirabilis' as 'a very good water to be maide', and this required distillation, of salendine [celandine?], melilot, cubebs, galingale, nutmeg, mace, ginger and cloves.[53] Her interest in such distilled waters involving numerous herbal and spice ingredients may be judged by the inclusion of at least four versions of Doctor Stephen's Water, another cure-all preparation with many ingredients which was often recorded in recipe collections.[54]

Some recipes contained fewer ingredients and, amongst the simpler recipes that Margaret appreciated, were the 'Comfortable Cordial to chear the heart' and the 'Cordial for wind in the stomack' which she described as 'A pretty receite for the winde' and 'A pretty cordiall for the stomacke and head' respectively.[55] Another recipe containing honey boiled with linseed and milk was listed as 'A very good receite for a bruis[e] and for the eyes'; and the term 'very good' was also added to the title for an 'Approved medicine for the yellow Jaundies' which included muscadine, barberry bark and goose dung.[56] From the *Queens Closet Opened* she noted the 'receipt to help digestion' involving ale, mint, sage and cinnamon as 'A very pretty receite for disgestion'.[57] Thus Margaret revealed her views about which recipes she sought out. She did appear to be influenced by efficacy statements, often repeating words like 'good' or 'special' where they were included in the original printed title. Although clearly interested in the distilled waters, most of the ingredients in the recipes she chose to record were herbs and culinary ingredients, with few exceptions likely to be available in the household or readily sourced from the local apothecary. Some of the recipes suggested an interest in more recently introduced imported or chemical items, and two recipes in the *Queens Closet Opened* were included that would have required apothecary purchases of china root and spirit of tartar respectively.[58] Margaret was also interested in the benefits to digestion of some of the items, as she particularly noted the 'pills for quitting the stomach and helping concoction' in Read's *Most Excellent And Approved Medicines* as being 'very pretty', these requiring purchase of powdered aloes to make.[59]

Overall, Margaret was highly selective in her choices from printed texts as, for example, she picked out less than 20 per cent of the recipes in the *Choice Manuall*, selecting sixty-one out of 357 possible recipes. Even fewer recipes were selected from the other texts, for example just twenty-four from 457 recipes (5 per cent) in the *Queens Closet Opened*. As Margaret did not record the detailed content of these recipes, it seems likely that she expected to have further access to all four texts. Although influenced by efficacy claims, the criteria that she used most demonstrated interest in ease of preparation, availability of ingredients, and safety of action. Her notes included relatively few cure-alls and omitted names of high status that were in the original titles. Although, sadly, there is little surviving evidence of correspondence between Margaret and others, there is one letter addressed to her in Cornwall from her sister that implied that she was involved in treating local people, observing that she was 'much imployed about the sick'.[60] Thus Margaret may have selected recipes which were intended for use both in and beyond the household.

Repeated recipes in household collections

In another early modern household, that of Lord and Lady Clifford in Devon, we can see a somewhat different perspective on what made a good recipe. Within the private archives of Ugbrooke House, Chudleigh in Devon, there are three leather-bound volumes of recipes, labelled 1689, 1690 and 1691–1752.[61] The Clifford family were an aristocratic Catholic family, and their archives provide an opportunity to examine links between the recipe collections compiled by several generations. Unlike the recipe collection of Margaret Boscawen, which had frequent additions, the three volumes of the Clifford household appear to have been assembled around the same time. The writing hand within each of these volumes shows some noticeable differences. In the volume labelled 1690, the oldest hand appears, with use of the secretary hand and abbreviations no longer seen towards the latter part of the seventeenth century. From internal evidence based on duplicate recipes in the other volumes, it appears that the earliest recipes are in this volume labelled 1690, and selected recipes were copied into the volumes labelled 1689 and 1691–1752.[62] Thus, the volume dated 1690 may have been compiled initially by Elizabeth (d. 1709), wife of Thomas (1630–73), the 1st Baron Clifford. The volume dated 1689 was probably compiled by Anne, wife of the 2nd Lord Clifford, Hugh, and bears many resemblances in format and hand to the third volume dated 1691–1752, which may have been a continuation of the 1689 volume. Both Elizabeth and Anne, as mother and daughter-in-law, were living on the Ugbrooke estate at Chudleigh in the 1690s and so they could readily have shared information and medicinal recipes.

The primary focus of the Clifford volumes of medicinal recipes was on digestive, musculo-skeletal and surgical complaints, and these account for over 39 per cent of all their recipes. Overall, the Clifford family collection included slightly more recipes for treating aches, ague, bruises and consumption when compared to other household collections. Many recipes were repeated and, within the Clifford recipe collection, there were 110 recipes which were repeated one or more times, giving a total of 239 duplicates.[63] Amongst the most popular repeated recipes were 'A powder to prevent a miscarriage', 'For stopping in the stomach' and 'A bruise in the body'.[64] Some recipes were copied from three to five times and appeared to be particular favourites, accounting for nearly one-fifth (18 per cent) of all repeated recipes (see Table 2.2). On some occasions the repeated recipes, particularly the preparations with numerous ingredients, were given with some ingredients omitted. The

TABLE 2.2 *Repeated recipes in Clifford household recipe collection*

Recipe title	Preparation type	No. of occurrences	Min. no. of ingredients	Max. no. of ingredients
A good surrop for a consumption	Syrup	3	14	21
A medicine for an ulcer in the womb	Drink	3	11	11
A medicine for people subject to miscarry	Powder	3	4	4
A purgeing ale	Ale	3	9	9
A receipt for the green sickness	Pottage	3	5	5
A water for after throwes	Water	4	5	7
An excellent good water for faint women especially women in travell	Water	4	4	4
An excellent green ointment for ache, bruise, lameness, stiches, gouts, spleen, ague, canker etc.	Ointment	3	6	7
For a bruise in the body by Mrs Holder	Drink	4	4	4
For a dropsey aproved	Drink	3	15	17
For a running nose	Snuff	3	2	2
For a stoping in the stomach	Pills	5	4	4
The green ointment	Ointment	3	38	42

Source: The Right Honorable the Lady Cliffords Booke of Receipts, 1689; The Lady Cliffords Boake, 1690; Receipts of All Kinds, 1691–1752, Clifford Family Archive.

reduction in ingredients appears to have resulted from copying errors rather than deliberate omissions. All of the favourite recipes were for internal use apart from two ointments, and four recipes were related to women's conditions such as miscarriage, childbirth and green sickness.

The proportion of the repeated recipes which were simples – that is, based on a single key ingredient – was slightly lower than average at 17 per cent compared to the overall Clifford collection incidence of 19 per cent. The number of repeated recipes which were polypharmaceutical – containing more than the average number of nine recipe ingredients – was higher at 30 per cent compared to the incidence of 26 per cent in the overall household collection. As can be seen in Table 2.2, some favourite recipes contained many more ingredients on average, while others were much simpler recipes with fewer than six ingredients. Repeated recipes in the Clifford collection were more likely to be internal remedies (62 per cent) than external remedies (38 per cent), and this proportion was similar to the overall Clifford household collection. The most frequent preparations selected for duplication were drinks, waters and ointments. It is noticeable that certain types of preparation were not chosen for duplication and these included juleps, possets, plasters for the temple, throat and wrist, purges or vomits. Regarding ailments treated by the repeated recipes, these preparations were much more likely to be polychrests for a wide range of conditions. A total of twenty-two (or 71 per cent) of all of the thirty-one polychrests in the original 1690 volume were copied into the other household volumes of recipes. Some cure-all items were to be made in substantial quantity, for example:

An E[x]cellent Green oyntment for Aches Bruises Stiches Gowts Spleen Ague Cankers

Take of Sage and rue halfe a pound of wormwood and Bay leaves of Each two pound of Ships [sheeps] Sewett put from the Skin three pound sweet oyle of olives a pott to Chop the hearbs very Small and then stampe them and shred the Suet and put them alltogeather then Stamp alltogather till the Seuet be not seen put it into a fare pott and put the Oyle to it and Cover it Close and let it Stand in A Moist plase the Space of tenn dayes then take it forth and Break it into a brass pan Sett it on a fast fire when it is halfe boiled put to it fower ounces of oyle of Spicke and allwayes Stirring till the hearbs be Cracking take it of and Straine it throw a wide Canvis Cloath into an Earthen pott soe keep it for those torment[?] ackes when you shall use this oyntment take a woole that Growes between the Sheeps leggs and Card it into Broad flaggs and bast it uppon a linnen Cloath and keep them alwayes to aches Bruses Lameness.[65]

Evidently, such a recipe would have made a large amount of ointment for external application, a cure-all preparation which could have been in frequent use for the range of complaints indicated, from aches to agues.

Overall, the recipes selected for copying in the Clifford family recipe volumes had a focus on recurrent problems related to childbirth and minor injuries and chronic digestive, respiratory and circulatory complaints. There was much interest in polychrest recipes suitable for a range of complaints, and polypharmaceutical recipes containing large numbers of ingredients, although a few of the duplicate recipes had relatively small numbers of ingredients. Issues of ingredient sourcing, ease of preparation and safety appeared to be less of a consideration for the Clifford household compared to the previous example of Margaret Boscawen's recipe listings, and possibly the larger aristocratic household could rely on servants for much of the labour involved in preparations. The Clifford household recipes that were repeated were identical almost word for word in subsequent volumes of recipes, with few additions. As a Catholic household in the seventeenth century, the family could have been affected by political and social changes, and the extent of possible networking for the collection of further recipes may have been limited to known and trusted sources. However, the likelihood of self-reliance on previous family generations for recipes was not solely based on religious persuasion alone, and differences in medical practice based on religious beliefs are extremely difficult to identify since both Catholic and Protestant medical practitioners were active in the seventeenth century.[66] In the case of the Clifford family there may have been a certain amount of insularity which resulted in the persistence of older recipes and fewer new additions to the recipe collections. The lack of further additions to the recipe collection might also have been a result of increased use of medical practitioners and purchases of prepared apothecary medicines, and the spending patterns of households are further explored in Chapter 3.

Recipe ingredient sources

The availability of recipe ingredients which were commonly found in kitchens or available in gardens has been flagged up in some studies of recipe collections.[67] As in the following example, some recipes could be made up entirely from ingredients derived from the kitchen or garden, particularly in a larger household where a range of staple products was available. One such recipe appeared in the Clifford household collection at least four times, suggesting that it was popular. The recipe for 'A water for after throws' was probably intended to provide relief from pains after childbirth:

A Water for after throws

Take peny Royall two handfulls Issop [hyssop] two handfulls Groundsill two handfulls pick and wash them very cleane in faire water Spread them all into an Earthen pott togather put to them a quart of Spring water Cover them and let them stand twenty fower howers then distill them in a Close Still then lett the bottle of water stand in the Sunn two Months Give a Gill of this water Milke warme with some Suggar Put to the patient before Sleep after delivery being layd in bed first.[68]

This recipe could have been in demand on numerous occasions, given the frequency of pregnancy and childbirth in early modern times, and involved the collection of pennyroyal, hyssop and groundsel.[69] Significantly, and unlike many other recipes in the Clifford household collection, this recipe could be made solely with plants cultivated in the garden or collected nearby in fields, although it would have required some advance preparation since these plants were not always in season. This raises a question as to whether many recipes could be readily made from plants and other items readily available to households and without recourse to the apothecary or another supplier. The analysis in Table 2.3(a) considers all of the medicinal recipes for the number of ingredients which were likely to require purchase.[70] Thus, the first column gives the percentage of household recipes requiring no purchase, the second column gives the percentage of recipes requiring purchase of at least one ingredient and so on until the last column which indicates the percentage of recipes needing eleven or more purchased ingredients.

Overall, in 6,352 medicinal recipes considered (where ingredients were given), just over 23 per cent of recipes did not require an additional purchase, a slightly higher proportion in printed recipes and slightly lower in the household recipes (Table 2.3(a)). Thus, the majority of medicinal recipes, over three-quarters (76 per cent) required one or more purchased ingredients. There was some variation in different households, the aristocratic Clifford family having over 90 per cent of recipes involving additional purchases although, as a substantial household, they may not have required additional expenditure being likely to have had equipment for distillation of spirits, labour for gathering plants, sugar and spices for making up conserves and other resources. The Fortescue and Clarke family recipe collections had varied proportions of recipes requiring purchased ingredients which ranged from 56.9 per cent to 85.5 per cent.[71] If a named contributor for a medicinal recipe was recorded then that recipe was even more likely to involve one or more purchased ingredients, since only 16.5 per cent of named contributor recipes in the recipe collections could be made without purchased ingredients (Table 2.3(b)). Closer examination suggests that female contributors were slightly less likely than male contributors to give recipes which would require purchase of one or more ingredients. These figures are only suggestive since most recipe collections had few named contributors, although it is tempting to consider whether women may have been more aware of the costs of ingredients, or at least of the availability of garden, household, kitchen or wild ingredients. Further studies of recipe collections could provide more opportunities to identify named contributors and to assess whether recipe ingredient sources really were considered differently according to the gender of contributors. However, the overall point of this analysis is to show that the majority of medicinal recipes did require additional purchases beyond the resources likely to be available in the household. These estimates of ingredient purchase requirements are based on a fairly substantial household with a

TABLE 2.3 *Medicinal recipes and purchased ingredients*

a. Proportion of manuscript and print medicinal recipes and ingredient purchases needed.

						No. of ingredient purchases needed						
	0	1	2	3	4	5	6	7	8	9	10	11+
Manuscript recipes, % (*n*=2,761)	21.9	25.2	17.9	11.7	8.2	4.8	3.2	2.8	1.5	1.1	0.6	1.3
Print recipes, % (*n*=3,591)	24.4	27.6	16.4	11.3	6.0	3.7	3.5	2.3	1.3	1.2	0.7	1.6
All recipes, % (*n*=6,352)	23.3	26.5	17.1	11.4	7.0	4.2	3.4	2.5	1.4	1.2	0.7	1.5

Note: the total number of recipes analysed is reduced from 6,513 as some recipe titles were given without ingredients.

b. Proportions of manuscript and print medicinal recipes from named contributors and ingredient purchases needed.

| | No. of ingredient purchases needed | | | | | | | | | | | |
	0	1	2	3	4	5	6	7	8	9	10	11+
Manuscript recipes, % (n=466)	17.4	22.5	17.0	13.7	9.4	7.3	2.1	3.4	2.1	2.1	0.4	2.4
Print recipes, % (n=397)	15.4	17.1	15.4	10.1	7.6	6.0	8.3	4.0	3.5	3.3	2.5	6.8
All recipes, % (n=863)	16.5	20.0	16.2	12.1	8.6	6.7	5.0	3.7	2.8	2.7	1.4	4.4

Source: Stobart, Recipes and Expenditure Database.

range of culinary supplies, and the labour and equipment available for processing, so that many prepared ingredients such as ale or syrup of roses could have been homemade. However, households of lesser status and wealth or in urban settings might not have had the resources of equipment and labour to have prepared ingredients readily available, or the facilities to keep many prepared medicinal items in stock. If the calculations are revised to also include the necessity of purchase of all prepared items, then the proportion of medicinal recipes feasible without a single purchase drops even further to about 15 per cent. Thus, overall, it appears that some 85 per cent of medicinal recipes needed one or more purchases of medicinal or prepared ingredients if they were to be made. This figure could be an underestimate, however, since the assumption has been made that the ingredients requiring purchase excluded all items which might reasonably be home-produced in a substantial household which was self-sufficient in animal fats and seed oils, bee products, flour and grains, meat and dairy supplies. Thus, it would be reasonable to expect some purchases of medicinal ingredients to be visible in household accounts if many of the medicinal recipes were being used, and this is further explored in Chapter 3.

How were medicinal recipes used?

Although selections and duplications of recipes do suggest those that might have been favoured in the Clifford and Boscawen households, they do not provide conclusive proof of actual use. Medicinal recipes were sometimes annotated 'probatum est', suggesting that the preparation was approved, or proved in use. However, this phrase may have been found in the original recipe and was then copied. For example, the 'purging ale', a recipe repeated in the Clifford recipe collection, ended with 'probatum est' in every one of the three copies made in the Clifford recipe collection. Similarly, there was a comment in the recipe 'A drinke to cure the ricketts often approved' in the 1690 volume of Clifford recipes, stating that 'I have cured severall that have bine farr gone in the ricketts without any ointment'.[72] Although this was a claim of actual use it was not necessarily made by the person who contributed the information or the person who wrote down the information. A study of efficacy phrases, such as 'probatum est', reminds us that they derived from medieval texts where proof was based on theoretical discussion rather than actual use.[73] Such phrases, and other similar stock phrases like 'it healeth', were not essential to the recipe and were declining in importance by the end of the seventeenth century.[74] But, if recipes were not definitely used to make preparations they could have had other significant roles in the seventeenth century. Leong and Pennell cogently argue that household recipes provided a form of medical education, whether for the household practitioner or for the patient seeking advice and remedies.[75] The nature of early modern medical education through popular advice books and other medical texts is further discussed by Irma

Taavitsainen in relation to the spread of humoral understanding.[76] For many families the medicinal recipes could have provided a window on medical knowledge. More specifically, the genre of recipe books may have provided numerous examples of how medical care could be framed, particularly in a humorally-based manner. The rationale of many medicinal recipes focused around a 'cure' for an illness, and many of these were based on humoral understanding with titles such as 'How to make the lyme water good for the Kings Evil, dropsey and all moist humours', 'A medicine to purge and amend the harte, stomack, spleene, liver, lungs and brain', 'For the coffe or a rhume' and 'To voide phlegm'.[77] The format of household recipe collections meant that they could be readily augmented with new items, and this is self-evident in many compilations where further additional recipes were appended and inserted at the end, or in spaces between other recipes. This might have provided a mechanism for new ideas about medicine to be spread, such as the addition of recipes for the complaint of rickets which are mentioned in Chapter 6. Equally, as David Goldstein suggests, whilst some compilers might record innovation others might 'cling on to older recipes'.[78]

Although medicinal recipes could promote medical knowledge, those considered in this study rarely identified details of other aspects of healthcare such as prevention, diet and lifestyle.[79] Even though information about diet might have been given in letters of advice from both lay and learned individuals, this was not always incorporated in the recipe compilations. The general incidence of dietary advice in recipe collections was less than 2 per cent.[80] Medical practices, such as bloodletting, that were widespread and had long-standing use within household self-help[81] were not mentioned in the recipe collections: such practices were commonplace and likely needed no specific mention. It is also noticeable that charms and spells were few and far between in the recipe collections; just fifteen (0.2 per cent) items involved incantations or amulets in the 6,513 medical recipes analysed.[82] Such omissions in recipes might be viewed as indicators of boundaries on acceptable medical knowledge,[83] but the majority of these items occurred in recipe books associated with learned sources in the latter half of the seventeenth century.[84] These recipe inclusions might not have reflected fully medical intentions since, as Helen Smith comments, written items could be perceived as prophylactic or curative by some and then recast as entertaining tales.[85]

The value of recipes

Recipes were highly valued and many recipe collections were carefully handed down through generations, as indicated by the inscription on the inside cover of one recipe book: 'Our Great Grandmother Hodges her receipt book. She was mother to Mrs Priaulx who was Grandmother of Mrs Sarah Tilley by Mrs Howes marrying her daughter Mrs Mary Priaulx'.[86] For some early modern individuals, the knowledge available in a recipe might be convertible into cash. Recipes were acknowledged to have monetary value, as is suggested in the recipe entitled 'An Excelent and approved Medisen: for the collick: and Stone' where 'it is said that a women got above a 100 by this Medison: therefore it being a poor womens livelyhood it was to be kept secreat'.[87] This recipe for the colic and the stone advised use of a powder derived from fish and eggshells to be drunk in white wine and, dated March 1675, it was entered in Margaret Boscawen's large book of recipes.[88] Some other medicinal recipes were described in terms of secrets. For example, a letter to Margaret drew attention to the possible concealment of a remedy for 'madness', revealing an awareness of boundaries in the provision of healthcare by women. Margaret received the letter from her sister who suggested that there was an understanding between the two women about their medical practice. Her sister wrote of her 'cheefe medicine which reaches unto madness', saying 'which I will not conceale from you, also considering your practise being at too great a distance to prejudice mine'.[89] This correspondence suggests that both Margaret and her sister provided local healthcare, although they were far enough apart to share medical secrets without discomfort. Valued recipes might otherwise be worth concealment.

Some individuals explicitly sought medical information despite expressing their understanding that there were limitations to their role. For instance, Isabella Duke (fl. 1673, d. before 1705) of Otterton in Devon wrote to John Locke in 1686 asking for details of how to cure ague with Jesuit's (Peruvian) bark, explaining to him that 'an abundance of my friends and Neighbours now suffer and I would be glad to be able to give them that relief'.[90] Such medicinal information had potential value in maintaining or raising Isabella's status in the community. But she was evidently aware of overstepping some kind of boundary as she added 'if you think this request ridiculous, let my Charitable intentions atone for my Ignorance and indiscretion'.[91] It seems that Locke did not readily provide the required information and Isabella sent at least four further letters in the subsequent six months, complaining of his lack of response. When Isabella did finally hear from Locke, he provided her with a critical reply including 'advice against my reading and tampering with physick'.[92] Denied access to information, Isabella could not presume to 'give relief' to her friends and neighbours, and gain status with acquired medicinal knowledge of a particular remedy. Although Isabella attempted to claim charitable intentions as a woman, this was not sufficient to gain the support of a male (and famous) learned medical practitioner.[93] The response that Isabella received from Locke provides an indication of the difficulty that women might have had in attempting to augment their standing by gaining knowledge of newer medicines.

Self-improvement and networking

Other reasons for gaining advantage from medicinal recipes are not hard to find, particularly when the gift of medical information could be advantageous to the donor as well as the recipient.[94] A number of letters in the Fortescue family papers testify to the willingness with which individuals followed up on opportunities to provide medical advice, remedies and services to a wealthy family. Such opportunities arose because, from childhood, Bridget suffered from the condition widely known as the King's evil or scrofula, a chronic complaint affecting the neck glands.[95] In 1679 Elizabeth Penhallow wrote to Mistress Harvey, the Boscawen family housekeeper, about a cure for Bridget's neck sores. Elizabeth's letter offered information on a certain herb:

Kind mistris Harvey

According to my promise I have indeverd to know the names of the hearbes and use of them which I tould my lady of and you . . . the name of the hearbe is white arkeangle [archangel] which is to be boyled a littell quantity . . . with stale beare and drink it the first in the morneing and the last at night . . . I will send upon her Returne the hearbes that my lady may see them and if my lady thinke fit to make use of it or will have the younge woman to come and fit the things as she did for the child, shee will be very willing to waite on my lady . . . your loveing freind to serve you Elizabeth Penhallow.[96]

In her letter Elizabeth recorded the extent of her efforts made to gather exact information, to confirm its 'truth', and her willingness to arrange attendance on the sick child. She added that she could arrange to provide and prepare the herb. The potential benefits of ongoing association with the Boscawen family could have been substantial.

Networking with others through sharing medicinal recipes also appeared to be anticipated within the Boscawen household since copies of favoured recipes were made ready for others to take away. The archives contain three identical copies of a lengthy recipe for an 'excellent' diet drink for 'scorbutick dropsy and gout', and all were in the same hand (Figure 2.3(a)).[97] The diet drink involved an impressive list of ingredients (Figure 2.3(b)).[98]

An Excellent Dyet drink for a Scorbutick Dropsy and Gout

Jallop/ Fine Rhubarb/ Sen[n]a of Alexandria/ Indian Wood or Lignum Vita[e] Cortex/ Sarsaparilla/ Bayberryes/ Sassafras wood/ Epithemum/ Saldonella [bindweed?]/ Polypodie Rootes/ Ashen Keyes/ Elicompane roote/ English Liquorish/ Fennell/ Annis/ Commin [cumin]/ Carriway/ Coriander Seeds/ . . . Wilde Sage/ Bettony/ Scurvy Grass/ Germander/ . . . Topps of Wormwood/ . . . Horse Rhadish rootes.

Take 3 gallons of Wort boyled without Hopps and in the boyling putt all your things About Except the herbs and the Sena Rhubarb Jallop and Epithemum; which four Ingredients must be put in presently as it is taken

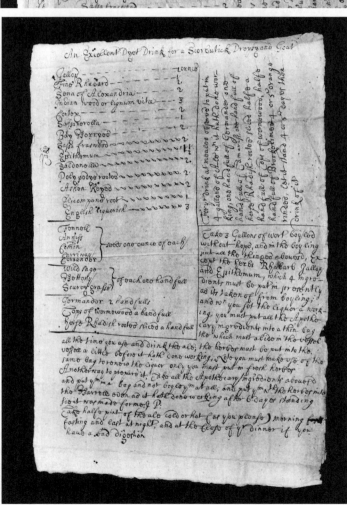

FIGURE 2.3 *Diet drink recipe: (a) three copies of the same recipe; (b) 'An Excellent dyet drink for a Scorbutick Dropsy and Gout'. Fortescue of Castle Hill papers, 1262M/FC/8, Devon Heritage Centre (courtesy of the Countess of Arran).*

off from boyling, and when you sett your Liqor a working you must put all the Apothecary ingredients into a thin bag, the which must abide in the vessel all the time you use and drink the ale; the herbs must putt into the vessell a little before it hath done working Now you must make use of the same bag to renew the liqor only you must put in fresh herbes. Another way to prepare it, Take all the Apothecary Ingredient about and put them in a bag and not boyle them at all and put them with the herbes into the [barrell?] oven as itt hath done working after 6 dayes standing; soe it was made for me J P.

Take halfe a pint of the ale cold or hott (as you please) morninge fasting and last at night and at the Close of your dinner, if you have a bad digestion.[99]

This recipe was further augmented by an additional note, 'For your drinke at meales', in the margin. It is hard to imagine any other reason for making three copies than that these were to be given to selected guests or acquaintances. In her study of cookbooks, Janet Theophano points out that 'to give a gift is to exercise a form of power', and that giving a recipe implied an expectation of reciprocity.[100] The 'gifting' of a range of items including foods did play a part in the maintenance of neighbourly and family networks,[101] but gifts in the records of elite households were more often unusual or distinctive items.[102] This recipe for the diet drink was certainly distinctive in length and number of ingredients. As we will see in Chapter 3, the household accounts also provide indications of gifting through occasional entries showing payments to messengers as bringers of gifts. Medicinal recipe collections provided ideal repositories for gifted advice which could enable a relationship to be further established. However, not everyone expressed favour in relation to proffered medical advice and remedies, and there might have been some anxiety about receiving such items, especially if a reciprocal favour might be expected.[103] Mary Clarke gave her view that she had 'no faith' in the 'little meddicens' suggested to her by friends. She wrote to her husband in 1696, 'I am told severall little meddicens by my frends that say they have cured many peaple when the famous Doctors prescriptions have done no good but I have no faith in them nor shall never trye'.[104] For Mary, the 'gift' of medical advice from a lay person appeared to be unwelcome. Furthermore, she might be expected to reciprocate in some way if she accepted advice and ever did 'trye' one of these remedies. Thus, although recipes were often eagerly shared, as shown above, there were some instances of rejection of proffered remedies.

Conclusion

We have seen that medicinal recipes were widely sought after in the seventeenth century and carefully passed on. Household manuscript recipe collections reflected the shared networks and many sources from which advice and recipes were sought, alongside printed works which in turn also drew on household collections. In general this necessarily brief analysis of selected household recipe collections suggests that medicinal recipes were sought for a variety of reasons apart from the nature of ailments indicated, including ease of preparation, safety and efficacy, availability of ingredients and potential use as cure-alls. Recipe-sharing could also provide a basis for acquiring medical knowledge, and many collections accumulated new additions alongside old recipes, although the addition of new medical knowledge was not guaranteed. Some women indicated their awareness of the boundaries of their healthcare involvement through their care taken in sharing recipes, regarding them as akin to secrets. Some recipes had particular value for exchange and promoting advantageous connections. Overall, we see that both lay and professional advice in the form of recipes might be sought and offered, but could also be withheld or even declined. If we look again at Read's *Most Excellent and Approved Medicines*, we can see that he readily acknowledged several possible forms of treatment, referring to 'physick' for every individual 'patient' or a 'medicine' for every 'disease'.[105] Recipes thus provided an emphasis on medicines, although these were clearly not the only remedies expected in healthcare in the seventeenth century since a range of other advice including diet and lifestyle recommendations could also be given. Whilst recipes have been considered in this chapter as information sources, we now turn to further explore details of the material resources available for household healthcare in Section Two, and the next chapter investigates household expenditure on health.

SECTION TWO

Resources

The second section of this book explores resources available for self-help healthcare in a number of seventeenth-century households. Here, I consider some material factors which could influence the making of medicines at home and self-help. Accounts for earlier and later seventeenth-century households are compared in Chapter 3 for healthcare-related purchases of medical supplies. The accounts show that a few favourite preparations were made in quantity at home or made up for the household, while purchases of other prepared medicines and medicinal recipe ingredients were often made in small quantities. Patterns of expenditure on medicinal supplies and medical services suggest that self-help and medical practitioner treatments were not always mutually exclusive. There were some concerns about healthcare costs, but I show that these household accounts recorded less than 1 per cent of annual budgets on healthcare-related supplies and services. Chapter 4 further considers ingredients in medicinal recipes, particularly plants. Prices of medicinal items varied and imported medicinal items remained costly throughout most of the seventeenth century. Few native plants, although used in folklore, were as well represented in medicinal recipes compared to exotic imports and spices. Native plants were often available locally, although gathering them could incur a cost, and familiarity with all plants was not assured. There was differing opinion about whether native plants, as simples, or exotics were preferable as medicines. Gifts of exotic items provided a way to find out about new medicines, yet there was also some increasing interest in simples in the latter part of the seventeenth century. In Chapter 5, kitchen resources, from foods to utensils, are further considered. Foods were important in healthcare, either as possible medicines or as causes of illness, but advice on diet was becoming variable and I show

how foods were challenged as a hindrance to medical treatment, or even ridiculed as a form of self-help. Equipment resources available in the kitchen were suitable for making many medicinal preparations, although distillation required additional resources, and other equipment might be needed for administration of medicines. Some recipes provided alternatives to the demanding process of distillation. For a range of reasons, household medicine production was undermined but the widespread availability of prepared medicines for purchase could enable continuing self-help in healthcare.

3

Early Modern Spending on Healthcare

Household accounts in the seventeenth century provide a rich source of detail of expenditure on healthcare, from purchases of medicines to payments for medical services. Seventeenth-century household accounts are considered here in three ways. First, what range of medicinal items was purchased, from prepared medicines to recipe ingredients? Second, how did different households compare in their health-related expenditure in terms of self-help and use of medical practitioners? Third, did households have any concerns over health costs as part of their overall budget? In this chapter we will see that the relationship between medicinal supplies and medical practitioners varied in different households, and higher levels of spending on self-help medicines or recipe ingredients did not necessarily preclude use of medical services. For larger households, the cost of healthcare identified in household accounts was a small percentage of their overall budget, although concerns were still expressed about unpredictable costs and quality.

There was no standardization of records for household expenditure in the early seventeenth century, nor was instruction given although some advice books stressed the wife's role in relation to household finances.[1] As Todd Gray points out, 'each household devised its own system', and the producers of accounting records could range from trusted servants to a head of household.[2] Alice Clark noted that although wives of farmers and tradesmen were often actively involved in family business, it was fairly unusual to find elaborate accounts kept by such women.[3] In the later seventeenth-century gentry households considered here, the accounts were maintained by Mary Clarke and Bridget Fortescue, while the household accounts for Lord and Lady Clifford appear to have been compiled by a steward. These household accounts did vary in the extent to which foods, wages, taxes, repairs and other incidental costs were recorded, some being primarily kitchen accounts listing mainly domestic purchases, others being disbursement accounts including the wages of household servants.[4] The level of detail about medicinal supplies also varied in the household accounts: some items were specified by name and others were listed vaguely as 'drugs' or 'things from the apothecary'. For analysis, the household expenditure records on healthcare were categorized as either medicinal supplies or medical services. Medicinal supplies included both individual 'raw' recipe ingredients and prepared items purchased from apothecaries and others, while medical services involved payments for the attention of a medical practitioner, such as a physician, apothecary or other healthcare provider. There may have been some overlaps between these categories – for example, an apothecary could be paid to provide a service of bloodletting – but every purchase was included only once in the analysis. One problem, when interpreting the household accounts, was to determine which items might have been purchased for medicinal use. Items categorized as medicinal for the purpose of this analysis included all those specified as medicines or medicinal recipe ingredients, most distilled waters and spirits, mineral waters, many herbs and spices, and imported or unusual fruits, nuts and oils. The Glossary provides detail of the nature of items which are not explained in the text. As we will see in Chapter 5, many common food items might have been considered to be medicinal in some way, but these were not included in expenditure totals unless specified as for medicinal use. Medicinal services are often more readily identified in the household accounts but particular caution has to be exercised in interpretation of payments to women for medicinal supplies or medical services as, even when a woman was named, an expenditure item was less likely to indicate status and medical role that would be given for a man.[5] A further problem with household accounts is that they may not provide the whole picture of healthcare, since some records could be incomplete, especially while household members were away. The household accounts do not fully represent health-related activities that were not readily recorded as expenses, such as care by relatives or servants, or items not involving payment such as gifts,[6] or ingredients brought in from the garden or hedgerow.[7] However, since substantial tips were expected in higher-status households for messengers bearing gifts, there were occasional payments of such rewards: an example can be seen in the early seventeenth-century personal accounts of Margaret Spencer (d. 1613), where payments of 12d were entered 'to the woman that my Grandmother sent with butter and medlars' and to the 'man for bringing of oringes'.[8] Some health-related assistance which was gifted might have reduced expenses considerably but could also have brought expectation of reciprocal favours. For example, there was little expenditure on physicians in the Clarke household accounts since this family sought medical advice from their learned friend, John Locke. A return of favour was provided by Edward Clarke through frequent assistance to Locke with his business concerns.[9] However, Locke's advice may not have reduced costs on every occasion as he sometimes suggested seeing another physician.

Early seventeenth-century households

The aristocratic household accounts of the Earl and Countess of Bath in the first half of the seventeenth century provided details of numerous purchases that could have been used as medicinal supplies. The quantities recorded were sometimes substantial and include, for example, large amounts of ginger, eringo roots, red roses and cassia. A purchase of 3,000 red roses at Michaelmas 1651 was accompanied by a large quantity of thirty pounds of sugar, specified for making conserve of roses.[10] Amounts of three pounds' weight or more of preserved eringo roots and cassia were purchased 'for my Lord'.[11] Such large quantities would have ensured that sufficient stores were available for regular use in large doses[12] or over an extended period, but in other cases the amounts purchased were often much smaller and thus likely for immediate use. The most frequent purchases of this kind were of eringo roots, oranges and caraway seeds. Further purchases mentioned at least three times were for aniseed, brimstone, cinnamon, citron and scurvygrass. Readymade preparations were also commonly bought and included conserves, syrups, strong or distilled waters and spirits. Occasional items were listed as bought individually from apothecaries, such as a 1651 purchase of syrup of gillyflowers. Other medicinal purchases were from herb gatherers who were often women: for example, on 21 January 1645/6 a purchase was made for 1s and recorded as 'given to a woman for scurvy grass'.[13] Within the personal account book of the Countess of Bath there were also substantial payments to a 'herb woman' and for 'herbs' of around 12s per week in May and June 1639, while another purchase on 16 January 1642/3 was recorded as 'to Mrs Tarry by bill and for spirit of balm £1 8s 6d'.[14] Thus, some purchases were for prepared remedies, even though this substantial household likely had facilities for carrying out distillation. Medicinal supply purchases for the Bath household, where individual ingredient costs were given, totalled £25 14s 3d over the period 1639 to 1655, an average expenditure of 11s 8d per year. During the same period, a further total of £146 1s was recorded as spent with apothecaries: this amount was paid out over 34 occasions, with an average payment of £4 14s per occasion. Such large payments to the apothecary were not typical, the average being exceeded on just nine occasions, but it is clear that the apothecary bill could add up to a significant amount over a fairly short period. Overall, the Bath household accounts listed at least forty-three different medicinal items, and of these fourteen were prepared remedies of some sort, and the remaining two-thirds were raw materials within the household.

An account from a much smaller merchant household in the early seventeenth century can be found in the 'financial diary' of John Hayne, son of a serge merchant, who became bailiff of Exeter in 1609 and Sheriff in 1635.[15] Almost all of Hayne's medicinal purchases appear to have been from apothecaries, including Humphrey Bidgood (d. 1641), an apothecary of Exeter who also supplied the Bath household.[16] Some of Hayne's other purchases were for medicinal ingredients and the services of making them up: for example, a diet drink in 1634, 'Aug. 5, Paid for Harts [horn] 1s. to make Gellie, with 12d given goodwife Fish for boyling it, and 3d for seeing my diet drink boiled'.[17] Hayne was married (twice) and he paid his wife fortnightly 'house expences', but it does not seem to be the case that he or his wife prepared these medicines.[18] Indeed, further purchases suggest that the household put out raw ingredients to be finished both for medicinal supplies for self-help use and for sale alongside fruit and vegetables in front of the house.[19] In 1639, a substantial payment was made for making comfits: 'Aug 17, More xxij s. I paid mr Wiles the Comfit maker for 8 lb of divers sorts of Comfits at 22d the pound, and one pound of Eringo rootes at 8s'.[20] Purchases of other pills and cordials in Bidgood's apothecary shop were made by Hayne in most years, and a further purchase was made of bottles for holding medicinal waters in 1640.[21] The Hayne household also purchased relatively recent medicinal introductions at the apothecary, such as guaiacum, or lignum vitae from the tropical Americas, and china root from Asia.[22] These accounts show that a range of exotic imports could be readily obtained outside London towards the middle of the seventeenth century. Overall, the Hayne household account included purchases of at least twelve different items with likely medicinal purpose, and two-thirds of these were to be prepared in some way by others. There were some similarities between the large aristocratic household and the smaller merchant household; both Bath and Hayne households bought diet drinks and large quantities of conserves and comfits, or had them made, and there were similar kinds of ingredients purchased. The smaller household may not have had the facilities, equipment, labour or personnel to make many preparations, but the accounts recorded purchase of some exotic items. These were not always specified in the Bath household accounts, although they could have been supplied as part of apothecary purchases.

These early seventeenth-century household accounts bear similarities to some other published studies of household expenditure, both in the making up of certain preparations and in purchases of prepared medicinal items. The aristocratic household of Edward Ratcliffe (c. 1559–1643), 6th Earl of Sussex at Gorhambury, indicated in its accounts that there were significant purchases of roses: for example, seven and a half bushels were purchased for 15s in June 1638, accompanied by nine glass bottles costing 4s 4d.[23] In Alice Le Strange's (1585–1656) accounts, some ninety-one different medicinal ingredients and preparations were purchased and, although thirty-four were 'raw' ingredients, many items were bought in ready prepared form including aqua vitae, syrup of lemons, conserve of roses, mithridate, Dr Mundford's water and powder for worms.[24] In the smaller spinster household of Joyce Jefferies (c. 1570–1650), medicinal supplies included some 'raw' ingredients such as liquorice and elecampane roots, but most purchases were of prepared items such as aniseed water, aqua vitae, syrup of coltsfoot and other items from the apothecary.[25] Both smaller and larger households purchased prepared items, from comfits to syrups and distilled waters, even though they may have differed in the resources available for making up medicines.

Later seventeenth-century household expenditure

Accounts for the latter half of the seventeenth century also recorded many medicinal purchases. Sets of medicinal items could sometimes be grouped together in a single purchase from the apothecary, while at other times specified individually. For example, Elizabeth Wentworth (m. 1671), who kept accounts from 1655 to 1708, included purchases almost every year of 'things' from the 'poticary'.[26] A few items were recorded by Elizabeth in more detail such as 'physicke hearbs' bought for 3s 6d in 1661, and there were occasional purchases of angelica water, almond milk, aqua vitae, brimstone and eye water.[27] Most of the named individual purchases were prepared items, and it is not possible to be sure whether 'things' were more prepared items or raw materials for making up recipes. In the following sections, the unpublished accounts from the Clarke, Clifford, Fortescue and Strode households are outlined to give a broader picture of the extent and range of medicinal supplies recorded in the later seventeenth century.

Clarke household accounts

Soon after she married Edward Clarke, Mary started a book of household accounts with an inscription 'Here follows an Accompt of ye House-hold Expenses since my comeing to Chipley on the 9th of May 1685', and these gentry household accounts were maintained in considerable detail for nearly eighteen years.[28] Included in the accounts were wages of household servants, and culinary and household items. The Clarke household account recorded substantial and regular purchases of dried and fresh imported fruits, spices and sugar. Oranges and lemons were bought frequently, sometimes a dozen at a time, and households could obtain advice as to the best times to purchase such items in John Houghton's monthly trade periodical available in the later seventeenth century.[29] Sometimes dried fruit was purchased for a particular individual, possibly with medicinal use in mind, such as 22 May 1701 when '1 lb of figs for my little Master at Holcombe' at a cost of 4d was recorded.[30] Frequent purchases were made of several ounces to half a pound of spices, including allspice, cloves, ginger, mace, nutmeg, black and white pepper. Cinnamon, aniseeds and mustard seeds were also bought occasionally, as was garlic. There were also frequent purchases of other items with medicinal properties including caraway seeds, caraway comfits, aniseeds and aniseed water which were purchased in most years. Syrup of roses was a popular apothecary purchase, bought at least twice a year up until 1696 (see Figure 3.1).[31] Rhubarb was first recorded in 1690 and was then bought every year till 1696 and then again in 1701, while liquorice was purchased at least once every two years, and brimstone was purchased up to

FIGURE 3.1 *Syrup of roses apothecary jar, seventeenth century (credit: Wellcome Library, London).*

three times in a year.[32] In addition to these specific items, the accounts recorded ten payments to apothecaries, including one in 1689 for pills 'derected by Dr Thomass'.[33] Another item in 1702 noted an apothecary payment for 'things had of him in the childrens sicknesse'.[34] One of the items included payment to the apothecary, Mr Cockrom, for letting blood, showing that he provided additional services beyond medicinal preparations of pills and other 'things'.[35]

In total the Clarke household account listed purchases involving seventy-one types of ingredients, of which twenty were prepared in some way. The majority of purchases bought were simples of a purging nature including rhubarb, syrup of roses and wormseed. Appendix 1 provides a list of medicinal purchases in the Clarke household account which were often itemized in sufficient detail to provide quantities, showing that many medicinal items were bought in fairly small amounts, likely intended for use soon after purchase.

Clifford household accounts

The aristocratic Clifford family maintained a set of household accounts from January 1692/3 until May 1702. A range of items including wormseed, brimstone, and preparations such as Hungary water, mithridate and London treacle were purchased at various times.[36] Mithridate and treacle or theriac were costly compound preparations originally made as poison antidotes in classical times.[37] In addition, there were regular purchases of spices, fruits, oils, brandy, sugar candy and chocolate. Some items were recorded more than once, including sal prunella purchased in April and October 1693; senna and gentian purchased in November and December 1700; and mithridate purchased in March 1694/5 and August 1701. Some items bought were called vaguely 'pouders', or 'druggs' and not identified.[38] Medicinal purchases in the Clifford accounts were rarely detailed in terms of quantities, though the amount purchased was more likely to be recorded if it involved a larger quantity. Most of these larger purchases could have had uses other than the purely medicinal, such as a pound of fenugreek bought 13 October 1693, half a pound of allum and a barrel of vinegar bought 18 July 1699, a pound of saltpetre bought 4 December 1699.[39] Further apothecary purchases were infrequently recorded in the household account, likely because the household received a composite account from the apothecary for supplies over a longer period such as a year.

In total, the Clifford household account listed purchases involving sixty-six medicinal ingredients, of which twenty were prepared in some form. Overall the household recorded purchases of a variety of remedies including simples, some minerals such as antimony, Bath waters and expensive prepared or compound preparations such as mithridate. No particular items were bought on a regular basis, though some years saw much more activity than others.

Fortescue household accounts

Bridget Fortescue regularly approved a household expenditure account at Filleigh in North Devon from 1695 to 1704. The gentry household account entries lack specific dates, although there were regular yearly purchases of fresh cherries from the summer of 1697 through to summer 1704. Cherries, mostly black cherries but sometimes red cherries called 'mazzards', were obtained every year in large quantities.[40] Indeed Bridget mentioned cherry beer in one of her letters: 'I forgot to writ you that I sent a hallfe Hogsed off chery bear'.[41] Using the first purchase of cherries each year, estimates of yearly expenditure can be totalled, albeit running from July to July. Regular and substantial purchases were made of fruits, sugar, spices and wines. As in the Clarke household, lemons and oranges were purchased in most years, sometimes in large quantities, such as 200 oranges purchased for 14s 6d in 1703.[42] Caraway seeds and caraway comfits were also frequent purchases.[43] Brandy was bought every year in quarts or gallons, sometimes alongside purchases of 'pipes' of wine, sack and other imports at Bideford in North Devon.[44] Oil of almonds, likely for health use, was bought frequently by the Fortescue family, and can be seen in the accounts every year, on as many as five occasions in 1702,[45] and in 1704 a purchase of almond oil was recorded from the apothecary.[46] Occasional mention was recorded in the Fortescue household account of butter being purchased for ointment making, in 1697 a purchase of 'butter for to make the ointment, 5d', in 1700 'for 3 pound of butter to make ointment, 1s' and in 1702 'to Mary Collins for cream eggs and butter for ointment, 3s 2d'.[47] These specific references to butter for ointment may have been for 'May butter', which was made by repeatedly melting fresh butter without salt until whitish in colour, perceived suitable as 'any simple Unguent'.[48] The quantities of butter bought for making ointment were fairly substantial, implying use over an extended period or use with a number of different people. In total, the Fortescue household account listed purchases involving seventy-four ingredients, of which twenty-four were prepared in some form. Altogether nine payments were recorded to the apothecary, occasionally specifying the prepared items purchased. Unlike the gentry household of the Clarkes, there were few purchases of prepared purging items such as syrup of roses or rhubarb. The household accounts suggest a few specific items were prepared in the household, particularly a butter-based ointment and a cherry water or beer.

Strode household account

Anne Strode of Parnham in Dorset, a wealthy spinster, recorded her personal accounts between 1679 and 1718. Her accounts are of particular interest because of her regular purchases of medicinal items and indications of Anne's charitable interests in the poor. Anne lived within the larger aristocratic household of her brother, and paid a regular quarterly sum for her keep, along with her maid, of £7 10s 'for my dyet'.[49] In some years Anne travelled away to London, Bristol, Sherbourne and possibly elsewhere, visiting family and friends. Frequent purchases of brandy, sugar, honey and butter were recorded in most years by Anne in her account. Brandy was bought in amounts of one to four gallons in all but six years, an average of nearly 11s expenditure per year on spirits. This was comparable to the amount of spirits purchased by the entire Fortescue household, and there were some additional occasional purchases of wine, claret or aqua vitae. It is possible that there were medicinal reasons for the brandy, and Anne evidently had access to facilities for distillation, this being indicated in one accounting entry in 1679: 'for brandy to still, 10s 6d'.[50] Alcoholic drinks were widely regarded as medicinal in earlier times, and Lynn Martin notes the increased use of brandy and consumption of spirits amongst elite women by the end of the seventeenth century.[51] Thomas Tryon (1634–1703) complained that brandy drinking was particularly increasing amongst women for any 'medicinal' reason:

Many English Women have betaken themselves to the drinking of Brandy and other Spirits, and have invented the Black-Cherry Brandy which is in great esteem, so that she is no body that hath not a Bottle of it stand at her elbow, or if ever so little Qualm or disorder be on the Stomack, or perhaps meerly fancied, then away to the Brandy Bottle.[52]

Sugar was another major expenditure item in Anne's account, purchased in almost every year, in amounts from two to six pounds, with an average expenditure comparable to brandy, amounting to almost 11s per year. Honey was purchased almost every other year in large quantities up to 18 pounds. The accounts show that these large amounts of honey were not all for her own use but for potting up to be sent to family in London, and some of the other items bought in quantity might also have been intended for gift purposes. Anne bought most other medicinal supplies in small quantities, her few larger purchases were for items such as gillyflowers and elderberries, that could be made into preserves, waters or syrups.[53] The smaller medicinal purchases were largely exotic or compound preparations, including costly items such as confection of alkermes, balm of Gilead, elixir proprietatis, leaf silver, gold litharge, mithridate, frankincense and Venice turpentine.[54] Some purchases of brimstone, unguentum basilicon, diapalma and other ingredients for ointments were also made. Anne bought imported items such as coffee from the 1680s: for example, a half a pound for 8s 6d in 1680; by 1683, the half pound of coffee cost 2s 6d.[55] Anne also bought some Jesuit's powder in 1708.[56] One pound of chocolate was bought for 2s 10d in 1710, and more bought in 1712 as 'West Indy chocolate'.[57]

The Strode accounts record repeated purchases that suggest Anne's direct involvement in the making of a poppy water: in 1686 'for things to put in to the poppy watter, 1s 1d', in 1687 'for poppys, 8d' and 'for seeds licorish and figs for my Poppy water, 6d'.[58] In *A Physicall Directory*, Culpeper gave a number of recipes using poppy flowers, juice or heads for a simple syrup which 'cools the blood, helps surfets, and may safely be given in Frenzies, Feavers and hot agues'.[59] Anne spent consistently at the apothecaries although, from the later 1680s, she recorded much less detail of her medicinal purchases, preferring to note down a catch-all phrase of 'for things from the apothecary'. The total recorded expenditure for these 'things' between 1679 and 1718 came to £9 10s 6d, which was almost as much as her total recorded expenditure of £10 4s 3d on physicians and surgeons over the same period. On these seventy-six occasions of apothecary purchases Anne's average expenditure was thus about 2s 6d per occasion. In total, Anne Strode's household account listed sixty-nine types of medicinal ingredients, of which twenty-five were prepared in some form. Overall it is apparent that Anne purchased many new and costly named items alongside larger quantities of a small number of items for making some specific preparations.

As we can see from the above examples of household accounts, purchases of prepared items were frequent in all households, amounting to a third or more of the medicinal items recorded. Another type of purchase which occurred in some of the household accounts and became increasingly popular in the seventeenth century was that of mineral waters. As Noel Coley describes, the use of warm springs at Bath and Buxton had been part of a revival of interest in medicinal waters in the sixteenth century, leading to considerable popularity in the seventeenth century. New spas at Epsom and Tunbridge Wells became fashionable resorts, attractive to the wealthy and these waters were a focus for the newer ideas of chemical physicians using Helmontian concepts.[60] Mineral waters could be sent to individuals to drink at home. The amounts of water consumed could be substantial, as recorded in a letter about Edward Clarke Senior: 'Thursday last he took three pints of Castle Cary water which did not worke with him 'till after wee had given him a clyster yesterday he took five pyntes of it which wrought with him, I believe, 10 or 12 tymes'.[61] More waters were advised when he became sick again in 1678.[62] Bridget Fortescue also took waters, and expressed her anxiety about obtaining further supplies from London. She wrote to her husband in London, 'pray dont forget to send mor[e] spaw waters'.[63] Thus, the household accounts not only give some indications of medicinal items that were bought prepared, or to prepare, but also suggest take-up of additional medicines. Having considered expenditure recorded in household accounts on medicinal supplies, we now turn to an overview of spending on medical services by these seventeenth-century households.

Spending on medical services by households

Varying amounts were recorded in the household accounts for the services of a range of practitioners including physicians and surgeons, midwives and wet nurses, as well as those tending sick people and providing health-related help. Substantial payments were made in the aristocratic Clifford accounts to a number of different medical practitioners. These costs ranged from 7s 6d for the bleeding of Lord Clifford, carried out by a surgeon, to the visits of various other physicians who charged at least £1 or £2 per visit.[64] In some years the cost could mount up: for example, in 1696, over £7 was recorded on such fees.[65] Payments were also made to individuals for sending to, and fetching items from, medical practitioners.[66] Midwives accounted for large sums in the Clifford household accounts, being summoned for births in most years, and they received payments which appeared to increase substantially over the years, ranging from one to ten guineas.[67] There were other costs associated with midwives, including payment to the person who fetched the midwife in addition to supplies required by her, such as a 'pint of sack'.[68] Occasional payments were made in the Clifford household account for tending or keeping individuals, such as on 3 October 1700, 'To Mr Symons keeper, 2s 6d'.[69] Overall, the healthcare spending recorded in the Clifford household account was dominated by expenditure on a variety of physicians, surgeons and midwives, and expenditure on medicinal supplies was low compared to amounts spent on medical services.

In contrast to the aristocratic Clifford family, the gentry household of the Clarke family recorded payments mostly to one medical practitioner, a Dr Parsons who was paid £1 for each of five visits between 1697 and 1700, largely for seeing the children. However, the family did not lack medical advice as they regularly consulted their learned friend, John Locke. In addition, some other local physicians were occasionally consulted, as shown by a payment to an apothecary, Mr Cockrom, for 'pills for Master' which was made on the instigation of a Dr Thomas.[70] Other medical services included tending individuals, such as in July 1686, when 'old Goody Jarnner' was paid 4s for 'being there with her when she had the measells a fortnight'.[71] Payments related to smallpox care were also specifically mentioned.[72] The Clarke household accounts did not record any expenditure on midwives, and this may be because Mary went to London for the birth of her children, and these costs may have been recorded elsewhere. Even fewer payments to medical practitioners were recorded in the gentry household accounts of the Fortescue family. This may have been partly due to a family tradition of avoiding physicians since Bridget Fortescue's mother, Margaret Boscawen, was reportedly reluctant to call on the services of physicians. A letter to Hugh Boscawen, in 1686, asking for news of Margaret's illness, noted that she was 'averse to Drs'.[73] However, occasional references in the Fortescue household account indicate that some medical practitioners were sent for by the household in 1699 and 1700, although no specific payments to physicians or surgeons were found to be recorded in the household accounts. The few healthcare-related payments that were recorded were for tending of individuals, fetching doctors and bloodletting,[74] but not for midwives or wet nurses. As with the rejection of medical practitioners, it is possible that

Bridget's mother had an inclination not to use wet nurses, as she came from the Clinton family of Lincoln. The family were noted for the views of Elizabeth Clinton (1574?–1630?), Countess of Lincoln, the authoress of an early seventeenth-century pamphlet, *The Countesse of Lincolnes Nurserie*, which made a strong plea for mothers to nurse their own children.[75] Overall, since there were so few payments for the services of medical practitioners and others, the Fortescue household account was dominated by the purchase of medicinal supplies, either as named ingredients or items from the apothecary.

The household account of Anne Strode, a wealthy spinster in Dorset, recorded numerous payments to physicians and other medical practitioners. The fees paid depended on who was seen by a medical practitioner; a visit for attending Anne was charged at 10s, rather than the usual 5s charged for attending a maid or other servant.[76] In 1701, numerous payments were made for additional services, when smallpox was rife and affecting the household and servants, and requiring much tending and cleaning: for example, 'to the Doctor for Nan, 5s', 'for things at the Apothicaries, 2s 10d', 'for Huckford for being a day with Nan, 5d', 'for a nurs 3 weekes for nan in the Smallpox, 9s' and 'for washing and cleaning the room, 4d'.[77] The Strode accounts suggest that, even in a small spinster household within a larger household, there was considerable cost and effort required to deal with the problem of a smallpox outbreak.

The above examples suggest differences in the spending patterns on medicinal supplies and medical services which can be seen in household accounts of the later seventeenth century. Two households, those of the Clifford and Fortescue families, were higher spending households on medicinal supplies although they differed considerably in their use of medical services. In all years but one the aristocratic Clifford household stands out with substantial spending on medical practitioners, with about one-fifth of expenditure on medicinal supplies from the apothecary or elsewhere. The gentry Fortescue household spent almost as much on medicinal supplies as the Clifford household, but had few records of spending on medical practitioners in this period. The Clarke and Strode households were the two lowest-spending households. The Clarke household account portrayed a more mixed expenditure, with earlier and later years focused on medicinal supplies and the interim years focused on medical practitioners and services. The Strode accounts concentrated on medicinal supplies in the earlier years, the later years being largely based on medical practitioner services. So was there any evidence of different patterns of household spending associated with healthcare? We can consider this in several ways. First, was there a connection between the use of physicians and apothecaries? We can look at the relationship between physician/surgeon expenditure and that of all other expenditure on apothecaries. Some early seventeenth-century records suggested that there was link between payments and activities of physicians, surgeons and apothecaries. For example, in the early seventeenth-century Bath household accounts from 1639–55, there were at least fifteen occasions in as many years when the payment of a physician's bill coincided within a month of the payment of an apothecary bill. On some occasions, an apothecary and physician were closely linked, for example in 1643 a payment was made of £3 10s to 'Mr Shelbury Sir Morris Wilyam's apothecary'.[78] However there were also some twenty occasions when an apothecary payment did not coincide with payment of a physician, and it is possible that some of these times were opportunities for the apothecary to act in an extended capacity, providing a medical service rather than just medicines. For example, the 10s given to 'Roger Jeffreys the apothecary the 22 Oct[ober] when he came to my Lord in the night' or when Jeffreys came to give a glister to his lordship several months later in December 1648.[79] There were at least five payments in the Bath accounts to surgeons, mostly for letting blood, but none of these were linked to payments of apothecaries, though they did occur within a month of a physician's payment and so may have been consequent on a physician's advice. In contrast, in the later seventeenth century household accounts there were very few occasions when the apothecary and physician payments appeared to coincide. This accords with the findings of Pirohakul and Wallis in relation to account disputes presented to the Prerogative Court of Canterbury from the 1670s onwards, in which there appeared to be a move away from using a physician and apothecary together.[80] In the Strode account, which includes seventy-six apothecary payments over a twenty-year period, there were only four years in which both apothecary and physician payments were made.[81] In this account it was again the apothecary who appeared to readily take on additional duties such as 'out of hours' calls and bleeding. So, the later seventeenth-century household accounts confirm that more medicines and services were being purchased from apothecaries without necessarily being advised by physicians.

Second, we can consider the relationship between purchases of medicinal supplies and all medical services, not only physicians and surgeons but all other payments for healthcare services. Yearly totals for medicinal supplies and medical services were available for all four households in much of the 1690s. During this period there was a positive correlation between combined categories of spending, suggesting that greater expenditure on medicinal supplies was connected with greater expenditure on medical services. However, when broken down into separate households, there were different patterns evident. Two household accounts, for the Clarke family and Anne Strode, showed a tendency to increase spending on both medicinal supplies and medical services. However, the Clifford household tended to spend far more on medical services than on medicinal supplies, while conversely the Fortescue household spent far less on medical services than medicinal supplies. Given these variations in spending, we cannot presume that greater levels of use of medical practitioners in the later seventeenth century meant less self-help or vice versa. The view that self-help was an alternative to medical practitioners was not readily apparent in these household accounts.

Overall household expenditure on healthcare

How did expenditure on healthcare signify as a proportion of the overall household budget? Some examples show that recorded expenditure on healthcare was a very low proportion of the household account spending in most years. The aristocratic Bath household in Devon was a fairly large enterprise, costing approximately £1,200 per year to support in the first half of the seventeenth century; for example, some thirty-six servants were employed in 1638.[82] Based on the published household accounts, the average total expenditure on medicinal supplies and medical services was just over £31 per year, and this amounted to less than 0.3 per cent of the estimated annual household budget. Also in the earlier part of the seventeenth century, the much smaller merchant Hayne household allocated £3 per fortnight for 'house expences', this being a household with one domestic servant and occasional use of a nursekeeper, or sicknurse, during the confinements of Hayne's wife.[83] Average health-related expenditure in the Hayne household amounted to about 10s per year and, based on a yearly household budget in the region of £80, just over 0.6 per cent of household budget was spent on medicinal supplies.[84] Although healthcare appeared to take up small proportions of both household budgets, the smaller merchant household spent over twice as much on healthcare in proportion to its overall household budget.

Indicative running costs for the later seventeenth-century households in this study were also established. In the aristocratic household of Lord and Lady Clifford there were at least thirteen waged individuals, and expenditure recorded in the steward's accounts between 1693 and 1701 varied from a total of £919 to £2,247, an average household running cost of £1,638 per year.[85] During this period the household account recorded at least £14 per year expenditure on healthcare, representing 0.85 per cent of average annual household costs. Over one-third of all of this health expenditure was paid to physicians over the period from January 1700/1 to May 1702, including a substantial figure of £56 6s 9d to Dr Walrond for his bill. This payment was noted in the account as 'above the constant family expence',[86] suggesting that such sums of money for healthcare were unplanned and regarded as over and above the usual costs of running a household. The substantial costs of physicians attending an illness were certainly the largest part of the Clifford household's spending on healthcare.

Gentry households were also fairly substantial in the seventeenth century in terms of the numbers of people present. Jean Hecht notes the estimate of one writer in 1717 that a large country house gentry family might entail some twenty servants.[87] In the Clarke household in Somerset, there were at least twelve servants in addition to the family in 1696.[88] Their household accounts indicated a total expenditure over 10 years between 1686 and 1696 inclusive of £6,720, giving an average household cost of just over £672 per year. Health-related expenditure identified in the Clarke accounts amounted to an average of £1 12s 6d per year, a proportion of less than 0.3 per cent of the yearly budget, and the highest level of expenditure in any one year amounted to £4 15s. These figures reflect a lack of recorded expenditure on medical practitioners, and the Clarke family likely obtained 'free' advice from family and learned friends. For the Fortescue household, the total household expenditure amounts spent on a yearly basis appeared to be somewhat similar to the Clarke household, and reimbursements recorded between 1699 and 1704 suggest that household costs averaged between £500 and £600 per year.[89] However, considerably more was spent on health since recorded costs in the Fortescue household for health-related care averaged £4 4s per year, close to four times more than the Clarke household, and mostly spent on medicinal supplies. Based on £600 per year for household costs, the proportion of the Fortescue household budget recorded as spent on healthcare averaged 0.7 per cent, over twice that of the Clarke household.

In the accounts of Anne Strode, sample totals of household expenditure for the three years of 1687, 1697 and 1707 gave an estimate of average yearly expenditure of around £75 to meet the needs of Anne Strode and several servants. Her 'household' was really a unit within her brother's larger establishment and most day-to-day costs were met by a regular fixed payment to her brother. Overall the Strode accounts show average spending of around 14s per year on medicinal supplies and medical services. Over 70 per cent of expenditure was on the apothecary and on medical practitioners, in roughly equal amounts, whilst named ingredients and other medical services made up the remaining 30 per cent. On average, Anne spent over 0.9 per cent of her outgoings on healthcare, a greater proportion than all of the other later seventeenth-century households considered here. As was the case for the earlier seventeenth-century accounts, it seems that the smaller household unit was likely to spend proportionately more of their budget on healthcare. Yet altogether, the accounts for the seventeenth-century households suggest that less than 1 per cent of household budgets was devoted to healthcare costs, a comparable proportion between both earlier and later seventeenth-century households.

A closer look at four of the household accounts in the 1690s suggests that more was being spent on healthcare year on year.[90] The size of increases appeared to be proportional to the household budget overall, the greatest increases being in the larger households and the lowest in the smaller spinster household unit. These changes may have been related to the 'life cycle' as the family 'aged' in the sense of increasing numbers of children and/or older people, and the family households typically growing more than that of spinsters. The named beneficiaries of healthcare-related expenditure are further explored in Chapter 6. It is not straightforward to identify a single explanation for increased spending on health-related matters. Pirohakul and Wallis claim in their analysis of medical debts from 1660 to 1800 that health expenditure was not significant as it amounted to less than 5 per cent of household resources in 80 per cent of cases, and they further argue that medical choices were based on preferences rather than wealth.[91] However, their analysis is focused on medical practitioners (five groupings which included physician, surgeon, apothecary, nurse or attendant, others including chemists and druggists) and does not appear to distinguish between medicinal supplies and medical services.[92] In the records drawing on unpublished household accounts which have been discussed here, differences in use of medicinal supplies and medical services *were* apparent between households even though the levels of recorded health-related expenditure consistently appeared to be less than 1 per cent of household budget.

Thinking about consumption and how household healthcare expenditure developed into the eighteenth century, we can compare the published accounts of Richard Latham (1699–1767), a Lancashire-based small-scale yeoman farmer and tradesman whose household expenditure totalled between £20 and £40 per year.[93] Within the Latham household accounts, there were frequent purchases of medicinal items such as liquorice, quicksilver, brimstone, senna, lead, aloe and vitriol, in addition to purchases of prepared waters (aniseed, Hungary, juniper and wormwood) and spirits of scurvygrass. Some purchased items were listed variously as physic, pills, cordial, salve and 'doctoring stuff' for members of the household, including animals. The Latham household may have had limited facilities for preparation of medicines, but there were many similarities in the purchases of medicines to the larger seventeenth-century households that have been considered in this book. Some years were more costly and in 1748, when their son died, the household accounts recorded a range of medical expenses which totalled over £1 6s, representing about 6 per cent of annual household expenditure. Whilst more studies are needed to thoroughly document household spending on healthcare, the example of the Latham household suggests that medical expenditure in the eighteenth century could demand a greater proportion of the household budget than we have seen in the seventeenth-century households. Indeed, by the middle of the eighteenth century, it was not uncommon to see huge apothecary bills, such as that sent to the Arderne family of Cheshire for the provision of some 570 items including distilled waters, purges, cataplasms and liniments.[94] An indication of the considerable range of commercial medicinal preparations that were available by then can be seen in a list of more than 200 nostrums published in the *Gentleman's Magazine* in the mid-eighteenth century, which were all 'kept a secret for the use of the proprietors, tho' advertised . . . for the benefit of the public'.[95]

Concerns about the costs of healthcare

Estimates made by contemporary commentators in the seventeenth century of the likely costs of healthcare were varied. Some writers described illness as an unpredictable event with households certain to incur expenditure of some kind. Mary Evelyn (c. 1635–1709) gave the following instructions on household management to a married friend in 1677:

> Of the £500 per Ann. (which you tell me is what you would contract your Expences to) and that you are to provide your Husbands Cloaths, Stables, and all other House-Expences (except his Pocket-money) I leave you £20 over, and for your owne Pocket etc £40 (In all £60) and that little enough considering Sickness, Physicians, and innumerable Accidents that are not to be provided against with any certainty.[96]

Mary's figure of up to £60 per year, or 12 per cent of household budget for unexpected costs including medical supplies and services, was relatively high in comparison with the household accounts considered above although, as Mary explained, this amount was supposed to cover other unexpected needs.

In family correspondence and recipes, the possibility of extra costs arising for healthcare was occasionally noted. A letter in the Fortescue papers mentioned the expenditure of 'many pounds', saying, 'I had occasion to speak with a Neighbour of mine who had a daughter which she had spent many pounds upon which had the Evill break out upon her in severall places'.[97] The high cost of some imported items due to taxation was also noted. A letter to Mary Clarke from Mrs Levens referred to 'the extraordinary dearness of sugar and spice' and claimed she had 'no thoughts of lying inn this winter now caudle is chargeable'.[98] Some writers explained how they had avoided extra expense by omitting or replacing ingredients in medicines. For example, a recipe for Gascoign's powder in one of the Clifford recipe collections incorporated a note to say that the expensive ingredient of beazor stone powder could be left out although an expensive ingredient of viper origin was still needed, as the writer explained that it would be sufficient 'to make a Gelly of vipers Skins and hartshorne which I find doth very well'.[99] Preparations based on vipers were noted as costly items, as Samuel Jeake recorded in his seventeenth-century diary that brandy was cheaper and 'much more speedy and effectual' than 'Volatile Salt of Vipers' when self-treating for a toothache and swelling in his jaw.[100] Despite the costs of some prepared compound medicines, a letter from London, written in 1688 to Richard Coffin (1622–98) in Devon, told of an apothecary who claimed that 'the panacea or generall remedy amongst the ordinary sort of people is a pennyworth of Venice Treacle in a Gill of Canary'.[101] It seems that there was ongoing interest in such costly prepared medicinal items amongst a wide range of people. This is consistent with Wallis's findings that imports of drugs increased so much in the seventeenth century that consumption of drugs must have extended far beyond the wealthy elite.[102]

Although there might be widespread willingness to pay for some prepared medicines, there were contemporary concerns expressed about the cost of apothecaries and physicians. Gregory King (1648–1712) thought the 'average' seventeenth-century person had four serious illnesses, and that the nation spent nearly £250,000 per year on health, of which 61 per cent was on apothecaries and 17 per cent on doctors and quacks, 13 per cent on 'kitchen physick' and 9 per cent on surgeons.[103] The 1688 estimate by King was based on 40,000 'sick persons' which gives a figure of £6 5s expenditure per sick person per year, an amount which exceeds the household account expenditures identified above.[104] The discrepancy might be partly due to under-recording of household expenditure on health, and partly due to increasing costs in the later seventeenth century. These figures suggest that apothecaries were providing considerable medicinal supplies and, probably, some medical services in the later seventeenth century. Apothecaries were thus major beneficiaries of illness; indeed some could make large profits as shown by a sample of inventories of fourteen apothecaries in London with average fortunes of over £2,000.[105] Physicians were also criticized for their interest in extracting money from patients in the seventeenth century. Amanda Herbert notes a recipe in Elizabeth Digby's collection, dated 1650, for 'winde in the Stomacke' which included the words 'this being knowne will breed health, and hinder gaine to the Phisitian'.[106] Lady Mary Chudleigh (1656–1710) wrote of 'Physicians with hard Words and haughty Looks/ And promis'd Health, bait their close-covered Hooks/ Like Birds of Prey, while they your Gold can scent'.[107] The promise of some printed texts containing recipes was that expensive physicians were no longer needed: for instance, Read's *Most Excellent and Approved Medicines* claimed 'Thou needest not Waste thy Estate, or spend all thou has upon Physicians'.[108]

Concerns about costs extended to questions about the quality of supplies. Imported goods carried high values although many imports, such as rhubarb, might have spent weeks or months in unprotected conditions leading to considerable spoilage.[109] Adulteration of costly goods was a recognized problem, and John Houghton (1645–1705), in his weekly newsletter from London, *A Collection For the Improvement of Husbandry and Trade,* noted of bezoar imported from India in 1694 that 'lately it has been sold for almost five pound the ounce' and for this reason was 'counterfeited and made up with powders, rosin and mucilage'.[110] Edward Herbert (1583–1648) recommended in his autobiography that a gentleman should 'know how to make these medicines himself', partly because 'no man can be assured that the said drugs are not rotten, or that they have not lost their natural force and virtue'.[111] The suggestion that people should make their own medicines did not necessarily prevent the supply of old or rotten ingredients, but perhaps such deficiencies were more easily covered up in compound preparations which were available for purchase.

Apothecaries were not the only suppliers of medicinal items to attract criticism for supplying adulterated or spoiled medicinal items. Herb women appeared to be a particular target for suspicion as to the authenticity and quality of their items for sale. Burnby reports the comment of Thomas Johnson (c. 1600–44) in *Journeys in Kent and Hampstead* (1632), 'For the doctor relies on the druggists and the druggists on a greedy and dirty old woman with the audacity and capacity to impose anything on him'.[112] Arguments for better recognition of medicinal plants contributed to the establishment of botanic or physic gardens where plant identification could be practised. In 1670, Christopher Merret (1614–95), a well-established physician and member of the Royal Society, claimed that every student of medicine should spend time as 'Scholar to the Gardener of the Physick Garden' in order to learn features of plants and prevent themselves 'being outwitted by the Herb-women in the Markets'.[113] This statement suggests that native plant supplies were often obtained though markets from women herb gatherers, and such supplies are further considered in Chapter 4. A few studies have helped to clarify the particular nature of pedlars, itinerant and theatrical mountebanks in the supply of medicinal goods.[114] But Steven King notes a shortage of 'systematic regional studies of the medical marketplace or patient strategies', and his study of eighteenth-century drugs in Lancashire and Northamptonshire identifies a complex mixture of suppliers linked to transport routes and personal supplies provided by medical personnel over considerable distances.[115]

The household accounts do not always provide extensive detail of what the apothecaries supplied. Thus, we cannot know if some of these households did attempt to maintain stocks of certain purchased medicinal items. And items such as medicinal herbs were of little value or did not keep well, so that stocks did not appear in inventories of the deceased.[116] Occasionally, studies have pinpointed individuals with a range of items available for medicinal use, such as Elizabeth Freke in Norfolk who kept various strong waters, including aqua mirabilis, elixir salutis and Hungary water.[117] There were some advisory lists of the kinds of medicaments which a household should consider having available in case of need in the seventeenth century. A 1634 translation of a French physician, Philbert Guibert, gave a lengthy list which was recommended for wealthier households, with over seventy items, of which thirty-eight were prepared items (see Figure 3.2).[118] This advisory list contained a large number of items which would have had to be purchased at the apothecary, although Guibert preferred to encourage patients to prepare their own remedies under a physician's direction.[119] The list offered by Guibert pales into insignificance when set against the 270 or more items recommended by John Woodall (1556?–1643) in the 1617 publication of *The Surgeon's Mate*, with advice intended for sea voyages.[120] Evidence of such an extensive range of purchases was not readily available in the household accounts, but the idea of a set of medicinal items being available in the household did develop further in the eighteenth century with the introduction of medicine chests which were commercially available and increasingly popular.[121]

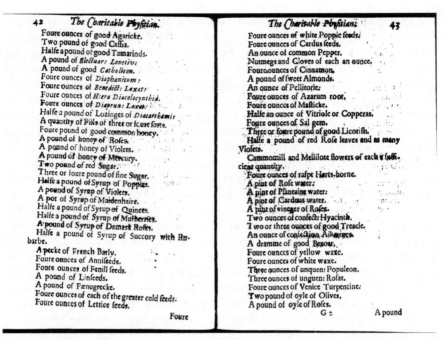

FIGURE 3.2 *List of medicaments from Philbert Guibert,* The Charitable Physician with the Charitable Apothecary *(London: Thomas Harper, 1639), pp. 42–3 (courtesy of Proquest/ Early English Books Online).*

Conclusion

Household accounts provide much detail of health-related spending on both medicinal supplies and medical services. Based on the seventeenth-century household accounts seen in this study, it appears that there were some medicinal preparations which were favourites in households and made on a repeated basis, sometimes in quantity, such as an ointment in the Fortescue household and flower water made by Anne Strode. Many prepared medicinal supplies were also purchased by the seventeenth-century households in smaller quantities, suggesting that they were used as needed rather than kept in stock. In some households the accounts suggest increasing reliance on apothecary purchases, and show less detail of individual items. The costs of visits of medical practitioners and midwives were high in comparison to the costs of medicinal supplies, while other less costly medical services included tending and nursing for serious outbreaks of illness, such as smallpox. There was variation between the households in the balance of expenditure on medicinal supplies and medical practitioners, suggesting different styles of healthcare and more or less self-help elements. The aristocratic Clifford family accounts indicated that considerable sums were spent on medicinal supplies and medical services, as was the case in the smaller household of Anne Strode. The gentry Clarke household bought many prepared items and made extensive use of 'free' learned medical advice through their connections with John Locke and London friends. The Fortescue household also appeared to rely more on the apothecary than the physician, and they spent considerably more on medicinal ingredients than the Clarke household. Not explored here were the longer-term impacts or ensuing costs of illness or accident in terms of loss of labour, disrupted production and impact on the rest of the household. There is no doubt that the immediate costs of healthcare in illness or accident would have been devastating for lower status households such as those of labourers and the poor.

This exploration of household healthcare expenditure has demonstrated that there were significant purchases of medicinal supplies, including prepared medicines, in addition to medical services from the early seventeenth century onwards. Although the proportion of household budget spent on healthcare tended to increase as size of household decreased, overall expenditure recorded on health remained at less than 1 per cent in all of the household accounts considered. There was variation in how much self-help was employed and these households did not consistently show that greater use of self-help was accompanied by a reduction or increase in use of medical practitioners. In relation to the eighteenth century, Porter and Porter have argued that medical self-help and consumerism did not compete against each other; rather that they proved 'mutually reinforcing',[122] and the increased purchasing of medicines could be viewed as part of an overall surge in demand for material goods.[123] Although there seemed to be room for further spending in the seventeenth-century households, there was some evidence of concerns about the unpredictable costs of medical services and the quality of medicinal supplies.

4

Animal, Vegetable and Mineral: Medicinal Ingredients

This chapter focuses on the medicinal ingredients, or materia medica, in both household and printed recipes. The range of ingredients indicated in recipes was wide, from animal to mineral and vegetable items, and the sourcing of medicinal ingredients is considered in terms of suppliers. Many ingredients were imported and had to be purchased from the apothecary, while native plants could be grown or gathered from the wild (foods as recipe ingredients are further considered in Chapter 5). Although native plants might have been expected to be free to collect, there could be costs associated with the labour of 'gathering' native plants, as well as problems with plant identification. Preferences are discussed in this chapter for different kinds of medicinal recipe ingredients. Popular ingredients in recipes included spices and more exotic items and, as we shall see, there were variations in preferences for medicinal recipe ingredients which may have been related to gender and status. During the seventeenth century there was debate about the use of exotic or native plants, and some increase in interest in simples. Finally, purchases of combinations of medicinal items in the household accounts are explored to see if they were intended for making recipes, and it seems that they could reflect self-help or be the result of medical practitioner advice. Overall, this chapter shows that sourcing of medicinal items was not always a straightforward matter for seventeenth-century households and evidence for use of recipes is not always easy to identify.

Ingredients in the medicinal recipe collections were analysed, and from a grand total of 34,864 named ingredients listed in 6,352 recipes (averaging between five and six ingredients per recipe), the vast majority were found to be of plant origin (27,311 or 78 per cent). There were also many animal and mineral ingredients, representing 12 per cent and 7 per cent of the total respectively, while the remaining 3 per cent of ingredients were either compound items or not readily identifiable.[1] Frequent sources of animal ingredients included bees (honey and wax), chickens (eggs), cattle (milk, ox gall), deer (antler), pigs (grease), sheep (dung, suet, tallow), snails, swallows, woodlice and worms but sought after rarer items included ambergris, bezoar stone and spermaceti.[2] Mineral ingredient sources ranged from everyday items such as alum and brimstone to valuable gemstones, gold and silver and imported mineral-like materials such as coral and powdered earths.[3] A substantial proportion of the recipe ingredients (25 per cent) were 'prepared' in some way, such as conserves, cooked items, juices, oils, syrups or waters. Occasionally, recipe ingredients were deemed magical, such as in a recipe with a title or text including mention of a charm or spell, and there were fifteen recipes of this kind in the collections studied. One example, 'Another [recipe] for the bleeding of a wound', briefly stated 'Write these four letters, *AOGL* with the blood of the wound, about the wound', while another recipe described an amulet against ague.[4] Tanya Pollard explains a spell is 'a set of words, a formula or verse, supposed to possess occult or magical powers; a charm or incantation'.[5] Apart from plants, the ingredients in magical recipes were varied, from animal-like elements of afterbirth, blood, swallows and urine, to mineral-like elements of amber and ashes. Thus in a magical recipe, although these ingredients might be animal, mineral or vegetable in nature, they were also, like the words of a spell, imbued with symbolic meaning and power. These overtly magical items were few in number compared to the overall body of recipes, but this should not be taken to mean that powerful symbolic attributes were unrecognized for other recipe ingredients. These examples serve to remind us that the boundaries between magic and science were not always readily distinguishable in the seventeenth century; indeed most of these recipes for charms or spells were found in the recipe collections associated with the latter half of the seventeenth century, particularly the printed collections with learned associations.[6] As we shall see later in this chapter, there was ongoing interest in the seventeenth century in medicines which claimed to contain powerfully acting ingredients.

For the further analysis of the ingredients used in the household manuscript and printed book recipes, a source species was identified for every ingredient. Altogether there were 4,107 different ingredients which could be linked to 954 source species, including 576 different plant species, and different parts of a plant were all grouped together under the same source species name.[7] Thus a range of different preparations based on both elderberries and elderflowers (Figure 4.1) were all combined as one source species of 'elder'. Many plants were identified by a single name, but there were 122 plants with more than one name, some having numerous alternative names: for example, coltsfoot was indicated by the names elfer hoof, foalfoot, leave foote, turnsole and turnfol. In total there were fifteen plants like coltsfoot which were listed by as many as four or more alternative names.[8] These plants were bindweed, catmint, dock, dodder, hawthorn, herb robert, holly, horseradish, knapweed, meadowsweet, mullein, nightshade, pennywort, plantain and turnip.

FIGURE 4.1 *Elderflowers (*Sambucus nigra*) (photograph by author).*

Knowledge of medicinal plants

Knowledge of many medicinal plants may have been passed on orally as part of traditional uses, customs and beliefs, although modern researchers have pointed out difficulties with identification of reliable records, particularly in relation to women.[9] A comprehensive survey by David Allen and Gabrielle Hatfield critically reviews folklore sources for evidence of around 200 plants used medicinally in England, Wales, Scotland and Ireland, finding that some common native plants have had long-standing use for medicinal purposes, although the uses can be verified only for a particular region due to incomplete records.[10] In addition to oral transmission, knowledge of plants was passed on in written medieval sources, some of which have been translated and evaluated.[11] Classical medical knowledge, derived largely from Greek and Roman writers including Dioscorides, Galen and Theophrastus, was also conveyed through repeated translations into Arabic and back into Latin, and these texts were sought after for learned instruction in scholastic contexts.[12] These texts included detailed plant lists that identified primary qualities of heating or cooling, and secondary qualities of drying and moistening, and the strength of these qualities was described in various degrees. However, views of the qualities and virtues of particular plants were subject to ongoing debate, and some scholars claimed that translations of classical texts had introduced errors.[13] While early published herbals drew predominantly on translations of European sources such as Gerard's *Herball*, some authors – including John Parkinson and William Turner – took great pains to collate more accurate details from direct observation and experience.[14] Printed herbals were very costly, and printed information about plants was limited in availability until the latter half of the seventeenth century when many more advice books arrived on the market, including the popular publications of Nicholas Culpeper.[15]

Although gentlewomen were widely expected to have some knowledge of the medicinal virtues of plants,[16] gentlemen were also advised to learn about 'herbs and plants': for instance, Edward Herbert (1583–1648), 1st Lord of Cherbury, wrote that it would gain much credit for 'a gentleman to have some knowledge in medicine' and 'to be a good botanic, that so he may know the nature of all herbs and plants, being our fellow-creatures, and made for the use of man'.[17] Some plant knowledge may have been regarded as less worthy, and Laroche notes that the word 'simples' was removed by John Parkinson in the title of *Theatrum Botanicum* (previously the 'Garden of Simples').[18] Physicians were criticized for their ignorance of simples by William Coles (1626–62), for leaving such 'small matters' to apothecaries, and being overly reliant on the 'words of the silly Hearb-women'.[19] Coles wrote at length of the importance of knowledge of the main qualities of medicinal plant simples, and he listed detailed 'signatures' by which such plants might be recognized.[20] Further widespread interest in the medicinal uses of plants prompted publishers to profit from books about herbs, and some aimed to attract an audience of women with titles such as *The Ladies Dispensatory* (1652), a book which claimed to provide 'an alphabeticall table of all the vertues of each herb and simple'.[21] Thus, plants which could be used for medicinal purposes appeared to have a rather mixed standing in the seventeenth century, from associations with sources of low status to virtues drawn from classical and learned sources. The question of how people viewed plants and expressed preferences for native or imported remedies is further discussed in the latter part of this chapter. Before that, however, we will look in more detail at the sourcing of medicinal ingredients for making up recipes in the Recipes and Expenditure Database.

Sourcing medicinal ingredients

Medicinal recipe ingredients could be obtained from a variety of sources: from the apothecary to the household and the wild. Some of the medicinal ingredients were most likely purchased from a household supplier other than an apothecary, or even made at home. For example, soap was an ingredient in forty-seven recipes although sometimes specified as black soap, which was an inferior kind of soap compared to soft or white versions.[22] These recipes were mainly for plasters and, for example, the *Choice Manuall* provided three recipes containing black soap, including:

For an ach in any Joynt

Take clarified Butter a quarter of a pound, of Cummin one pound, Black Sope a quarter of a pound, one handful of Rue, Sheeps suet [ounces] ii. Bay Salt one spoonful, bray these together, then fry them with the gall of an Oxe, spread it on a Plaister, and lay it on as hot as you can, and let it lye seven dayes.[23]

Black soap also featured in plasters for a thorn, felon, prick or wen, mixed with other household items such as lime.[24] Many variations of this type of plaster could be found in the household recipes, and were largely preparations for drawing out splinters, soothing irritated, itchy and inflamed skin or small wounds. Other household items that were commonly found in medicinal recipes included alum, an important dye ingredient which was present in 203 medicinal recipes, and turpentine, an oily resin found in 284 recipes. Although many recipes did require additional purchased ingredients, some recipes could be made entirely from plants that might have been available locally. Amongst the repeated recipes in the Clifford recipe books that we saw in Chapter 2 was an example of such a remedy made from herbs which could be readily found or grown in the garden.[25] However, most recipes required ingredients from a variety of sources including the garden, household, kitchen, apothecary or wild.[26] Overall, in the seventeenth century recipes analysed for this study, there was potential for sourcing almost 27 per cent of recipe ingredients from the garden, with the remaining ingredients split between household (3.7 per cent), kitchen (13.3 per cent), apothecary (38.4 per cent) and the wild (16.9 per cent) (Table 4.1(a)). Other sources for ingredients (0.8 per cent) were either not readily identifiable or were obtained in a specific location such as at the tanner or blacksmith who could provide things like tanner's 'ouze' derived from leather tanning, or smith's 'water' used in quenching hot metal.[27] The ingredient sources can be split according to whether recipes were associated with the first and second half of the seventeenth century,[28] and this analysis suggests that there was a slight decrease in numbers of kitchen and household ingredients, whilst the proportion of garden ingredients remained much the same. With regard to ingredients gathered in the wild, these were more likely to appear in the recipes of the latter half of the seventeenth century, as were purchased ingredients from the apothecary. If the sources of ingredients are compared only for recipes from named contributors then further differences are evident, the proportion of purchased ingredients (Table 4.1(b)) rising to almost 42 per cent in the latter half of the seventeenth century.

For recipes with named contributors, the proportions of purchased and wild ingredients were greater, while the proportions of kitchen, garden and

TABLE 4.1 *Medicinal recipe ingredient sources*

(a) from all recipes (n=6,513).

	Ingredient sources												
	Garden		Household		Kitchen		Other		Purchase		Wild		All	
Time period	n	%	n	%	n	%	n	%	n	%	n	%	n	%
Before 1650	4,223	26.9	673	4.3	2,280	14.5	149	0.9	5,893	37.5	2,489	15.8	15,707	100.0
1650 and after	5,149	26.9	632	3.3	2,374	12.4	124	0.6	7,490	39.1	3,388	17.7	19,157	100.0
All periods	9,372	26.9	1,305	3.7	4,654	13.3	273	0.8	13,383	38.4	5,877	16.9	34,864	100.0

(b) from recipes with named contributors (n=881).

	Ingredient sources												
	Garden		Household		Kitchen		Other		Purchase		Wild		All	
Time period	n	%	n	%	n	%	n	%	n	%	n	%	n	%
Before 1650	685	25.8	93	3.5	299	11.3	31	1.2	1,049	39.6	493	18.6	2,650	100.0
1650 and after	909	25.2	88	2.4	353	9.8	26	0.7	1,572	43.6	659	18.3	3,607	100.0
All periods	1,594	25.5	181	2.9	652	10.4	57	0.9	2,621	41.9	1,152	18.4	6,257	100.0

Source: Stobart, Recipes and Expenditure Database.

household ingredients decreased. These changes were not dramatic, but when the named contributors are further divided between men and women, it becomes clearer that the increase in ingredients requiring purchase appeared mainly in male-contributed recipes, with purchased ingredients rising as high as 45 per cent of all ingredients, while the increase in wild-derived ingredients was found largely in female-contributed recipes. Such a finding might suggest that women had a preference for recipes and ingredients that could be sourced from the household and garden. However, a difference entirely based on gender should not be assumed, since these findings may be partly due to status; many of the male contributors were medical practitioners and therefore likely to have promoted items available at the apothecary.

Many of the medicinal recipe ingredients involved a purchase, and the household accounts can be used to estimate typical costs of particular medicinal items, from prepared remedies to individual recipe ingredients. Such estimates may be more realistic than valuations based on shop inventories which tended to give wholesale prices rather than retail prices, or personal inventories which showed differences in valuations that were based on the status of the deceased.[29] Retail prices can be considered more directly by looking at the household accounts for entries which recorded both price and quantity. Appendix 2 shows average prices in pence for ingredients based on units of quantity derived from such entries in the seventeenth-century household accounts. The household accounts show that some expensive medicinal items were purchased in very small quantities which were measured in grains or drachms (equivalent to 0.05 g and 3.54 g respectively). Occasionally the average costs were distorted by added costs for vessels such as bottles, or additional transport costs; sometimes different prices were charged in London or other places.

Many imported spices had medicinal uses and prices were variable during the seventeenth century. The Bath household in the 1640s and 1650s paid from 36d to 43d per pound for green ginger, while the cost of ginger in the last twenty years of the century ranged from 8d to 12d and reached a high in 1700 of 20d per pound. In the 1690s cinnamon cost from 96d to 108d per pound, while cloves cost from 8d to 14d per pound. Mace increased in cost from 12d to 20d per ounce from 1685 to 1695, and nutmegs rose from 6d to 18d per ounce by 1701. Newer and fashionable introductions could be very costly, and coffee cost 96d per pound in 1693 while chocolate cost 48d per pound in 1700. Other medicinal items that were imported also varied in price: for example, in the 1630s and 1640s the Hayne household paid 16d per pound for china root, while the Bath household paid 18d per pound for cassia. Rhubarb was usually imported and purchased in quantities of less than an ounce, costing between 32d and 60d per pound in the 1690s.[30] Rose-based preparations were often based on imported supplies. Conserve of red roses cost 36d per pound and conserve of rosemary 60d per pound, these prices possibly reflecting the high costs of sugar in the earlier seventeenth century. The prices of some sugary medicinal preparations appeared to reduce in the 1680s to 1690s, although syrup of roses could still cost from 1½d to 3d per ounce. Other ingredients for making up medicinal preparations could be expensive. For hartshorn, the Clarke family paid the equivalent of 48d per pound in 1691 and the Clifford family paid 36d per pound in 1694. Turpentine cost 18d per pound in 1693. Mineral-like ingredients varied, between 4d and 5d per pound for verdigris in 1693, 4d to 6d per pound for red or white lead, 14d per pound for lapis calaminaris, and 48d per pound for bole armeniac in 1695. Other household items were generally lower in cost, such as resin costing from 2d to 7d per pound, black soap 8d per pound, brimstone from 6d to 15d per pound, allum 4d a pound, saltpetre 12d a pound, and tar at 14d per pitcher. For native plants, purchase quantities were rarely listed in sufficient detail to identify unit costs, although they were sometimes listed as handfuls for a few pence.

During the seventeenth century there were some additional costs to bear due to taxes, particularly customs duties paid on imported spices, tobacco, spirits and wine. Inland taxes, or excise, were introduced from 1643 on beer, wine and tobacco and on various commodities made or grown in England including strong waters.[31] Homemade strong water or aqua vitae was charged at 1d per gallon and, if imported, the rate was 4d per gallon (in addition to customs duties). Further revenues were raised in the later seventeenth century on coffee, spices, sugar and tea, although considerable efforts were made to avoid payments of dues through smuggling both by merchant companies and individuals.[32] Comparison with prices per pound from London druggists, as shown in Gideon Harvey's (1636?–1702) *Family-Physician*, suggests that slightly higher prices were recorded in the household accounts.[33] However, comparison is not straightforward as many of the purchases in the household accounts were for relatively small quantities. Wallis has argued, using port books and customs records as evidence, that there was a considerable increase in imports of exotic medicinal items in the latter half of the seventeenth century although strong demand meant that prices remained buoyant.[34] The household accounts seen for this book suggest that although some exotic and culinary items did tend to reduce in cost over the seventeenth century, many medicinal items and spices maintained a high price or even increased in cost at the end of the century. Purchases made in larger or smaller quantities did not appear to reliably alter costs, and perhaps there was little incentive to purchase larger quantities or stocks if keeping qualities were not always reliable.

During the period of our study, London was a major centre for consumption of medicinal supplies, with clusters of well-appointed apothecary shops.[35] The Port of London received a great variety of goods in the seventeenth century, and the Book of Rates of the Customs House listed some 1,400 imported commodities, of which nearly 300 were medicinal items.[36] Most of the families considered in this book had frequent contact with colleagues and friends in London. For instance, Anne Strode regularly sent gifts of produce, including cakes and pots of butter.[37] She also travelled to London herself on a number of occasions since payments were made for the carriage of her trunk, bed and glassware, and she had supplies brought from the capital, such as a box of peaches, chocolate and oil.[38] Medical services were thought to be readily available in London, and some considered that these were of a superior nature. Long-distance supplies from and to London were also commonplace for the Clarke family. For example, a letter dated 13 June 1696 from Edward to Mary mentions a hamper from London with '11 bottles of such anniseed water as I used to buy formerly' plus a bottle of 'double annyseed water' and a bottle of 'aqua mirabilis'.[39] Mary visited apothecaries when in London and, after several stays there, particularly those of 1691–93 and 1697–99, few local apothecary purchases appear in the Clarke household accounts in Somerset. Thus a lack of recorded purchases may have been due to medicinal supplies carried over from London visits.[40] As Katharine Park points out, many medicines could be sourced from the countryside, so that urban and rural areas were not necessarily isolated in terms of healthcare.[41] Outside of London, physicians, apothecaries and other medical practitioners were readily available and increasingly formed a 'sizeable community' in major towns.[42] Imported medicinal supplies also became more widely available in the regions through towns and, for instance, detailed apothecary inventories show at least two-thirds of the medicinal supplies purchased by Sarah Fell of Swarthmore Hall in 1673 could have been obtained locally in Lancashire.[43]

Gathering medicinal plants for free?

It might be thought that many of the plants needed for medicinal recipes could be grown in the garden, or readily harvested from the fields or hedgerows. In a 1679 printed almanac, the entry for May stated: 'Now every Garden and Hedge affords thee Food and Physick; Rise early . . . Clarified Whay with Sage. Scurvy-Grass Ale and Worm-wood Beer are wholsome Drinks'.[44] However, the presumption that growing herbs or gathering from the wild might provide a ready and 'free' source needs to be carefully examined. Some of the household account entries show that plants from the fields were gathered to be sold direct. Purchases made by the Clarke household suggest medicinal items were purchased from individuals who came to the house. The Clarke household accounts for July 1685 show an entry for 'Centrey and Poppyes' at a cost of 2s 1d.[45] Centrey (centaury) and poppies were bought in several years in June or July when supplies of fresh plants could have been available: for example, an entry in 1700 records 'To a poore woman for popyes, 4d'.[46] Another payment in 1700 was to 'Goody Carpenter for Egremony [agrimony], 4d'.[47] However, not all entries for gathered plants matched the period when they should have been available fresh and this suggests that there were also purchases of dried herbs. For instance, in 1689, handfuls of elderflowers were purchased in December and

January, when these items could not have been in season: 'Pd for 4 handfulls of elder flowers, 6d'.[48] Such purchases of dried herbs might have been made from a herb woman rather than an apothecary. Amanda Herbert cites a recipe for a 'wound drinke' made with fresh herbs in Mrs Carr's recipe book dated 1682 which advised 'if you have occasion to use this drinke in winter you may buy the herbs ready dried of the herbwoman all winter long'.[49]

The Clifford family also recorded purchases of items collected by individuals, and some of these payments were for herbs and flowers that could have been grown in a substantial garden or field: for example, large quantities of gillyflowers costing 2s and angelica costing 1s.[50] Other items were probably collected in the wild, such as the broom buds picked in March 1696 by 'nurse Hollett' for a shilling.[51] These records show relatively large payments of a shilling or more which may have reflected the standing of the individuals involved rather than the quantities collected. Some plant supplies were bought in significant quantities by Anne Strode. In the earlier years of her accounts, there were payments for 'gathering of herbs' bought in quantity: for instance, in 1680 'one thousand of clove gillyflowers' was purchased for 2s.[52] As well as this, poppies, cherries, fennel, pennyroyal and elderberries were collected and the gathering of such items was repeated over a number of years.[53] On some occasions purchases were noted as specifically for making a water, such as in August 1688 when 'spices saffron and figs for the blossom water' cost 2s 9d.[54] Thus, the gathering of herbs took time and effort and might well involve a cost, either in the sense of payment for someone's labour, or a gift to a poor and deserving person, or a gratuity for the favour of bringing a gift. Some of the above entries recorded payments to individuals associated with the households, possibly a recognition that the gathering of plants was not always considered part of usual duties. Thus, we may not assume that garden or wild medicinal plants were always available to households without cost. Further payments in the household accounts were for plants that were available through cultivation or gathering in fields and woods, including broom, buckthorn, dodder, elder, elecampane, fennel, melilot and violets. These purchases are not all easily interpreted as they could have been for items which were usually gathered by household members but were out of season or of which existing stocks had run out. The main point to appreciate here is that gathering was not always free as it often involved consideration of the labour involved.

One way to secure medicinal plant supplies could have been to grow them oneself in the garden. Printed advice books gave details for culinary herbs, such as the 1631 edition of the *English House-Wife*, which included the sowing, cultivating, harvesting and drying of herbs.[55] This advice claimed to provide 'Knowledge of all sortes of hearbes belonging unto the Kitchin, whether they be for the Pot, for Sallets, for Sauces, for Servings, or for any other Seasoning, or adorning'. However, rather than providing detailed instructions to the housewife on growing these herbs, it was stated that this 'skill of Knowledge of the Hearbes, shee must get by her owne true labour and experience'.[56] Thus there was little detail beyond a list of which months the herbs were to be sown in, and some general suggestions.[57] Other publications were similarly lacking in detail: in *Natura Exenterata*, garden advice was included in a section entitled 'Certain Secrets of Hearbs not Commonly to be found in any Common Herbal', which gave a brief description of the uses of some fourteen plants including colewort and onion.[58] Other costly works, such as Gerard's *Herball* and Parkinson's *Paradisi in Sole*, catered for the wealthy elite, and it is not surprising that publication of cheaper popular gardening manuals increased in the seventeenth century.[59] There was more help in 1664 from books such as *The Compleat Gardeners Practice*, in which Stephen Blake offered a listing of 'Plants either for food, physick or pleasure' with some details of means of propagation.[60] Further studies of garden history are needed to address some of the practical issues that were involved in establishing and maintaining a source of medicinal plants. As Malcolm Thick notes, there is a paucity of evidence on how plants were sourced and more research is needed on the practicalities of early modern gardening.[61]

Recognizing plants

Successful gathering of plants from the field, hedgerow or woods presupposed that the required plants were readily identifiable by the collector. However, details of how to recognize wild herbs also tended to be minimal in the printed recipe books. Some all-purpose advice on gathering plants was included in *Natura Exenterata*: 'From the 25 of March till Midsomer the leaves and flowers are in Season: from Midsomer till Michaelmas the Crops and Herbs are in Season: and from St Andrews to the 25 of March the roots of Herbs are in force'.[62] One surviving handwritten example of interest in gathering medicinal plants is Margaret Boscawen's 'plant notebook', a small twelve-page booklet with notes about plants including flowers, roots and seeds to be gathered, saved, dried and distilled.[63] Brief details of many plants were entered in the notebook, mainly drawn from Culpeper's *English Physitian Enlarged*.[64] Many of the notes related to trees and plants which could be found in the countryside, such as agrimony and eyebright, whilst other notes related to plants which might be readily grown in the garden, such as succory and sorrel.[65] Written in Margaret's hand, there were also notes recorded in her 'large book' of recipes with distinguishing characteristics of wild plants, including several types of agrimony.[66] A clear distinction was made by Margaret between the common agrimony (*Agrimonia eupatoria*) and water agrimony (either *Bidens tripartita* or *Eupatorium cannabinum*).[67] These unrelated plants were both listed as ingredients in medicinal recipes, having a reputation for curing liver complaints.[68] The two plants appeared in Culpeper's *English Physitian Enlarged*,[69] and it seems that Margaret made detailed notes from this printed book over a lengthy period. Her notes were highly selective, and she did not include many details available in the printed book regarding the virtues of each plant. This effort to record descriptive details and avoid confusing plants with similar names suggests that recognition of plants was particularly important for Margaret. In her plant notebook, Margaret also listed some plants which she did not have, and she particularly noted that she should send to London for items such as horseradish root, gentian root, citron rinde and the bark of the black alder tree.[70] Some of these items could have been grown in the garden or found locally in the countryside, but Margaret seemed to rely on the information provided by Culpeper. For example, the details that she would have located about the black alder in the *English Physitian Enlarged* stated that it was to be found 'in St John's Wood, by Hornsey, and the woods on Hampstead-heath; as also in a wood called Old Park in Barscomb, Essex, near the brook's side'.[71] Hence Margaret decided to send for the 'barke of the blacke alder tree' from London, possibly being unaware that the same small native tree could be widely found in her own locality and indeed across the rest of England.[72] Bearing in mind the points above about London supplies, it is also possible that Margaret knew that the black alder bark was available locally but deemed that a London source would be preferable, based on the details supplied in Culpeper's publication. Drawing from this example of an educated gentlewoman of high status, it seems that interest in medicinal plants could extend beyond their qualities to details of how to recognize and obtain them, and knowledge of some plants could be heavily dependent on the printed sources that were readily accessible.

Preferences in medicinal ingredients

How did people view medicinal recipe ingredients and did they have any preferences? The twenty most frequent plant ingredients occurring in all of the medicinal recipes are shown in Table 4.2. It can be seen that plants of Mediterranean (rosemary and sage) and exotic (cinnamon and nutmeg) origin were frequently found ingredients. These were not native plants to England, although plants such as rosemary and sage could be cultivated in gardens.[73] Some of the most frequently mentioned plant species were found in many different forms or preparations: for example, rose could be found as cake, conserve, honey, oil, spirit, syrup, vinegar and water. Sometimes rose was further specified as the musk rose, red rose, or white rose, the main species in use being the damask rose which was frequently made into conserve-like purging preparations for purchase from the apothecary.[74]

Likewise, Elaine Leong finds the top ingredients in her study of early modern recipe collections to be rose preparations, sugar and wine which were found in about 3 per cent of entries, whilst honey, egg, milk, vinegar, sage, rosemary, cinnamon, nutmeg, fennel, aniseed, liquorice, cloves and rue

TABLE 4.2 *Top twenty plant ingredients in household medicinal recipes (n=2,909)*

Source species	Frequency, *n*	Frequency, %
Rose	367	2.90
Rosemary	255	2.01
Sage	226	1.78
Liquorice	210	1.66
Aniseed	198	1.56
Nutmeg	195	1.54
Cinnamon	187	1.48
Wormwood	186	1.47
Fennel	179	1.41
Rue	176	1.39
Ale	175	1.38
Borage	160	1.26
Chamomile	152	1.20
Betony	142	1.12
Plantain	136	1.07
Clove	132	1.04
Saffron	132	1.04
Raisin	129	1.02
Mint	122	0.96
Balm	114	0.90
All top 20 plant ingredients	3,573	28.18
All plant ingredients in household recipes	12,677	100.00

Source: Stobart, Recipes and Expenditure Database.

were found in 1–1.5 per cent of entries. Leong suggests that many of these ingredients could be readily obtained in the household or from the garden, although she notes that 43 per cent of all recipe ingredients were pre-prepared in some way, appearing in the form of oils, syrups, waters etc., and thus were more likely to have been purchased.[75]

In Chapter 3 we saw examples of the most frequently recorded purchases of items of possible medicinal use in the later seventeenth-century households of the Clarke, Clifford, Fortescue and Strode families. Apart from regular purchases of sugar and dried fruits, some items did correspond with the more popular plant ingredients in medicinal recipes, such as aniseed, clove, nutmeg, rose and liquorice. Some of these items could be used as simples, usually bought in prepared forms such as comfits or syrups, but they could also have been used in more complex preparations such as distilled waters. Other popular purchases were of exotic fruits such as figs, lemons and oranges, and of other spices such as allspice, ginger and mace. Of course, many of these purchases could also have been for culinary use, and in Chapter 5 the links between foods and medicines are further discussed. The question still remains as to whether popular purchases in the household accounts can confirm whether any of the household recipes were actually used. If some recipes were in use, we might expect to see specific medicinal ingredients in household accounts with repeated purchases or, perhaps, the purchase of a combination of ingredients related to a particular preparation. For example, the household account of the Eyre family of Salisbury showed that Anne Eyre specified purchases of groups of ingredients to make particular remedies:

26 June 1641   Ingredients to make a diet drink, 11d
17 July 1641   Honey to make a salve, 2s 0d and other ingredients, 9s 3d
11 June 1642   For ingredients for a drink against the pox, 6s 6d
1 July 1643   To ingredients to make the green ointment, 4s 0d.[76]

However, like many of the accounting records, the ingredients purchased by Anne Eyre were not always detailed separately. Other examples of grouped purchases of ingredients can be seen in the household accounts of Sarah Fell at Swarthmoor Hall. Repeated purchases were recorded in the 1670s of a set of ingredients to make 'Janes drink', these ingredients being saffron, treacle and turmeric.[77] Although a specific recipe is not possible to identify, many distilled waters for plague and other conditions contained saffron and treacle, and preparations for various types of jaundice often contained saffron and turmeric. The household also bought many other medicinal items including aniseed, cinnamon water, diascordium, hiera picra, jalop, juniper berries, mithridate, turpentine, wormseed and stomach water for the use of various individuals. Apart from 'Janes drink', many of the frequent prepared and combination purchases appeared to be for animal treatments rather than household members, including 'brimstone and quicksilver for some horses', 'sugar candy and alum and white wine for Ri. Ratcliffe's mares eye', 'sugar candy for calves', and 'treakle, anniseeds, diascordium and other things for a cow and a calfe of Mothers'.[78]

Other household accounts were examined for groups of specific ingredient purchases. Such purchases were rarely mentioned in the household accounts of the Clarke family, and most medicinal items in their household accounts were recorded as individual purchases on separate occasions (examples which specified amounts and prices are given in Appendix 1). Occasionally, a group of medicinal items were listed together: for example, in August 1695, a purchase was made of half a pound each of 'rosin 3d', 'lapis calaminaris 7d' and 'bole armanack 2s'.[79] Lapis calaminaris was used as an absorbent item, often in preparations for inflammations of the eyes, and was an ingredient in some versions of the Paracelsian plaster for wounds which appeared in many recipe collections and consisted of various gums, lead, olive oil, turpentine, myrrh and frankincense heated, stirred and kneaded in a lengthy process.[80] Bole armeniac was used as an astringent, especially for bleeding, and also widely used in plasters.[81] There was only one wound recipe in the Clarke household recipe collection containing both lapis calaminaris and bole armeniac:

A salve for an old ulcer

Take of olibanum, Lapis calaminaris, bole armonick, letharge of lead, of each 2 ounces yellow waxe 4 ounces oyle of York 3 ounces disolve the oyle, the wax on a gentle fyer of small coales, or imbers receanting a spoonefull of the oyle, wherein dissolve camp[ho]r in powdred 2 drams. Put it into the oyle and wax thus boyling the former powders, and soe let it boyle with continued stirring untill be of a good forme. It is no matter with every camphor being disolvd, be put in after or before so former be done, but only for a walme that powringe it into water, make it up as the former This is not to be spreade, But fitt itt, to the bignesse of the wound, the thicknesse of an halfe crowne or better, So lay it on a bollster and every day mixe it and furn[ish] the contrary side. When it is dry work it with oyle of Roses, or put on a new Feather.[82]

The purchase of resin, lapis calaminaris and bole armeniac recorded in the household account would have been sufficient to make up the recipe at least four times. So these three items, purchased together, could have been used for treatment of wounds, as in the above recipe. Alternatively these ingredients might have been used in other ways, and the date of purchase, August 1695, was significant since Mary experienced a miscarriage about this time. She wrote to Edward, 'when you have made me with child I am more fretful and impatient at then than at another time',[83] but, sadly, a letter one week later was endorsed 'Mr Clarkes letter I receved a little before I miscarried'.[84] Thus, the purchase of these items at about the same time may have been connected with efforts to deal with a miscarriage, although no recipes were located in the Clarke family recipe book which were specific to miscarriage.

Almost a year later, in June 1696, a further group purchase of medicinal ingredients was made by the Clarke household, mostly purging items listed as 'powder of wormwood, powder of Rhubarb, powder of Corolina, Burnt Hartshorne of each one drachm', a purchase totalling 8d.[85] Within the Clarke recipe collection there was no single recipe containing these three items. Wormwood and rhubarb were regular purchases in the household as purging remedies. Burnt hartshorn was an ingredient in a number of recipes in *Dr. Lowers, and Several Other Eminent Physicians, Receipts* including items for purges, fevers, looseness and one for worms which also included rhubarb and herb corallina.[86] There was one entry for a recipe containing corallina which was on a single sheet inserted into the Clarke recipe collection:

For a woman that cannot be delivered

Take as much corraline in small powder as will lie on a shilling put it in 3 or 4 sponefulls of milke warme from the cowe put upon to a little hony and give fasting for 3 or 4 morneings togeather Let her use to safe some reason of the sunn stoned fasting morneinge give her onse in a mouth on a ounce of syrupe of roses made into a farine this will gently purge phlegme whch is the cause of wekness.[87]

Thus the four items purchased together, may have been used as purging remedies for worms, but they may also have been intended for use in connection with a further miscarriage or difficult pregnancy. However, on further investigation in the archives, it turns out that these purchases were not necessarily intended for Mary's benefit. Within the family correspondence, there is a letter from John Locke, dated 17 May 1695, which advised the putting of 'rhubarb' and 'coralline' into small beer for one of the Clarke's daughters.[88] This was not the first time that the Clarkes had purchased ingredients at Locke's suggestion. The purchase previously mentioned of four handfuls of elderflowers out of season, appears to have been another example based on medical practitioner advice.[89] In December 1689, Locke wrote with advice for the household steward, John Spreat, saying that he should work into four gallons of small ale '1 lb of common dock roots, half lb of dandelion roots, 4 handfulls of elder flowers', and then drink a glass morning, afternoon and night.[90] So the purchase of four handfuls of elderflowers may have been made for the benefit of John Spreat. It is worth noting here that the term 'handfulls' does not necessarily indicate only lay use of the medicinal herb, as the handful was an apothecary measure, *manipulus*, in the sixteenth century.[91] Thus, a number of groups of purchases made in the Clarke household accounts, although possibly significant as medicinal recipe ingredients, were actually related to the recommendations of the family medical adviser rather than to the recipes at hand. Preferences for medicinal recipe ingredients and other medicinal purchases can be identified to some extent through establishing frequent and visible occurrences in recipes and accounts, although these findings are not always readily differentiated as self-help or medical practitioner instructions.

Exotic or native plants?

In the later sixteenth century, wild-gathered native plants were portrayed as superior in Partridge's *Treasurie of Commodious Conceits* (1591), claiming that 'those hearbs that growe in the fieldes are better than those that growe in the Townes and Gardens'.[92] Such plants were promoted as alternatives to imported drugs: for instance, in 1620 the parson-poet George Herbert (1593–1633) wrote that 'for salves the wife seeks not the Citty, but prefers the garden and the fields before all outlandish gums'.[93] Although some payments were recorded in accounts for gathering herbs or purchasing dried plants, the frequency of household purchases tells us little about whether there were any preferences for native plants used for medicinal purposes. Many native plants can be seen in folklore studies of beliefs and practices, based on knowledge of a lengthy or widespread tradition of use which was passed on orally. For comparison with exotic plant ingredients in recipes, a sample of forty native plants was selected from those that had traditional indications for use in more than one part of the British Isles.[94] These native plants could be regarded as having a long-standing tradition of use which was largely independent of classical or learned uses, though they were not exclusive to a folk tradition. If households drew on folklore traditions in their recipe collections then we might expect to see some or all of these plants appearing with greater frequency than average. Overall, these forty native plants accounted for just over 11 per cent of the plant ingredients in the recipes, and twenty-one of them appeared more often than the average of forty-seven occasions. Plantain (1.32 per cent) and betony (1.03 per cent) were the two most frequently occurring native plants, appearing almost as often as the popular culinary and spice ingredients of rosemary, sage, cinnamon and nutmeg seen in Table 4.2. Other frequently occurring native plants of significance were mint, mallow, poppy, comfrey, elder and hart's tongue (Figure 4.2).

Considering the commonly mentioned uses of the most frequently mentioned native plants, it seems that a key role of plant substances in folklore records was for external use to dry up bleeding and other bodily discharges. Plantain may have been especially prominent because it had a dual tradition of use in both folklore and classical sources, and several varieties of plantain were listed in recipes for distilled waters. In folklore sources, plantain was noted as a great 'wound healer' able to stop bleeding and ease rashes, stings and other skin complaints.[95] Within the learned tradition this plant was also 'reckon'd a great Cooler, and stopper of Fluxes, particularly of Blood, whether from the Nose, Mouth or Uterus'.[96] Betony too had a substantial standing in both folklore and classical medicine and was favoured as a distilled water with many uses, being included with other herbs in a number of polypharmaceutical plague and cure-all waters. John Quincy in his *Pharmacopoeia Officinalis* noted that there were a number of possible confusions of betony with other plants, but that it was 'accounted

FIGURE 4.2 *Hart's tongue* (Asplenium scolopendrium) *(photograph by author).*

a great Dryer' especially for 'rheums' and wounds affecting the head.[97] Some other frequently mentioned folklore-related plants had similar astringent actions to plantain and betony, and they were used to dry and dispel unwanted fluids from bleeding of wounds to phlegm. In addition, cooling and soothing properties were shown by some of the more frequently occurring plants, such as mallow, comfrey, coltsfoot and hart's tongue. Quincy noted that mallows of various related species provided 'a very soft mucilaginous Substance' useful for soothing a variety of urinary, respiratory and digestive complaints, and known particularly amongst the 'good Women, with whom it is in esteem for the Gripes in Children'.[98] Folklore use of coltsfoot for soothing coughs and colds has been shown, and coltsfoot was frequently mentioned in recipes for coughs, colds and related conditions.[99]

Although they did feature as ingredients in recipes, some of the native plants were dismissed by later medical authors. For example, hart's tongue was regarded by Quincy as not 'much in use', although Allen and Hatfield note the widespread use in the west of the British Isles of hart's tongue for diverse conditions including coughs, colds and skin eruptions.[100] John Pechey's *Compleat Herbal* (1694) recorded the use of hart's tongue for 'Mother-fits and Convulsions' taken in small beer, posset drink or as a conserve,[101] and this plant also appeared in numerous recipes for the rickets, which may help to explain its frequency in the household recipes compared to the printed recipes. Other native plants appearing in recipes provided a different kind of action, a warming action which was also regarded as helpful to digestion in learned sources. Mint was regarded by Quincy, in all

its varieties, as a 'great Strengthener of the Stomach'.[102] Such use differed
from the folklore sources where, according to Allen and Hatfield, a digestive
use of mint was secondary to its principal use in colds and coughs, while
Pechey noted additional uses, including relief for 'Hardness of the Breasts'
and also the distilled water in use to 'cures the Gripes in Children'.[103] In the
household recipes, mint was widely used in cordial and distilled waters,
these accounting for over a third of its occurrences, but it was also employed
for disorders relating to the head such as melancholy and palsy, as well as
some women's complaints. Thus, the reasons for greater inclusion of native
plants appeared to be varied, ranging from recognition in both folklore and
learned traditions to use for specific ailments amongst women and children.
The least popular native plants in the medicinal recipes, being much under-
represented in recipes with five or fewer mentions overall, included buttercup,
foxglove, lesser celandine and pennywort. These were plants of a notably
acrid or irritant nature, especially buttercup and lesser celandine which
widely figured in folklore records as counter-irritants used as external
preparations in a range of skin conditions.[104] These plants were also
considered insignificant by Quincy, for example lesser celandine was 'hardly
ever used in Medicine'.[105] Overall it seems that the recipe collections did
feature some native plants, and the most favoured native plants were used
both as simples and in compound preparations. Although dismissed by
medical authors, some of the native plants appeared in advice from lay
advisers for use as simples towards the latter half of the seventeenth century,
and elder provides an example. Earlier in the seventeenth century, elder was
widely listed in recipes for burns and sores as well as plague and ague
remedies, and credited with the ability to draw out infection and clear hot
humours. By the later half of the seventeenth century elder was frequently
recommended for the complaint of the King's evil in recipes contributed by
friends and advisers of the Fortescue family[106] to help expel excess corrupted
humours. The reinterpretation of the uses of this plant, the elder, possibly
fitted with humoral understandings of the King's evil complaint, rather than
reflecting newer understandings of disease. The weeping neck sores of the
King's evil patient were thought to be a means that the body used to eliminate
undesirable humours.[107] The recommendations of relatives and friends
which focused on the use of elder draw attention to the ongoing adaptation
of recipes by lay individuals.

Despite perceptions that native plants were more appropriate in some
conditions, there was continuing interest in new and exotic remedies in the
seventeenth century. Exotic items might be first encountered as gifts. The
Clarke family received presents from John Freke (1652–1717) in London;
for instance, he sent a gift of chocolate in December 1695. Edward wrote
with the instructions for using the chocolate:

Mr Freke's way of making Jocalett is this, Hee allowes two ounces of
Jocalett to a Quart of the best and softest water and putts the Jocalette

when scraped or cut thin into the water when cold and then setts it over the fire, where there must be great care taken, that it does not rise up, and runn-over (as it will be verie apt to doe) untill it comes perfectly to boyle, for if it runns over then the best of the Jocalett will be lost, then lett it boyle gently for halfe an houre or more, and sett in the Chocalett Pott open and uncovered till the next morning, when being again heated, it will bee fitt for drinkeing and Hee sayes that all Jocalett is the better for being made over night.[108]

The example of chocolate shows that instructions for use were needed for novel items. Such items could be incorporated into self-help use of remedies. In 1696, Mary wrote to Edward complaining that some items from London had not arrived in Somerset, 'I find you have mentioned a great many things that are in the hamper but have sed nothinge of the Hungary water, chocolett and storgion which makes me feare it is forgott'.[109] Hungary water and chocolate were evidently desired by Mary for her own use, as she added, 'I have a great vallew for finding a deale of good in my extreem weekness by the Hungary water and since in the chocolett, which I really thinke now doss much increase my stomack'.[110] Mary clearly appreciated the new and exotic preparation, originally received as a gift from a friend, and she took care to ensure further supplies.

Some people first came across the exotic remedies when they requested them from physicians. Long-standing interest in medicines brought from afar was indicated by Philip Moore in the sixteenth-century publication *The Hope of Health*, where he criticized those who sought out exotic items for the smallest complaint: 'But if their finger dooe but ake a little. . .they covet to have a medicine that is brought out of India, or from the furthest parte of the worlde'.[111] Such demands continued into the seventeenth century; Mary Clarke, for instance, complained of a lack of 'troppicall remedyes' from one of the physicians that she consulted.[112] The demand for imported exotic items made them costly, and the acquisition of curiosities from afar, including medicinal items, was highly desirable and a particular interest of some early modern medical practitioners.[113] Harold Cook describes the introduction of remedies like Peruvian bark, china root and ipecacuanha, which were widely favoured by physicians as 'specifics' against named diseases.[114] As Amy Tigner points out, 'New World' plants were thought to cure diseases which had originated from overseas.[115] These plants, often strongly purging in nature, could still be understood largely in a Galenic framework,[116] so that medical explanations of their effects did not have to change completely. Some commercial preparation promoted purified preparations as universal cures and incorporated exotic ingredients, such as the patented medicine, Daffy's Elixir.[117] A recipe for 'Dr Lowers tincture commonly called Daffys Elixir' contained senna, guaiacum, liquorice, elecampane, coriander and raisins in aqua vitae.[118] This remedy was widely sold from the 1670s into the eighteenth century with extensive distribution networks beyond London, involving many booksellers and others: for example, George May, bookseller of Exeter, received six dozen half pint bottles to sell on at least five occasions each year between 1680 and 1682.[119] However, there was probably much confusion about which items were native and which were not, as even printed material could be unreliable as to which medicines were native plants. For instance, in the eighteenth century, the *Dictionarium Domesticum* (1736) made a selling point of including 'qualities and uses of physical herbs and plants of English growth', for 'British Constitutions', although the alphabetical listing of ingredients in the dictionary included a large number of imported and exotic items such as Virginian snakeroot for ague and amber for cordials.[120] While there was considerable focus on imported medicines, native plants were also being rediscovered as specific medicines by physicians through information gleaned from 'illiterate practitioners' including 'midwives, barbers, old women, empericks'.[121] Some changes in the way that simples were regarded can be seen in seventeenth-century advertising materials for commercially available preparations, which emphasized the methods used to promote and purify their powers. Nancy Cox, in her study of early modern retailing, notes the importance of choosing suitable names to make items more easily recognizable and desirable, leading to the widespread use of terms like 'balsam', 'elixir' and 'cordial'.[122] Simples and their virtues had appeared for centuries in herbals, but it was Helmontian physicians who argued for the 'power of simples' in opposition to Galenic medicines which were 'blended and confused'.[123] Such an approach could involve both native and exotic plants, and considerable claims were made in support of purified simples as cure-alls which were promoted by commercial suppliers.[124] Amongst the loose recipes in the Fortescue papers was a printed advertisement for 'Spirits of Scurvygrass' (Figure 4.3) sold by Charles Blagrave (fl. 1680), 'Chemical Physician of London', a remedy which was 'faithfully prepared' by the author and claimed to 'answer your desire in most curable Diseases'.[125] The Spirits were claimed to cure a vast range of conditions, including 'the Kings Evil, Scabes, Itch' and to 'carry away all sorts of Salt Humors', at a cost of 1s per bottle. Bottles of these spirits were widely available at various booksellers, fruiterers, perfumers, milliners and fishmongers in London.[126]

There was widespread promotion of the potential of purified chemical medicines to prolong life, although David Haycock suggests that beliefs in a 'universal medicine' were waning by the end of the seventeenth century.[127] Nevertheless, towards the end of the seventeenth century Thomas Mace (d. 1709?) advertised his 'English Priest's Powder' at 10s per ounce as a 'Universall-Physical-Medicine' which as a 'Chymical Prepar'd Powder', although expensive, could be re-used thus offering considerable savings.[128] As a 'pure Tincture' with 'the Operative Power to stir and bring away the Poysonous Humours in Mens Bodies' it had 'no Body, can leave no Malignity, or Danger behind it', and it had the added benefit that the 'ordinary Housekeeper might Easily Purchase, and not only have the benefit of it for

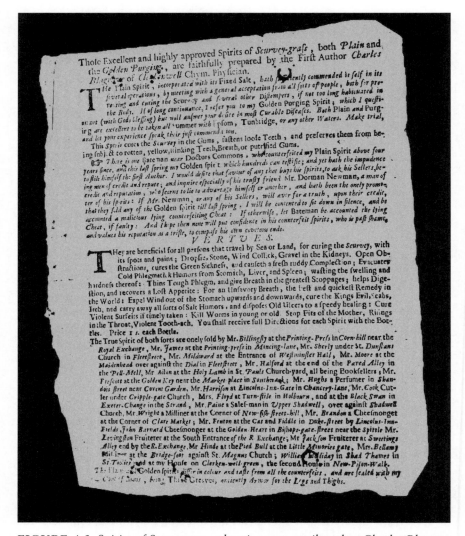

FIGURE 4.3 *Spirits of Scurvygrass advertisement, attributed to Charles Blagrave of Clerkenwell chymical physician, c. 1680. Fortescue of Castle Hill papers, 1262M/ FC/8, Devon Heritage Centre (courtesy of the Countess of Arran).*

himself and his whole Family, during his Life, in all common Sicknesses, and Diseases, but might also be assisting to all his Poor Sick Neighbours round Him'.[129] Thus it was claimed that any 'ordinary Housekeeper' might by this single purchase cure all of the family and neighbours, without needing to source ingredients, prepare medicines, provide nursing care or pay for the attentions of a medical practitioner. Given the concerns about potential costs which we saw in Chapter 3, the claims of a 'Universall-Physical-

Medicine' may have continued to offer an attractive proposition for a wider range of lay household healthcare practitioners. If beliefs in efficacy could be promoted and sustained, despite increased scepticism, then such prepared commercial medicines could provide a significant contribution to self-help efforts in healthcare.

Conclusion

Analysis of household and printed recipes shows an extensive range of plant ingredients alongside animal and mineral ingredients. When analysed by supply source, we have seen that purchased ingredients were rather more likely to be found in recipes from named contributors. There may have been some differences in favoured ingredient sources according to gender and status which deserve further investigation. The costs of individual medicinal ingredients could be high, particularly for spices and imported items, and such items were often purchased in small quantities for immediate use. Some items were readily available in the garden or in the wild, although the gathering of these items involved time and effort, and the household accounts suggest that this had to be paid for on occasion. There could also have been some problems in ensuring the right plants were selected, especially if there was insufficient knowledge for recognition of some plants. Medicinal items including prepared remedies were widely available, especially in London, and could be obtained in many towns.

Although many native plants had considerable evidence of folklore use, few native plants were included as frequently as imported ingredients such as spices in medicinal recipes. In the household accounts there were some groups of medicinal ingredients or 'combination' purchases which might have been related to use in household recipes. But the evidence for purchase of medicinal ingredients for use of the household recipes is not always easy to identify, and combination purchases of medicinal items may have reflected medical practitioner advice rather than actual use of household recipes. There were varying perceptions of the value of native and imported remedies. The use of some common native plants as simples was denigrated by some but appeared to develop in the seventeenth century, through adaptation of recipes by lay people and the promotion of the use of prepared simples by medical practitioners, and as cure-alls by commercial sellers.[130] The availability of prepared remedies with great claims further consolidated the role of medicines in the treatment of illness, whether purchased for self-help or recommended by medical practitioners.

5

'Butter for to Make the Ointment': Kitchen Physic

To what extent were household items like butter used for making medicinal preparations? An item recorded in Bridget Fortescue's household account book in 1697 was for 'butter for to make the ointment, 0s 5d'.[1] This item, along with other similar entries, tells us that ointments were being made over a period of at least five years within the North Devon Fortescue household in the later seventeenth century. The Fortescue household recipe collection contained some sixty recipes for ointments for many conditions including bruises, burns, itch, rickets and worms, and twelve of the recipes specified the use of butter. Many such ingredients for making up ointments and other external preparations were readily available from the kitchen. Foods and other household items also figured significantly as ingredients in medicines that were taken internally. In addition, the kitchen provided a range of utensils and equipment which could be used for making medicinal recipe preparations, although more specialist resources were needed for recipes involving distillation. This chapter explores the resources of the kitchen for making medicines, and the range of preparations which could be made at home, particularly considering the relationship between foods and health and how kitchen physic was affected by changing perceptions.

The phrase 'kitchen physic' was used in a variety of ways in the seventeenth century, at times suggesting foods and household ingredients used in the prevention or treatment of illness, while at other times describing healing based on household members. To modern readers, 'kitchen physic' might suggest the domestic treatment of illness and the production of medicines by women. However, this gendered perspective may not fully reflect the origins of the term, which derived from the close interplay between food and health in classical medicine. Sixteenth-century printed medical advice indicated that the 'chefe physicke' came from the 'kytchyn', instructing that 'the physycyon an[d] the coke for sycke men must consulte togyther for the preparacion of meate for sycke men'.[2] Ken Albala points out that these words show that diet was an essential part of health rather than the cook and physician needing to liaise regarding the preparation of foods.[3] A cook at that time in a high-status home was likely to be male, and dietary advice was expected from a male learned physician as to how certain foods could be beneficial and others could do harm in the body. In the sixteenth century, the idea of the kitchen as a source of medicines was also evident in printed books, such as *Bullein's Bulwarke of Defence against All Sicknesse,* of 1579, which claimed that a 'A good Kitchin, is a good Apothicaryes shop'.[4] The association of 'kitchen physic' with women became firmer as household management of food preparation and the kitchen became definitively part of the female domain. The links between food and health persisted although they were more focused on the care of a sick person and their recovery. Indeed, a modern definition specifies 'kitchen physic' as 'nourishment for an invalid',[5] a definition which does not wholly reflect the varied uses of the term in the early modern period.

Diet and health

In order to understand the way that early modern foods and medicines were linked, we need to clarify how people thought of food in relation to their bodies. Many kinds of food and drink could provide both nourishment and medicinal actions. Broadly, foods were regarded as items which were ingested and acted upon by the body to produce nourishment, while medicines could be capable of acting upon the body and changing its state.[6] Thus a cordial drink could be regarded as a medicinal item since it was recommended to lift spirits, comfort the heart and stomach, and was often flavoured with spices or herbs.[7] Some items could be culinary *and* medicinal according to the context. For example, candied preserves intended for eating at the end of a meal were culinary items associated with higher-status households, particularly since sugar was an expensive commodity in the seventeenth century, and considered beneficial in aiding digestion.[8] Some foods were specifically intended as restoratives for the chronically sick or weak, and such preparations were more likely to be given in a individual context, such as the sickroom or bedroom, reflecting a physical displacement of the ill person, separating them from their usual social context. As we shall see in later discussion of the 'broth', restorative items are of particular interest in relation to household healthcare since they represented a continuation of overlapping links between foods and medicines.

The medicinal effects of foods were associated with a humoral view of the body that was widely promoted in the Galenic revival of the Renaissance.[9] Ideas about food and health had been formularized by Galen (CE 129–210), although many of the principles that he expounded were expressed previously in Hippocratic and other works.[10] In the Galenic framework, the liver was believed to alter nutriments and to make blood continually, supporting the body in the formation of natural spirits which then became vital spirits in the heart and lungs, and were conveyed to the brain where they became animal spirits.[11] The initial process of digestion, or 'concoction', in the stomach required a certain amount of heat, in order to avoid the production of unwanted humours or corrupted matter which would interfere with health. 'Rheum' or 'choler' referred to the humours of phlegm or yellow bile in the body, and these humours were understood as imperfect forms of blood, alongside black bile which consisted of the dregs of blood.[12] Thus digestion was regarded as a key factor in the maintenance of health, and individual foods had 'qualities' that were indicative of how readily they could be digested. All foods had some degree of warmth or cold, moistness or dryness. Foods that were 'fine' were considered easier to digest, such as bread made from pure flour, new milk and young flesh, while 'gross' foods – such as old flesh and unripe fruit[13] – were harder for the body to break down. These ideas about foods persisted into the seventeenth century with little alteration and maintained a focus on bodily constitution, especially the strength of digestion. As John Archer (fl. 1660–88) explained in 1671, 'common sense tells us, that heat in man is predominant over the other qualities' and he explained differences in temperaments based on these qualities: the ideal hot and moist sanguine temperament; the hot and dry choleric temperament; the cold and moist phlegmatic temperament; and the cold and dry melancholy temperament.[14] Thus, Archer argued that everyone should recognize their own constitution and could benefit from knowing the 'nature of what he eats'.[15] Different types of foods were associated with greater or lesser ability to digest so that, for example, persons of high status could take only fine foods, thereby linking diet and identity in early modern England and enabling distinctions between urban and rural lifestyles: these beliefs about food and health made dietary change somewhat risky.[16] Some changes did occur over time in the kinds of foods that were more widely accepted: for example, the edible greens previously thought suitable only for gathering by country people became increasingly palatable to the better sorts.[17] Children were regarded as having a different constitution to adults, being more moist and warm, and so they needed an adjusted diet to match their young bodies. Indeed, blame for illness in children might be laid on nurses and keepers for allowing a 'poor' diet. In 1647, Sir Ralph Verney's wife, of Claydon in Buckinghamshire, wrote of their son, Jack, that 'his leggs are most miserable, crooked as ever I saw any child's', and she thought this was due to his diet, saying 'they lett him eat anything he hath a mind toe, and he keepes a very ill diett'.[18] The nature of a 'poor' or 'ill' diet was understood as a diet which did not appropriately correspond to a person's particular constitution.

Printed advice on diet

An inappropriate diet could produce corrupted matter, and this was widely expressed in printed material. Dietary advice, both as a preventative measure and as a medical treatment, was available through printed regimens from the sixteenth century, such as those of Sir Thomas Elyot (1490?–1546), *Castle of Helth* (1539), and Sir John Harington (1560–1612), *Regimen Sanitatis* (1607).[19] The regimens provided detailed rules on what to avoid: for example, since plain food was thought to be easier to digest, banquets were associated with excess and surfeits, and the order of eating foods also had implications for successful digestion.[20] A survey of dietary regimens and advice books of the late sixteenth and early seventeenth centuries, showed a 'continual balancing act striving for tempered mediocrity', contrasting with previous courtly fashions which had allowed many tastes and pleasures.[21] Much of the advice was further promulgated through popular print, including almanacs. Within the almanac *Riders (1679) British Merlin,* there was printed advice about diet and health for every month: for instance, the entry for May stated, 'Abstain from meats that are hot in nature, and salt in Quality', and the almanac owner inscribed additional notes on the inside cover, writing 'temperance the best Phisick', providing further emphasis on the need for moderation.[22]

Food was thus potentially dangerous, and Shigehisa Kuriyama points out that a significant fear of the period was concerned with the poisonous nature of trapped corrupted wastes in the body, leading to constant anxiety about purging.[23] In order to deal with corruption, regimens included much more than advice on the management of food as, more accurately, they described an entire lifestyle, referring to management of the six 'non-naturals',[24] namely air, food and drink, sleep and waking, movement and rest, retention and evacuation, and emotions.[25] Thus, household environment, daily activities and personal hygiene were all important parts of a regimen for good health.[26] Even arrangements for sleeping were based on notions of the dangers caused by cold air at night, so that enclosed beds were recommended.[27] The Galenic orthodoxy was to manage the nature of bodily fluids through diet and these other means, including prophylactic bloodletting, all activities which were largely based on promoting a 'hot' regimen and removal of excessive humoral matter. Some changes were introduced in ideas about regimen during the seventeenth century and these were based on increasing interest in a 'cool' regimen: this approach brought a fashion for exercise and 'balneology', involving treatment with baths and medicinal springs, bringing the body into harmony with the British climate.[28]

Physicians were closely associated with advice on diet and regimen, and their approach based on individual constitution distinguished them from empirics or others who treated on a symptomatic basis.[29] Some physicians argued for the use of diet to be tried before further treatments such as physic of a purging nature. This perspective can be seen in Robert Burton's (1577–1640) *Anatomy of Melancholy*: 'A wise physician will not give physic, but upon necessity and first try medicinal diet, before he proceed to medicinal cure'.[30] Thomas Muffet (1553–1604) referred to a general principle regarding diet for the sick: 'When any man is sick or distempered, let his meats be of contrary quality to his disease: for health it self is but a kind of temper gotten and preserved by a convenient mixture of contrarieties'.[31] However, since ideas about diet and health were more widely available in print, almost anyone could treat themselves through self-help. Indeed, diet was claimed to be an alternative to physic for both the 'rich and poor'.[32] The use of foods for medicinal purposes could also be associated with those of lesser status. Thomas Cock published *Kitchin-Physick: Or, Advice to the Poor* in 1676 'for the better enabling of Nurses, and such as attend sick people' to 'prevent sickness, and cure Diseases by Diet, and such things as are daily sold in the Market'.[33] These publications claimed the use of foods as cheaper medicines, especially for the poor. Yet some of the recommended foods were not recognizably cheap, as the *Kitchin-Physician* of 1680 demonstrated: it was claimed that ailments would be helped by good wine and nourishment 'with good Victuals like chicken broth and other nourishing, soft and delicate foods'.[34] Dietary advice could also be used as a vehicle to advertise medical remedies for sale: for instance, in *Every Man His Own Doctor*, Archer took the opportunity to promote the availability of his own pills for numerous complaints.[35] Thus, some of this advice was rather disingenuous as it relied on the ability of the sick individual to purchase pills or more expensive food items.

Foods as medicines

Considerable detail on the specific qualities of individual foods was readily available to those who could afford printed texts. In Muffet's *Healths Improvement*, every kind of food was listed according to various degrees of heat, cold, dryness and moisture, for example, from the easily digested flesh of warm and moist young pigeon to hardly digestible cold and dry old beef, from vegetables such as onions and leeks which were hot and drying to lettuce which was cold and moistening.[36] Many of these individual food items could be deemed beneficial to health due to their qualities. Despite earlier concerns that some fruits might be overly cooling and moist in nature, by the early eighteenth century Quincy noted that cherries were 'a very wholesome Fruit, and grateful to the Stomach', strawberries were regarded as 'moderately cooling and cleansing', and quinces could 'cool and strengthen the Stomach'.[37] Fruits from foreign parts were long thought to have some medicinal properties. For example raisins were used in many preparations 'to promote Expectoration', although currants were not so much used 'unless sometimes in Gruel or Broth, to cool and relax the Bowels'.[38] Of lemons, oranges and citrons, it was claimed that all 'much agree in their Medicinal Virtues', the lemons being the 'sharpest and most efficacious' and used for nausea, diarrhoea and other stomach complaints.[39] The range of uses for spices and other condiments from a medicinal perspective was wide, many having warming qualities. Nutmeg was a 'great comforter of the Head and Stomach' and mustard was 'mighty efficacious in stimulating the Fibres and loosening and discussing Viscidities'.[40] Sugar was regarded as a medicinal item in the early seventeenth century being 'hot and moyst' and agreeing 'with all ages', unlike honey which was thought overly heating and drying.[41] Sugar varied in its effects according to its 'fineness', the brown sugar being sweetest and oily in nature and so 'most opening' and 'best to use in purgative Syrups, as also in Glysters', while finer sugar had a more binding quality.[42] However, by the end of the seventeenth century, although sugar was thought useful for its 'opening' qualities in 'purgative Syrups', it could 'occasion many Scorbutic symptoms' being of a 'fermentative nature' and not appropriate in fevers.[43] Other new and exotic introductions found favour in the seventeenth century and were described in terms of both culinary and medicinal qualities, such as chocolate which was claimed to be a 'nourishing Food' being 'oily and soft' and suitable for 'weakly and decaying Constitutions', helping as an emollient by 'lubricating and relaxing the Passages'.[44]

Many of these food items might have been regular purchases in a wealthy household, as we saw in Chapter 3. However, the range of foods available for medicinal purposes to households of lesser status was likely much more limited, and this affected the dietary choices and recipes which could be readily made without additional purchases. Analysis of all the medicinal recipes found that many included food items but less than 2 per cent could be made up entirely from common household food items alone, such as ale, milk, butter, eggs, salt, vinegar, flour and beans. Household food items which were likely to be available, such as bread, eggs and apples, were also used to administer remedies in various kinds of preparations. For instance, in a Fortescue household recipe for a powder to be given for worms, the instruction was provided that 'you may give this powder in the pap of an apple: stewed prun[e]s or any conserve'. Orchard apples were thought to be 'cooling' and to assuage thirst, but may not have had any key medicinal action in a recipe for worms other than their use as an attractive vehicle for administration to children.[45] Roasted apple was also used as a base in a recipe advising how to 'draw out an Earewig of the eare',[46] and for an external application the soft and moist consistency of cooked apple would have been ideal for reaching into smaller crevices. In addition wild or crab apples, although very sour and bitter, could provide astringency with drying effects for many inflammatory skin complaints.[47]

Dietary advice in recipes

We have seen that dietary advice was given as part of medical treatment provided by physicians, and it became more widely available in printed sources during the period of this study. Yet dietary suggestions did not appear with great frequency in the seventeenth-century recipe collections analysed in this book: in fact they occurred in less than 2 per cent of both household and print recipe collections, and several printed recipe collections and one household recipe collection contained no dietary advice at all. Where it did appear, the advice varied considerably and was not always consistent. Almost half of the items including diet advice in the household papers mentioned drinks in some form, sometimes advising 'drink no other drink' and yet in other places suggesting 'drink no beer or wine'. Some recipes recommended a spiced drink or broth, while others suggested oxymel, thin water or water gruel, but advised avoidance of strong drink, wine, cider and hot waters. Regarding foods, there were also variations ranging from recommendations to abstain from a wide variety of items, such as salads, spices, beans, gross flesh, waterfowl, fruit, cheese, butter, salt meats and fish broths, to recommendations to eat specific foods. These recommendations featured in recipes for all types of ailments, from purging preparations to those for various conditions including fever, pox, stone, women's complaints and the itch. Some humoral justification can be seen in the household recipes with instructions like 'keep a good diet eat no sallets or phlegmatic meats' included in a recipe for a 'purging dyett drink', suggesting a concern to restrict intake of moist 'phlegmatic' drinks and foods like salad and green herbs.[48] Often the advice appeared to be to avoid items which might prove hard to digest and produce more phlegm, an undesirable humour in the body.

A humoral basis can also be seen in the recipes containing diet advice within printed books. Most of these recipes were for internal preparations, and some specified foods to be avoided or sought out. Dry and roast meats were recommended for gout, consumption and inward ulcers and a warm diet or drink was recommended for ague and inward bruising, whereas windy, cold and moist meats were to be avoided in convulsion fits and the stone. Drinks were also mentioned in over half of these printed recipes and strong drinks and old beer were to be avoided in fever and hot urine respectively. Four of the recipes were explicitly for purging diet drinks: for instance, the 'diet drink for a fistula, or for a body full of gross humours'.[49] The printed remedies directly referred to qualities of accompanying food and drink, such as 'warm broth', 'hot spices', 'moist meats', 'cool posset ale' and 'sour and sharp meats'. Significantly, unlike the other recipes constraining diet, one later seventeenth-century recipe for the yellow jaundice noted that the patient could 'walk and eat usual food and white wine'.[50] Perhaps this recipe indicated that there was an alternative to the close connections previously understood between food and health.

In the Clifford household recipe collection, dietary advice largely originated with recipes from named physicians. A recipe from a Dr Purnell was given for consumption, made from turnips and apples with herbs, to which was added 'This with a good dyett and keeping yourself warme is next to Infallible'; another recipe for Dr Sharcock's wound drink instructed that 'all the time that you use it forbear wine and keepe to a Spare dyett'.[51] Advice books such as Muffet's *Healths Improvement* gave some indication of the nature of different diets in health and disease, and a 'thin diet' was 'never to be used' unless 'violent disease' undermined the body's 'vigour'.[52] These suggestions were expected to be understood without much further explanation. Another Clifford household recipe was more specific about which foods should be avoided; an 'approved remedy for the dropsy' consisting of herbs infused in sack added 'when you take it forbeare all white meates'.[53] Such advice would be consistent with a humoral approach, in this case avoiding moist foods for a phlegmatic condition. Another recipe, a balsam, also for consumption, dropsy and lung complaints, stated 'whilst you drink this you must not drink any wine nor eate any Salt meats nor hoggs flesh'.[54] A rationale for this advice was less clear, as pork was regarded as moist, whereas salt meats were generally drying.[55] Overall the dietary advice in the Clifford recipe collections did appear to be largely drawn from named physicians, and it mainly consisted of specific instructions related to specific conditions. In the Fortescue household recipe collection, diet recommendations came from a wider sort of people, and not only from physicians. Some recipes gave detailed instructions, such as a recipe for a 'raging pestilential fever' which involved abstaining 'from all wine, strong drink, hott waters as aqua vitae, and hotte spices untill the strength of the disease bee over'. In addition, the recipe further advised use of 'cooling broths'; when these became 'tedious', alternatives included 'panade, sugar sops', and for drink 'let it be of middle strength and you may use milke possets and sorrell possetts'.[56] Such advice would be consistent with attempts to reduce heat in the body. Other recipes in the Fortescue household collection included one for 'the pox and to dry up rhumes' which came with a letter instructing that the patient, 'must not tast no meate but mutton: dry Roseted without salt they must eate spareingly and forbeare suppers: if they can: and onely eate handfull of Reasons of the sune'.[57] In another letter, with a purge and a drink for 'Bridget's sores', the writer insisted 'she must eat no milk nor cheese nor no swines flesh and eat light meats and no fish'.[58] Much of the diet advice in the Fortescue household papers came in letters containing recipes from lay advisers as well as physicians.[59] The advice received in the household suggests that there was no exact consensus as to which foods were problematic, although a humoral basis could still be discerned in frequent expressions of concern about qualities of dryness and moistness in particular foods.

Why was relatively little advice on diet found in the seventeenth-century medicinal recipe collections? Some dietary counsel was given in the letters that accompanied recipes but it may have been omitted when recipes were compiled. It seems unlikely that foods were considered unimportant for health, given widespread appreciation of the humoral basis of ill health. It is possible that since diet was usually identified with the advice of physicians, the compilers of recipe collections attempted to distinguish themselves from those who claimed medical authority by omitting dietary details. Another possibility was that dietary rules were so widely known that they did not need to be written down – but then we might expect not to see any dietary advice at all, or at least more consistency in suggestions. In the next section some closer examination of other aspects of food-related recipes suggests that there were further changes affecting the role of food in relation to health and illness in the seventeenth century.

The changing role of food

Foods and medicines seemed inseparable within the Galenic tradition, yet when advice was included on dietary measures in recipes, it was often suggested that food was a problem. Cock instructed that 'sickly and tender people' should eat little and often, and criticized women and chemical practitioners who 'continually encourage the sick say the Physician what he will, to be eating one good thing or other'.[60] Remedies were often specified to be given on an empty stomach, which involved 'fasting' for a short period prior to administration. Some household recipes included recommendations for fasting after taking medications. For example, the Clarke household recipes included 'For the paine in the bottome of the Belly', which involved taking a drink of herbs and beer in 'a reasonable draught morning, and evening, fasting taking a little suger after it'.[61] Another recipe for the 'yealow janders [jaundice]' involved herbs boiled in beer and drunk warm '3 mornings following fasting' with the instruction 'eat nothing in two houre after'.[62] Other recipes mentioned fasting, including the 'excellent restorative' made with rosa solis which was to be taken 'in the morning fasting a spoonefull',[63] 'A water for 'collick in the stomack' which was taken in the morning fasting, and a 'cordial water' which was 'usealy taken upon an empty stomack'.[64] In general, an empty stomach was regarded as desirable for taking medicines since the remedies were believed to work better without the distraction of digestion.

Fasting alone was perceived by some to be sufficient for curing a range of complaints.[65] It was widely believed that the ability to live without food was associated with piety, and reports of individuals surviving without food were much debated in the seventeenth century.[66] The regimen advice of Leonard Lessius (1554–1623), translated from the Latin and published in English in 1634 as *Hygiasticon*, was prefaced by a number of verses, one of which ends 'But Fasting will cure almost all, alone'.[67] In the *Kitchin-Physician*, an entry to strengthen the stomach noted that 'the best Remedy is fasting'.[68] Excessive eating was blamed for health problems, and some contemporary sources suggested that parents were responsible for illnesses of their children as a consequence of providing too much food. In 1682, Thomas Tryon wrote of practices which made children more subject to diseases than in any other country, saying, 'our Children are generally weak, puling, Rickety, and Sickly, so the occasion thereof is too evident, since they are almost made Gluttons from the very Cradle, their Mothers gorging and Feeding them till they loath their Victuals'.[69] Here, the specific individuals deemed responsible were women. Even foods which were considered suitable for those who were ill began to be portrayed in a different way, as is shown in the following example of broth.

The role of a broth

Given that food could nourish but could also contribute to illness, the diet of those who were recovering from illness necessarily had to be different than normal.[70] Archer, for example, warned that someone who had been cured of the pox should 'be careful not to return to a full Dyet speedily'.[71] Use of foods that were nourishing and easy to digest was regarded as appropriate for the sick or weak, and included broths and other restoring preparations.[72] Thomas Dawson's *The Good Huswifes Jewell*, 1587 edition, included recipes with a specified restorative purpose, such as a 'strong broth for sick men' and a 'broth for one that is weake'.[73] In Partridge's *Treasurie of Commodious Conceits*, there was 'A receit to restore strength in them that are brought lowe with long sicknesse' which was in the style of a broth involving meat stewed with dried fruit, nuts, spices and bread or other grains.[74] In the early seventeenth century, the making of simple broths was described in Markham's *English House-wife*, although not in direct reference to provision for the sick.[75] Broths featured in mid-seventeenth-century publications attributed to women – for example, *Queens Closet Opened* and *Natura Exenterata* – and sometimes the broth had a more specific purpose than restoring weakness, being used as a remedy for a particular complaint such as a consumption or fever. Broths of this latter type differed from earlier versions due to the inclusion of exotic ingredients such as china root and sassafras.[76] In the later seventeenth century, the broth appeared again in Wolley's *Accomplish'd Ladies Delight*, in a medicinal recipe with china root, and as a 'Cordial strengthening broth' which included pieces of gold in the ingredients, while basic broth recipes such as a 'barley-broath' were included in a separate culinary section entitled 'The Compleat Cooks Guide'.[77] There was a divergence developing in the way that broth was portrayed in these printed texts: the broth had medicinal value in the later seventeenth century when it contained expensive or exotic ingredients, but otherwise it had become a food item for which no medical claim was made. The role of broth as a treatment became less significant in printed medical advice except as a vehicle, although it continued to have restorative value as a digestible food in the care of the sick and weak.[78] Changes in the way that broths were described in print could also be seen in the household recipe collections. In the Fortescue household recipe collection there was a restorative recipe 'To make a Cock Broth or Cordiall Broth for the weekest'.[79] Of the other broths in this recipe collection, two were unspecified in purpose and the others contained purging and clearing items which were for dropsy, King's evil, rickets and sweetening the blood.[80] The household recipes included both the use of broths for restorative support for the ill and weak, alongside broths which incorporated exotic drugs to treat specific illnesses. A different perspective on the broth could be seen in the mid-seventeenth century, when it was ridiculed in print in relation to medicine, as one of a number of 'strange and excellent Receits' in *The English Mountebank*, a satirical pamphlet printed in 1652.[81] This pamphlet included a recipe for making 'Cordiall Broath', involving 'three dozen of sheep Trotters', liver and oatmeal boiled for two hours, strained through a 'hair sackcloath' and then drunk a gallon at a time to 'appease grumbling in the Guts, or a wambling stomach'.[82] The author added that 'I am of [the] opinion that he hath read Gerards Herball',[83] and included other strange food recipes, scoffing at medical knowledge based on plants and Galenic theory. The broth and other elements of diet were portrayed as ridiculous, undermining the role of kitchen physic in medicine. Foods and medicines were increasingly distinguished in the seventeenth century, partly due to Helmontian ideas which focused closely on chemical and mechanical explanations of digestion.[84] Physicians were accused by Helmontians of an erroneous focus on diet to disguise their lack of effective medicines, reflecting the 'huckstery of the kitchin' and old-fashioned dogma: they expressed contempt for the 'cook-physician'.[85] The contrast between foods and medicines was made further explicit in the view of Everard Maynwaringe (1628–99?) that 'Physicians endeavour to raise up their weak Patients by Restauratives, Jellies, and nourishing Broths' but that this was mistaken as 'Foul Bodies the more you feed them with high Nourishment, the worse you make them'.[86] In this example, Maynwaringe still drew on Galenic ideas of the production of corrupted matter as being the reason for avoidance of certain foods for health reasons. As food was castigated, dietary advice fell in status; for instance, Cock suggested that notions of treating the poor and advising on diet might be 'below the state and Grandeur of a Physician, and more fit for some waiting Gentlewoman, Nurse or Master of the Pantry'.[87] As Pelling points out, physicians had some difficulties in establishing their professional role in relation to dietary advice which was denigrated in this period.[88] This was not entirely a clear-cut trend, as some writers continued to promote dietary practices which they regarded as healthier.[89] However, we have seen that the role of foods in the prevention and treatment of illness was becoming much less straightforward in the seventeenth century. The contribution of the kitchen to healthcare was undermined apart from a continuing role for easily digested foods in recovery from illness. As we will see below, the resources of the kitchen in terms of equipment for making medicines might also have been found wanting in the seventeenth century.

Kitchen resources

Kitchens could provide a focus for the preparation of medicines in the household, and the resources of utensils and other equipment determined the range of processes possible. However, details of the resources available in early modern kitchens are somewhat limited as studies of domestic technology are largely restricted to general descriptions, or to developments which took place later than the period of our study.[90] Typical cooking utensils included 'iron pots, skillets of brass or bronze, long-handled frying pans, earthen cooking pots including pipkins [small pans] with handles', and many items were repeatedly mended for continuing use.[91] Increasingly specialized cooking equipment was introduced in the early modern period: for example, there was a change from the use of a vessel hanging over an open hearth to various devices for controlling heat based on the use of flat-bottomed utensils.[92] There was a growing impact in the later seventeenth century of domestic iron casting and brass founding which provided a variety of kettles, pans and mortars, the latter enabling more effective grinding and powdering.[93] For the larger household, a specialist item offered by George Hartman in his publication *The True Preserver and Restorer of Health* of 1682 was his 'engine' which was a still that was 'also very convenient for boyling and stewing all Sorts of meats and Fricasies, etc', thus providing for a range of culinary and medicinal preparations.[94] The physical resources available in the kitchen included a range of utensils and containers for mixing and heating which would have been necessary for medicinal preparations. Many household medicinal recipes could be assembled using relatively simple heating methods, and processes such as beating, mixing, 'searcing' (sieving) or straining. Almost half (46.7 per cent) of all the medicinal recipes in the household collections involved some form of heating process. A further 11.6 per cent of recipes required distillation which necessitated more specialist equipment. The remaining household recipes involved mainly mixing ingredients (34.1 per cent) or otherwise no further processing (7.5 per cent). In printed book recipes, a similar proportion (47.9 per cent) of recipes involved heating while fewer involved distillation (9.7 per cent) and slightly more recipes could be based on mixing ingredients (38.9 per cent), and fewer recipes needed no processing (3.5 per cent). Recipes that involved mixing alone often included prepared ingredients, such as powdered items or readymade waters.

Although a significant proportion of medicinal recipes could be made up with kitchen equipment that was widely available, printed sources suggested that some additional equipment was needed for administration of many medicines. For example, an advice book of the early seventeenth century carried detailed recommendations as to the equipment which was needed by a household to provide healthcare for themselves and others:

First two syringes or bladders fitted with pipes to give Clysters, the one for great folks, and the other for children.

A little brasse pot to keep a Clyster in, and to warme it in.

Another bladder and boxe pipe to lend charitably to the poore.

Two sieves, one very fine to straine medicines, and the other to straine decoctions.

But instead of the said sieves you may use white linnen cloaths sitting.

Two pulping sieves, the one to pulp Cassia, Prunes, Tamarinds, etc. And the other to pulpe roots, hearbs etc. for Cataplasmes.

A set of weights of sixteene ounces in the pound, and a paire of scales to weight the medicaments.

Two Spatuls of iron, one bigger then another.
One wooden Spatule.
A Marble morter with a pestle of wood.
A brasse morter with an iron pestle or a pestle of the same.
A lesser morter with a pestle as before.
Pots, Pipkins, Skillets, Basons etc. To make the Ptisans, decoctions etc.[95]

Notably, this list, given in the 1639 translation of Philbert Guibert's (1579?–1633) *Charitable Physician*, included a bladder and boxe pipe (for clysters or enemas) to be lent to the poor. Guibert was Doctor Regent of the Parisian medical faculty and the title of this list of equipment for making up medicinal preparations indicated that it was expected of a wealthy household, 'A Treatise or Catalogue of Those Instruments which the Rich Ought to Have in Their Houses'.[96] Guibert's list was short by comparison with that of Thomas Brugis (1620?–51?) in the *Marrow of Physicke* (1640) which required, amongst many other things, a roller for lozenges, presses, an incision knife, forceps, galley pots, pledgets, cauteries, a limbeck (still) and a bathing chair.[97] Some of these items were necessary for bloodletting, to enable opening of the flesh and then staunching further blood flow with a pledget or small bandage. Other items were for storage of ointments and other medicines such as galley pots or gallipot jars. Substantial storage vessels would have been needed for households involved in making large quantities of some remedies. As Wear notes, the large-scale production of medicines by Lady Grace Mildmay, who made ten gallons of aqua vitae or metheglin at a time, would have necessitated attention to storage.[98] Leong also shows that Elizabeth Freke (1641–1714) listed many gallons of cordial waters and syrups in her early eighteenth-century inventories.[99]

The household accounts and inventories occasionally revealed purchases of the variety of more or less specialized equipment which could be put to medicinal use. In the Bath household accounts, there was a 'posset pot' in an 'inventory of plate' dated 13 February 1638.[100] The overlap between culinary and household tasks is evident in records of more general purchases for equipment for cleaning (such as brooms), general kitchen work and brewing (sieves, earthenware, funnels and bottles) and for dairy work (tin pans and ladles). In the Fortescue household accounts in 1698, there was a purchase of 'bouls scales and ladle and pipes' for 3s 10d. Shortly after there was a purchase of 'earthen potts for the dairies and a dish' for 1s, with further expenditure made for kitchen and dairy items in the following year.[101] A few entries provided details of specific items or equipment necessary for an episode of sickness which required extra cleaning: for example, the Fortescue accounts recorded that a bedpan was bought in 1697 for 3s 7d. On the same page of accounts, there was a reference to purchases of 'scouring sand and sand for the rooms' at 2s 6d.[102] Another item for medicinal use was paper used for treating skin wounds or complaints, and the Fortescue accounts mentioned purchase of 'is[s]ue paper' for 6d in 1704.[103] In the main, however, the range of equipment in households was rarely identified sufficiently to be sure about which preparations were likely to have been made in the home. Another approach to consider in identifying equipment needs and availability is to examine recipe collections for an indication of the variety of preparations that might have been made. Altogether 176 different kinds of preparation were identified in the household manuscript and printed recipes, and these were

TABLE 5.1 *Medicinal preparations in manuscript and printed recipes*

	Manuscript recipes		Printed recipes		All recipes	
	n	%	*n*	%	*n*	%
External preparations						
Bandage	5	0.2	24	0.7	29	0.4
Drops	68	2.3	101	2.8	169	2.6
Lotion	100	3.4	142	3.9	242	3.7
Ointment	439	15.1	625	17.3	1,064	16.3
Other	26	0.9	37	1.0	63	1.0
Plaster	466	16.0	673	18.7	1,139	17.5
Powder	28	1.0	53	1.5	81	1.2
Spirit	65	2.2	136	3.8	201	3.1
Internal preparations						
Drink	841	28.9	769	21.3	1,610	24.7
Food	39	1.3	81	2.2	120	1.8
Gargle	36	1.2	49	1.4	85	1.3
Other	17	0.6	26	0.7	43	0.7
Pill	92	3.2	118	3.3	210	3.2
Powder	195	6.7	247	6.9	442	6.8
Spirit	291	10.0	282	7.8	573	8.8
Suppository	29	1.0	36	1.0	65	1.0
Syrup	172	5.9	205	5.7	377	5.8
All preparations	2,909	100.0	3,604	100.0	6,513	100.0

Source: Stobart, Recipes and Expenditure Database.

TABLE 5.2 *Internal and external preparations during the seventeenth century*

Time period	Recipe format	External preparations		Internal preparations		All preparations	
		n	%	*n*	%	*n*	%
Before 1650	Manuscript	467	48.8	490	51.2	957	100.0
	Print	1,131	55.6	904	44.4	2,035	100.0
1650 and beyond	Manuscript	730	37.4	1,222	62.6	1,952	100.0
	Print	660	42.1	909	57.9	1,569	100.0
All periods		2,988	45.9	3,525	54.1	6,513	100.0

Source: Stobart, Recipes and Expenditure Database.

grouped in fourteen types of preparation as shown in Table 5.1, including both external and internal types of preparation. The most predominant types of preparation were ointments, plasters, drinks and spirits. Table 5.2 compares the frequency of internal and external preparations in recipe collections in the two halves of the seventeenth century.[104] For printed and household recipes of the first half of the seventeenth century, the proportions for internal and external use differed, the printed recipes favouring external preparations more than the household recipes. However, from 1650 the balance shifted noticeably in both household and printed collections towards internal preparations. Overall the proportion of recipes for external preparations in household collections decreased to less than 38 per cent of all recipes in the latter half of the seventeenth century. The reasons for this change in proportions of internal and external preparations in household recipes may be partly due to the frequent additions to recipe collections of recipes for diet drinks and other drinks for complaints such as rickets. This reflects a move away from plasters and ointments towards internal medicines.

Some medicinal preparations could have been expected to last longer than others, although preservation and storage of foods and medicines have been little studied in historical terms. Discussion of preservation methods by Una Robertson in her history of the housewife reveals the time-consuming efforts needed to resist putrefaction of food – involving drying, smoking, salting, pickling and potting with substances such as sugar and vinegar – and the need for storage away from insects and vermin.[105] Similarly, many medicinal preparations would have had very limited shelf lives without some form of preservation. This would be the case particularly for water-based lotions, plasters and drinks, as moisture provides opportunities for fungal and bacterial growth. Thus, the making of medicinal remedies could be especially time-intensive where items had to be repeatedly and freshly made every few days. Dried items, whether based on herbs or made as pills and powders, would have remained stable for much longer periods of several months or even years if they remained sufficiently dry and therefore deterred microbes. Other methods of preservation were possible: in sufficient proportions, sugar acted as an effective preservative for syrups and various conserves, while alcohol in spirituous waters could provide long-lasting protection of several years or longer.[106] One advantage of distillation was that it concentrated any alcohol or essential oil content in the distillate, and so distilled preparations might keep well for many years. The next section provides an overview of the kinds of equipment needed for distillation, and discusses the availability of such specialist resources in the seventeenth century.

Distillation of medicines

Distillation was flagged up in Chapter 2 as an interest of several compilers of medicinal recipes. Distillation has a lengthy history, and essentially refers to the technique of heating liquids to form a vapour in a container called a limbeck or still, and then cooling the vapour to produce another liquid.[107] Printed advice on distilling in England arrived with the 1527 translation of works of Hieronymous Brunschwyck (c. 1450–c. 1512), a surgeon of Strasburg.[108] A 'lute' ensured an airtight fit of the head of the still and cooling methods varied, including air, wet rags and water on a still-head. Sir Hugh Plat (1552?–1608) recommended various types of still, writing that, 'the manner of drawing or extracting of the oils out of Herbs or Spices, with all necessary circumstances' required a 'Copper body, or Brass pot, with a Pewter Limbeck, and a glass Receiver'.[109] Distillation equipment was generally large and expensive, and required a dedicated source of heat so that a separate area from the house or kitchen was advisable.[110] The still-house was an additional separate building or outhouse in a number of sixteenth- and seventeenth-century houses,[111] and this could be added as part of garden redesign.[112] Wilson describes the still-room as the successor to the still-house, part of a new fashion in the design of country houses, 'often next-door to the housekeeper's room' where the housekeeper could be 'directly involved in both distilling and preserving activities, assisted by the stillroom maid'.[113] Evidence shows the use of stills by women of aristocratic status in the early seventeenth century,[114] although distillation was probably being practised more widely by the middle of the seventeenth century: for instance, the clergyman Ralph Josselin's diary for 31 May 1646 tells us of the 'making of steeped hyssop' and the 'stilling of roses'.[115] Although it is sometimes presumed that distillation was mainly a female interest, some men were directly involved: it was John Evelyn who set out the details of the still-room at Sayes Court.[116] Stills were highly valued, and some were named in bequests in the seventeenth and eighteenth centuries: for example, as Sara Pennell notes, there was a bequest of a limbeck by Sarah Boult (d. 1732) near Reading to her daughters.[117] There was mention of stills in the Clifford, Fortescue and Strode household account records of the later seventeenth century but not in the Clarke household.[118] In the Fortescue household account, there was a payment for mending a still in 1700, associated with the purchase of additional pans and funnels.[119] A still continued in use in the Fortescue household in 1702 and 1704, when supplies of spirits were purchased for distilling, as well as gallipots for storage of distilled waters.[120] Anne Strode probably had access to distillation equipment, as she bought brandy in 1679 to 'still'.[121]

The use of a still appeared to be variable, possibly something of a personal interest amongst the better-off, rather than a universal expectation. When Lady Anne, Countess of Bath, died on 6 January 1638 there was a 'Still House' containing '1 cupboard, 1 chest, 2 little tables, 3 pewter stills, 2 glass stills, 3 brass pans, 1 limbeck head, 1 little scummer, 1 alabaster mortar and pestle, 1 green stool, vials, 2 glasses of May Butter'. A year or so later, an inventory of 9 March 1639 of 'all the household goods and furniture which is in every room and office in the House' showed that the equipment listed in the Brewhouse was more detailed than in the Still House which then had only '4 stills, 1 old table, 1 old limbeck'.[122] These records suggest that there was a decline in use of the still-house, and perhaps once Lady Anne had passed away there was a change in the level of interest in distillation. A still was also difficult or costly to repair and, although stills were shown to be in use in some households, findings from inventory studies suggest that not all stills were in frequent use or kept in good repair. A survey of inventories in Cornwall provides some indication of this between 1601 and 1745.[123] In all, sixteen stills (about 25 per cent) were either described as old in some way or were stored in a chamber out of use. Stills would probably have needed to be stored since large quantities of plant material could only be obtained at certain times of the year. They could be expensive to repair if damaged, but were too valuable to sell or throw out.[124] Another source, drawn from a recipe collection, provides a suggestion of changing perceptions of distillation. The Clifford household recipe collection included 'A very good Cordiall water without the trouble of a Still'. Closer examination of this recipe provides a further possible key to the way some viewed distillation towards the end of the seventeenth century. This cordial is the last but one of sixteen cordial recipes in the collection, 'The Right Honorable the Lady Cliffords Booke of Receipts', dated 1689.[125] The recipe lists ingredients for standing in brandy for a three-week period instead of the usual procedure of distillation:

A very good Cordiall water without the trouble of a Still

Take two quartes of brandy and keepe it in a great glasse with a Reasonable narrow mouth, put into it of Cloves, nutmegg, Cinamon, and Ginger, Cardemom-seeds, Corriander seeds, anes-seeds, liquorish, of each of these ['but a quarter of an ounce annes-seeds' added] halfe and Ounce bruised, Long pepper and grains of each of these ['half an ounce' crossed out] one drame bruised, Elicampane, 2 drams bruised. Lett all these steepe in the brandy a fortnight, then pour it out into another glass softly so long as itt will Run Cleare then put more brandy into the glasse where the Ingredients are, and lett that stand three weekes and so long as you find there is any strength in the Ingredients, still put in more brandy and let it stand every time longer and longer Then take your first two quartes of brandy which you poured of and put in it four ounces of white sugar Candy and so much Syrupp of Clove-Jelly-flowers as will well Collour itt with store of Leafe gold give 2 spoonfulls att a time: It is good in case of any Illness or Swouning to drive out any Infection and venemous humours, It is good for wind in the Stomack and to keep out Cold.[126]

Perhaps the reason for changing perceptions of the value of distillation lay in the demanding nature of the distillation process, not only the expensive equipment in need of repair, but also because of a need for servant labour. Jayne Archer records that Dame Margaret Verney (d. 1641) at Claydon House had a 'preserving room' and 'spicery with furnaces, brewing vessels and a brass skillet' and may have been assisted by at least six waiting gentlewomen.[127] Thus distillation activities might be highly labour-intensive, if not dangerous since stills were known to explode.[128] Distillation could also require considerable quantities of flowers or herbs and, if medicinal ingredients were to be grown or gathered, someone had to carry out the gardening labour involved. Indeed, William Lawson's (fl. 1618) *A New Orchard and Garden* referred to the work to be ordered of the gardener saying 'Your gardener must . . . distill his Roses and other hearbes'.[129] While some households may have had many servants with specific functions, in others the role of servants may have been changing with priorities in other areas than household distillation, especially since many distilled preparations could be readily purchased.

But who would have deemed a still unnecessary? The recipe above which avoids the 'trouble' of a still raises some questions about the perception of the need for distillation in seventeenth-century household medicine. The use of a still as a means of purification in producing a cordial was not easily dispensed with by those with 'chymical' knowledge for whom 'distillation perfects a substance'.[130] For those who saw the preparation of medicinal substances as symbolic of high status, an expensive and time-consuming preparation was particularly appropriate, and such individuals may have been unlikely to favour a recipe which suggested that use of a still was a 'trouble'. However, it was likely that household servants were tasked with making up and administering some medicinal remedies, including Mrs Harvey, the housekeeper in Margaret Boscawen's household, Dorcuss the cook in Mary Clarke's household and Mrs Ann in the preserving room in Lord and Lady Clifford's household.[131] These individuals may well have appreciated this new approach that was made possible by this recipe, in which prepared ingredients such as brandy were deemed just as suitable and effective as the products of distillation. In this recipe without the 'trouble' of the still, the contributor might not have regarded the personal supervision of purification by distillation as essential for the efficacy of the final product. Another recipe from a popular later seventeenth-century publication further demonstrates an interest in the end product rather than the process. Entitled 'An excellent sweet water', in the *Accomplish'd Ladies Delight* (1685 edition), this recipe claimed to provide an 'instant' sweet water, saying: 'Note that you may make a sweet water in an instant, by putting in a few drops of some distilled Oyles together into some Rose-water and brew them altogether'.[132] With reduced effort, the sweet water could be made 'in an instant' and yet it was still 'excellent' in comparison with other waters, no longer requiring the previous method of preparation by distillation which was time-consuming and messy. Recipes like this suggest that there were some changes brought about by the interaction of economic and cultural factors, paving the way for different kinds of medicines which could be more easily assembled from pre-prepared ingredients. Commercial manufacturers of waters were not slow to appreciate these new methods and the physician John Quincy noted the shortcuts of wholesale dealers who could 'in an instant, brew the largest Quantity' of Queen of Hungary water using 'chymical oil of Rosemary and that of Lavender, and this with a good assurance and a French Title, they palm upon the Nation for right French Hungary Water'.[133]

Distillation was not the only form of preparation which involved much effort and expense. Of the extensive list of medicinal items prepared by Elizabeth Walker (1623–90), it was said 'these cost Money, but more Pains and Labour to prepare them'.[134] Other processes were involved in making medicines which were portrayed as physically unpleasant, noisy and smelly. In 1670, Christopher Merret explained that a busy physician should not make his own medicines because he would be 'exposed to a perpetual disturbance by the noise of the Mortar, and have his spirits dampt by the unpleasant steems of Glysters, Oyntments, and Plasters'.[135] Such a 'grease, stinking Glyster-Pipe, and Plaister-Box Doctor', according to Merret, would not 'be endured in the presence of some delicate tender-scented Ladies, that are his Patients'.[136] For some ladies, it was suggested by Merret, no reminders were desired of the preparation processes of medicines. As economic conditions changed in the seventeenth century it seems relevant to ask whether the cost and availability of domestic labour could have influenced the nature and desirability of making medicinal preparations at home. This question would be a particular consideration in the town or city, where over half of households might have no servants.[137] In addition to the problems associated with some forms of preparation, annotations in some recipes suggested that ingredients were becoming increasingly obscure or complex. A recipe for 'diascordium' was followed by a note saying of the ingredients that 'the Apothecaryes will understand if you shew them the Receipt and will furnish you with them'.[138] This preparation could be made without even knowing what it contained since the processes of assembling the ingredients and of making up the preparation were effectively separated. These examples suggest that the family and household in the seventeenth century could be faced with increasing challenges in preparing their own medicines, and this is consistent with the purchases of prepared medicines identified in Chapter 3.

Conclusion

In the seventeenth century, the resources of the kitchen offered key components in self-help healthcare, providing foods as well as ingredients like butter for making up preparations such as ointments. By the end of the century, however, the contribution of the kitchen was being undermined in relation to the practice of medicine, as a consequence of changing views of food, greater interest in internal medicines, and different kinds of preparations. In the early seventeenth century there had been much overlap between foods and medicines, appropriately expressed in the term 'kitchen physick'. There was widespread understanding of the important role of digestion and how this could help or hinder health. Dietary advice and details of the qualities of individual foods were available in regimens and other sources, yet largely absent in recipe collections. Sensitivity about the boundaries of medical authority may have accounted for this to some degree, since dietary advice was expected from physicians. Dietary recommendations reflected some humoral understanding but were often inconsistent and this may have reflected changing understandings and some therapeutic confusion about the causes of disease. There was an increased emphasis that food could be the cause of health problems and conflict with the administration of medicines. The broth, a digestible preparation that linked food and medicine, shifted in the recipe collections to become a mainly culinary item easily digested in convalescence, and remained medicinal only if it was a vehicle for exotic drugs. This change in views expressed about food reflected a changing emphasis from concern with the humoral constitution of an individual to treating diseases with specific medicines. Food was becoming irrelevant in medicine and was even ridiculed as medical treatment. Such views undermined the status of the household in healthcare, especially the kitchen and women who were closely involved in food preparation.

Household recipes included preparations for both internal and external use, and internal preparations were becoming more significant in recipe collections in the latter half of the seventeenth century. Many items required powdering, mixing and heating, and these processes could be carried out in the kitchen with homemade or purchased ingredients, although distillation involved costly specialist equipment and extra help. Other elements of healthcare, such as the administration of glysters or bleeding and cupping, also needed specific items of equipment which might be found in a wealthy household, possibly for loan to poorer households. Examples of alternative ways of preparing distilled items with purchased prepared ingredients suggest that the use of distillation was regarded by some as troublesome and unnecessary since ready-distilled items could be purchased. Through the purchase of prepared medicines or prepared ingredients for recipes, the availability of medicines for much self-help healthcare could still be maintained without recourse to 'kitchen physic'.

SECTION THREE

Practice

The third section of this book explores practice in seventeenth-century household healthcare, drawing on examples of self-help treatment and relationships with medical practitioners. It focuses on therapeutic determination in household healthcare and builds on the information and resources highlighted in previous sections. In Chapter 6, I analyse named recipients in later seventeenth-century household accounts and find that the main priority was the treatment of children and household members, with little evidence of direct healthcare assistance for the poor. Comparison of medicinal purchases and recipes for children's complaints suggests that there were also some differences in approach between the households, although purging remained significant in the treatment of children. We can see examples of women determining therapeutic approaches, and household practitioners like Mary Clarke and Bridget Fortescue gained confidence in diagnosing illness and providing treatments for children. Self-help and medical advice from medical practitioners could be closely mingled as medical views were sought to confirm their approaches to treating the children. However, diagnosis of a child's complaint in a case of rickets could lead to criticism from the physician who sought to portray danger to the child from a lack of professional medical advice. Such criticism continued into the following century when physicians sought to limit domestic medicine to treating minor complaints and following the doctor's orders. In Chapter 7, I turn to consider a range of chronic complaints in later life and self-help for complaints of pain and melancholy. Ongoing nursing care involved a considerable variety of household tasks and, although there were some staunch defenders of housewifery, there were tensions relating to the role of women, as domestic responsibilities were regarded as a burden by some women, taking up much-needed time for other spiritual or intellectual activities. Difficulties in keeping servants, or other priorities for their labour, could also undermine household healthcare. We see how Mary and Bridget fared as patients in later life when suffering from their own chronic complaints, and how they used various strategies to achieve their preferred therapeutic approaches. These strategies reflected both practitioner and patient stances, varying from debating the suitability of medicines to non-compliance with medicines prescribed. The culture of medical practice was shifting in the seventeenth century, and therapeutic approaches were more diverse, ranging from Galenic to chemical and other frameworks, a diversity which extended into self-help healthcare. Medicines played a major role in both self-help and medical practitioner treatments and a preferred therapeutic approach could be reflected in the selection of medicines. Therapeutic determination through self-help was possible with either homemade or readymade medicines in the seventeenth century.

6

Therapeutics in the Family

Jenny have bin a little indisposed this day or 2 with those swellings in her face, as you have seen her have, but eats her meat very well and is up and down the house and I give her ruburbe and beare which I hope will carry of the humour as it used to do.[1]

Jenny was Mary and Edward Clarke's three-year-old daughter and, in her letter to Edward in 1697, Mary told of her therapeutic approach to treating the children. She assessed the complaint that Jenny suffered from, how it affected her in terms of appetite and activity, and she treated the child on the basis of past experience and understanding of health and illness. In this example, Mary was using rhubarb to 'carry off' an unwanted humour from the child's body. As we shall see later in this chapter, the Clarke family letters reveal other examples of treatment at home for the children, showing how Mary developed her confidence in diagnosing and treating illnesses, and how decisions were made by Mary and Edward on calling medical practitioners for help. This chapter also considers who was most likely to have received medicines and healthcare originating from the household. We shall see that the later seventeenth-century household accounts sometimes recorded named beneficiaries of health-related purchases, and these individuals were largely family members, particularly children and servants. The household accounts also provide some indication of the therapeutic approaches used for treating common complaints of children, and purchases are compared to household recipes for children. Although women became more assured in their attempts to diagnose complaints, there was criticism of these attempts which prefigured more tightly defined boundaries on the nature of self-help. The issue of who provided a diagnosis became significant in distinguishing the boundaries of lay and professional medicine and the term 'domestic medicine' came into more frequent use later in the eighteenth century. This chapter focuses on family care, particularly for children; household healthcare concerns in relation to pregnancy and childbirth are not considered here in detail, as there are studies of early modern midwifery practices and texts to which the reader may refer.[2]

Who received healthcare?

Some health-related payments in the later seventeenth-century household accounts specified named individuals in the Clarke, Clifford, Fortescue and Strode households. Altogether, these household accounts provided 896 health-related expenditure entries, and there were 66 (7.4 per cent) which were readily identifiable in terms of the recipients, either explicitly named individuals, or identified in terms of relationships.[3] Table 6.1 provides the status of all such individuals receiving healthcare in the household accounts, and it is evident that many were family members. Over one-third of these payments related to children, almost another third concerned servants or householders themselves and the remaining one-third related largely to other named persons associated with the households, including visitors.[4]

Over three-quarters of the payments recorded for named individuals referred to medical services, whether attendance of a medical practitioner, or for tending and related care. The remaining purchases were for medicinal supplies such as syrups, oils, worm powder, purges or other items from an apothecary. In two of the households – those of the Clarke and Clifford families – the total expenditure on named individuals amounted to almost a quarter of all health-related expenditure, ranging from just under 20 per cent to just over 24 per cent. In the Fortescue and Strode households, however, the total level of expenditure on named individuals was considerably lower. The average spend per named recipient varied widely from £1 18s 1d in the Clifford household to 2s 8d in the Strode household. The difference between these average amounts was largely accounted for by the costs of medical practitioner attendance which were substantial in the Clifford household. Apart from children and family members, other named recipients were mainly servants. Tradition required that a 'sick servant should be tended with every care', particularly in larger households.[5] The household accounts from the earlier half of the seventeenth century recorded efforts to provide for servants, including giving cash payments; for example, the Bath household accounts showed that Goodwife Redhead, a servant of the household, was helped in April 1644, a payment of five shillings being made when she was 'lying very sick', and further payments were made to her while ill.[6] In the later seventeenth century, advice books for women included reminders of the responsibility to make 'a sufficient and decent provision, both in sickness and in health' for servants.[7] Instances of servants in the Clarke family household at Chipley in Somerset being given treatment when ill were reported in the family letters. Treatment could involve medical advice, remedies and bloodletting, and these were all elements of healthcare which were much the same as ways in which members of the family would expect to be treated. John Locke, as a family friend, was asked by Edward Clarke for advice and treatment for various individuals associated with the family including the family steward, John Spreat, and the gardener's boy.[8] Mary Clarke provided frequent updates on the progress of servants who

TABLE 6.1 *Status of named recipients of healthcare in household accounts*

Status of recipient	Number of recorded payments				
	Clarke household	Clifford household	Fortescue household	Strode household	All households
Boy	1	6	1	0	8
Child	4	0	2	0	6
Cook	0	1	0	0	1
Girl	5	2	2	0	9
Lady	0	2	0	0	2
Lord	0	4	0	0	4
Maid	1	0	0	3	4
Man	3	8	0	0	11
Mistress	1	0	1	1	3
Mistress and maid	0	0	0	1	1
Other named	0	2	0	2	4
Self	0	0	0	1	1
Servant	1	3	0	1	5
Son	4	0	0	0	4
Woman	0	1	0	2	3
Recipients, named	20	29	6	11	66
Recipients, not named	257	152	189	232	830
All records	277	181	195	243	896

Source: Stobart, Recipes and Expenditure Database.

were unwell, sometimes expressing annoyance when caring for their health was expensive, unrecognized or inconvenient. She had provided much medical care for one servant, Isaac the coachman, and wrote to Edward: 'For these 3 dayes last past his legg and foot has bin soe swelled and painfull to him that he has with great difficulty gone from the fire to the bead'.[9] A few months later, Mary noted of Isaac that 'today [he] was let blood and is something better'.[10] Treatment for Isaac was lengthy and costly, involving bleeding and purging, and Mary suggested that he should show more gratitude and respect for the care and attention given to him.[11] In the same year, another servant in the Clarke household, Mrs Burgess the housekeeper, suffered accidental injury in falling off a horse and consequently this affected Mary in her plans to travel to London. As Mrs Burgess lay unwell in bed, Mary wrote: 'I begin to be a little backed in my undertaking of coming to London with her'.[12] Servants also brought further worry and problems if they caught smallpox, as Humphrey did in 1697, and he had to be moved elsewhere.[13] Mary wrote: 'Humphrey could never have had the small pox so inconveniently in all his whole service as now, which shall be a warning to me not to take any agen that have not had them, [even] if they are the best servants in England'.[14] Evidently Mary lost patience at times with all of the additional costs and trouble of dealing with illness amongst members of the household. In March 1704/5, she complained of little recompense from the French tutor, Mr Duboy 'for my care jurneys and medicens used in his illness att Chipley, one ginney which was all I ever received from him or any other persen on his account'.[15] The guinea was for the cost of medical attention, but Mary's comment suggests that she also arranged care and obtained medicines. Mary's experience reminds us of the example of Elizabeth Freke in late seventeenth-century Norfolk who complained bitterly about the costs of a servant in her illness.[16] Despite the inconvenience and expense, servants in the household were provided with medical treatment, and this reflected a continuing expectation of employers to provide such care, an obligation which could be reinforced by orders of the courts.[17]

Healthcare for the poor

For the people outside the household but in the locality, especially the poor, healthcare responsibilities might be viewed in different ways in the seventeenth century. Medical care for the poor was portrayed as one of the moral duties of wealthier members of early modern society, especially women. In *The Queens Closet Opened*, the reader was advised 'as for the Physicall part, what can be more noble then [sic] that which gives the rich such an opportunity of spending upon good works, while they succour the poor, and give comfort to them in their greatest distresses'.[18] In 1697, Timothy Rogers (1658–1728) referred to the 'physick' and 'medicines to relieve her poorer Neighbours' which might be provided by a 'vertuous Woman',[19] also distributing 'Money and Books, and Cloaths'.[20] Rogers added that such practice by a woman would receive a 'peculiar blessing' from God provided that she did not usurp the 'Advice of the learned' and used only items which were 'safe and innocent'.[21] Thus, the provision of healthcare by women was expected not to interfere with that of learned medical men. But increasingly physicians and others were paid to help the poor, reflecting a shift away from individual and clerical assistance with the formalization of parish poor relief, especially in the later seventeenth century.[22] Detailed analysis of parish poor relief from 1550–1750 confirms the extent of medical help included in casual or irregular disbursements at some 20 per cent of expenditure, with increasing amounts being spent in the later seventeenth century.[23] It is not entirely clear whether significant direct provision continued to be made by individual households throughout this period, though; indeed Reinarz and Schwarz state that 'apothecaries were the doctors of the poor', as well as the providers of medical aid in an emergency.[24] Some studies of charitable poor relief focus on reasons for individuals to help the poor, both religious and secular, but most studies highlight institutional provision, the latter often portrayed as a vehicle for increased professional control of medicine through the parish or the hospital.[25]

So was there any evidence in the household accounts for healthcare for the poor, particularly in the later seventeenth century? The Clarke household accounts recorded occasional cash payments to 'poor' individuals, such as 'to a poor woman 1d'.[26] The household account and family letters also graphically described the extensive provision of food for the neighbourhood on significant dates. For instance, on Christmas Eve in 1699, Mary recounted to Edward the huge effort involved in making provision:

> Satterday I disposed of near a hundred loaves and about forty peeces of beefe and now I am in expectation of 5 or 6 and thirty of the poor knaighbours and theyr wifes some that have bin and some that are workmen to the house and when all is over I beleve I must lye a bead a weeke to recover myselfe agen.[27]

In another letter in 1702, Mary again referred to such festivities involving food, explaining that 'we have 3 days work to bake bread for the poor'.[28] Although Mary wrote in detail of the extent of such culinary activities, she described no medical treatment involving the poor in her household accounts or letters. Several other households recorded assistance to the poor, such as contributions of cash or clothing in their accounts. The Clifford household accounts listed payments of small cash sums to poor individuals as well as payments towards the poor rates, a regular sum of £2 17s.[29] The wealthy spinster, Anne Strode, frequently bought clothes for the poor, especially shoes or cloth: in January 1685/6, she itemized 'for 15 yardes of cloth for poore folke, £1 1s', in December 1687, 'for the making my poore mans cote, 1s', and in January 1688/9, 'for a payr of shoes for a poor woman, 2s 2d'.[30] Although Anne detailed the purchase of clothing materials and making up clothes for individual members of the poor, she recorded no medical treatments for those struggling financially. Her payments to the apothecary were all clearly recorded as being for other household members, Anne herself, or her servants.[31]

Cash payments to the poor were also recorded by the North Devon household of Bridget and Hugh Fortescue, such expenditure items usually noted as 'to the poor', 'poor people', 'a poor woman', 'a poor man', in amounts varying from 1d to 6d.[32] Although medical treatment for the poor did not appear in the household accounts, Bridget claimed in her letters that she did provide such medical help to local people. Writing to Hugh, in February 1707/8, she described how she had treated many using her favourite 'snakeroot' remedy. She wrote 'thare are many pepel [people] have Agues hear about and I cuur [cure] many as infalibel as the Barke'.[33] Bridget compared her 'infallible' cure with the bitter-tasting Peruvian bark which was widely prescribed by medical practitioners.[34] However, no purchases of 'snakeroot' were found in the household accounts, and identification of this remedy remains uncertain.[35] Bridget also indicated her interest in using purchased medicinal preparations with the poor as, in March 1707/8, she wrote to her husband in London for some 'Vickers powders' to use with 'pore patients' saying: 'I wold be glad to have some for 2 or 3 pore patients that I wold trey it on one is a misarable obgek [object] of charity that is pore and cant help her self and is blind'.[36] Hugh evidently acted on Bridget's request, forwarding her letter with instructions: 'I send you this to read the good newes of my wifes being better: as also to read her latter parts of it relating to vickers; and desire you would goe straight to him and inquire'.[37] Thus Bridget received support from her husband in her efforts to obtain medicines from London suppliers to provide medical help for her poor patients.

From the examples given here, we can see that the later seventeenth-century household accounts did provide much detail of help for poorer people, such as cash, food and clothing, but did not often record medical treatment. Specific references to medicines for the poor were found in one household, that of the gentry Fortescue family, and this was the household that recorded the highest proportion of their budget on medicinal supplies. Provision of healthcare for the poor might have been made by other households, but it is unexplained why this was not recorded in later seventeenth-century accounts or letters where other help for the needy was mentioned in detail. Perhaps these households were relying instead on local collective arrangements of parish care for the health of the poor. Another slightly later household account suggests that when payments were recorded for medical treatment of the poor, they were payments for the services of medical practitioners or other attendants, rather than direct healthcare provision. In the early eighteenth-century account of Lady Cardigan, itemized payments included 'Paid Mrs Lambert for a nurse to attend sick people, 10s; Mary Bradley, £4 5s 0d for nursing Thomas Lee, postillion, for four weeks; Paid the woman that cured Roger White's child; Paid Maiching the surgeon for Widow Hawe's cure 15s; To Mr Baker, for physic for poor people, £11 15s 0s'.[38] At the level of the middling sort, attempts to increase distance from the 'settled poor' by organizational means are noted, particularly through the provision of school, apprenticeship, workhouse and almshouse schemes.[39] In a similar way, some of the households considered here may have avoided direct provision of medical treatment for the poor in the seventeenth century, and left this provision to others through poor rates and charity. Having said this, it is possible that some assistance for the poor was provided through the 'back door', that is some provision was made by household servants and associates which was not directly recorded in accounts or elsewhere.

Despite evident changes during the seventeenth century in the ways in which the poor were relieved, there was still a desire expressed by some writers to see the involvement of higher-status women in charitable activity related to healthcare. In 1673, Richard Allestree (1619–81) wrote of the need to 'see some of the primitive charity revive' where 'women of the highest rank' would attend the poor.[40] He argued for the personal involvement of ladies in 'dispensatories', claiming that they could prevent 'some abuses and frauds, which deputed agents may sometimes be tempted to'.[41] Thus, the expectation of higher-status women shifted from personally ministering to the poor to making a contribution of funds which they might then oversee. The previous emphasis on these women's direct involvement in healthcare for the poor was further undermined, for instance in 1714, when *The Ladies Library* gave the view that it was 'not of absolute necessity to the forming of a complete gentlewoman' to be 'the physician and surgeoness of the village'.[42] Perceptions of women's medical role in relation to the poor had changed, and this publication suggested that it was no longer an essential activity for women of standing, but perhaps a matter of choice.

Therapeutic approaches to children's complaints

Many purchases were specifically aimed at children's health in the Clarke and Fortescue household accounts. The most popular medicinal item for children seen in the Clarke household accounts was syrup of roses which Mary Clarke bought regularly, sometimes several times per year, between 1685 and 1696.[43] A recipe for syrup of roses was found in the Clarke family recipe book,

To make Syrrupe of Roses

Take 3 q[uar]ts of running water, 3 good handfulls of the buds of damaske roses crip, take an earthen pot and put this in stopt very close and keepe it warme night and day by the fier, you must every day straine them foor and add other damaske roses, as many and kept as before for the space of nine daies. you may add every day a handfull of mallowe flowers when you have strained the last day you must to every pinte of liquor that remaines, put a pound and halfe of suger and boile it to the height of a very thick sirrup clarifying it with the whites of 2, or 3 egges well beaten, and soe when it is cold you may keep it to your use. This is to bee taken 6 or 7 spoonefulls or more according to the strength of the patient with posset drinke, or clarified whay and an houre or two after the taking of it to drinke a draught of warme posset drinke. You must bruise your roses every morning in a stone morter, and straine them in canvas cloth, wringing it very hard. Prob.[44]

Whether the recipe for syrup of roses was ever prepared is not known, and there were no records of purchases of roses in the Clarke household accounts. Although the recipe may not have been used, it indicated the likely constituents and dosage for such a preparation. However, this recipe for syrup of roses might not have provided a totally accurate picture, as syrup of roses purchased from the apothecary was often prepared with the addition of senna for greater purging effect, which was regarded as an essential for children. The Clarke household account extract shown here (see Figure 6.1)[45] lists two medicinal purchases, one payment for powders of wormseed, rhubarb, corolina and burnt hartshorn, and the other payment for a bottle of syrup of roses. Purging was a key aim of many items purchased by the Clarke family.

Concern about worms in children was evident in the household accounts of the Clarke family; Mary paid for worm treatments of various kinds on frequent occasions. In 1689 she recorded: 'April 12 Pd Isacke what he laid out for the Children when they had the worms, 1s ½d'.[46] Two years later she recorded purchases of worm powder and wormseed, in 1696 more worm powder, wormwood and wormseed, and these items were purchased again in 1700 and 1702.[47] Further unspecified items could have been supplied by an apothecary as indicated, for example, by an item recorded in April 1702: 'Paid Mr Boson the apothecary of Wellington his bill of things had of him in the childrens sickness, 9s 6d'.[48] Medicinal purchases were also evident for the children in the Fortescue family. However, unlike the accounts of the Clarke family, the Fortescue household accounts included little

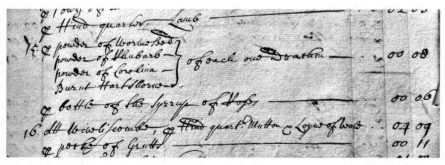

FIGURE 6.1 *Clarke household account extract, Sanford Family of Nynehead Papers, DD\SF/3304 Part 1, Somerset Heritage Centre (courtesy of Somerset Heritage Trust).*

mention of syrup of roses or worm powders. Bridget Fortescue did have recipes from her mother's collection for treating worms, including one entitled 'A powder to kill and purge forth the wormes, the small wormes in the Guts' containing wormseed, senna, coriander, hartshorn, rhubarb and rue, but she recorded only one purchase of wormseed.[49] Instead, the Fortescue household account recorded frequent purchases of oil of almonds which may have been intended for treating worms or fits in children. Oil of almonds appeared in the Fortescue recipe collection in 'A glister to kill the wormes', and also in two other recipes which were concerned with preventing fits in children.[50]

Further analysis of medicinal recipes which specified children as patients can help us to understand how children were perceived in terms of health and illness, even if the recipes were not necessarily in use. Hannah Newton has shown in her study of household recipe collections that almost all (91 per cent) included some recipes for children.[51] In the recipe collections studied for this book, 209 (3.2 per cent) recipes referred to children out of a total of 6,513 medicinal recipes, 81 (2.2 per cent) in 3,604 printed recipes and 138 (4.7 per cent) in 2,909 household recipes. Thus, proportionately, there were over twice as many household recipes aimed specifically at children as there were in print. Three particular ailments – convulsions, rickets, worms – made up over half of all recipes for children.[52] Altogether the recipe collections provided sixty-four recipes for convulsions or fits, and twenty-three (36 per cent) of them specified children.[53] Forty (65 per cent) of the sixty-two recipes for rickets, and thirty-one (26 per cent) of all 117 recipes for worms, mentioned children. There were also a variety of recipes relating to urinary difficulties in children ('bloody urine', 'cannot hold water', 'to make urine').[54] Purging treatment was particularly evident in medicinal recipes aimed at both young and old. 'A purge for children or old men' was one of the selection of recipe titles copied by Margaret Boscawen from the *Queens Closet Opened* and was based on spirit of tartar.[55] Another recipe for a purge that Margaret recorded as suitable for older persons or children was given to her by Mistress Booles, and was based on diaturbith and rhubarb which had purging properties. Elsewhere, she recorded recipes such as 'purges for a child very young' which included gentler ingredients such as aniseed.[56] Although dosage might be reduced significantly for children as in 'An excellent purge' (where the total number of twenty-nine grains for a man was reduced to twenty-four for a woman, twenty-one for a young man, thirteen for a child of six years and eight for a child one year old) the ingredients were often the same as those for adult use, including strongly acting ingredients such as antimony and tartar.[57] Newton further details dosage changes and other kinds of adaptations in the remedies given to children in recognition of their weaker and moister constitutions compared to adults.[58]

Certain ailments appeared to be specific to children according to the medicinal recipes; scalding urine (two recipes) and tender eyes (two recipes), for example, were only indicated as children's complaints.[59] Swellings in the belly and swollen or grown liver or hardness of liver were also identified in recipes specific to children. A swollen or hardened liver could be associated with worms, as in the recipe 'For young children that have the liver grown or the wormes' in *Natura Exenterata*, and Valerie Fildes notes that the London *Bills of Mortality* listed many deaths from 'liver-grown spleen and rickets'.[60] There were relatively few recipes for children's problems which might have been more widely encountered, such as teething, head lice and crying (six recipes in all). It seems highly unlikely that these conditions were infrequent, though they might have been dealt with by wet nurses rather than family members. It is possible that remedies for these problems were commonly suggested as part of knowledge passed on from generation to generation in an oral manner. Occasionally, such advice can be seen in family letters. For example, Bridget Fortescue's aunt wrote in 1693 of the benefit of Venice treacle which 'my Grandmother vere gave all her children and Grandchildren which are pretty numerous and none had convulsions'.[61] Venice treacle was a prepared electuary, with over fifty ingredients, available from the apothecary.[62] Thus, suggestions for remedies passed on independently of recipe collections did not necessarily equate to homemade or simple remedies, as some recommendations were passed on for medicines requiring purchase from an apothecary.

The recipes specific to children were further analysed for their medicinal ingredients. Table 6.2 refers to the fifteen most common ingredients listed in recipes for children's ailments, based on 209 recipes. These popular ingredients accounted for just over 30 per cent of all ingredients for children's ailments. Some of these ingredients were household staples (such as wine, butter, sugar and ale) and readily available in wealthier households. Popular prepared ingredients in recipes for children included distilled waters of succory, paeony and cherry and syrup of roses, and these would have been available from the apothecary, along with purging ingredients such as rhubarb and wormwood. Both hart's tongue and liverwort were frequent ingredients in remedies for rickets, and paeony was also a frequent ingredient in remedies for fits.

A comparison with Table 4.2, which shows frequent plant ingredients in all medicinal recipes, reveals that three of the top fifteen ingredients for children's recipes were similar, and these were rose, liquorice and wormwood. Spices such as cinnamon, cloves and other warming ingredients were less evident in the children's recipes. The reduced use of warming recipe ingredients is consistent with the perception of children as having warm and moist constitutions. While purging ingredients such as rhubarb figured strongly in both recipes and purchases in the household accounts, three other top recipe ingredients for children's complaints were not seen as specifically named purchases in the household accounts. These were hart's tongue, liverwort and paeony, all ingredients commonly found in recipes for rickets and convulsions, although it is possible that such ingredients might have been supplied by an

TABLE 6.2 *Ingredients in recipes for children (n=209)*

Ingredient source species	Household recipes, *n*	Printed recipes, *n*	All recipes, *n*	% of all ingredients
Cow	27	17	44	4.19
Wine	22	12	34	3.24
Deer	15	12	27	2.57
Hart's tongue	23	2	25	2.38
Sugar	13	10	23	2.19
Liverwort	19	3	22	2.10
Rose	17	5	22	2.10
Wormwood	13	8	21	2.00
Bee	8	10	18	1.71
Liquorice	8	7	15	1.43
Agrimony	9	5	14	1.33
Ale	11	3	14	1.33
Rhubarb	9	5	14	1.33
Succory	12	2	14	1.33
Paeony	12	1	13	1.24
All top 15 ingredients	218	102	320	30.48
All ingredients	710	340	1,050	100.00

Source: Stobart, Recipes and Expenditure Database.

apothecary without being specifically named. This brief survey of medicinal purchases and the recipes related to children's complaints suggests that the key concern relating to child health was the need to keep children from being 'costive' or constipated, and to remove undesirable humours through purging on a frequent basis. There was an emphasis on purging in many recipes, including those for convulsions, rickets and worms. Overall, while the household accounts might suggest differences in the nature of purchases for purging for children's health, the approach was largely one of conformity with the need for purging which was evident in the household recipes. The treatment of children in the household context thus appeared to be similar in both lay and learned hands, being strongly based on the long-standing Galenic humoral framework.

Confidence in healthcare for children

Whether medicines were purchased or made at home, women gained experience and confidence over the years in dealing with health problems amongst their children. Mary was directly involved in much of the healthcare relating to her children. She wrote to Edward frequently mentioning the children's health: for instance, 'I thank God we are all well here but Molly has a very sore mouth'.[63] Mary expressed confidence in dealing with everyday accidents of childhood, claiming this to be a far easier task in comparison to the problems of finding suitable marriage partners for her older children, when she thought that they required 'more carefull and diligent looking after then when 3 years old'.[64] Mary became more confident about common complaints, expressing her view that they were 'little' or minor sicknesses which would pass: for example, writing to Edward, 'it is very sickley all heareabouts but I thank God all our family holds well except a little cold or a sore throte or such a business'.[65] By the time that Mary had her tenth child in 1694, she was evidently more relaxed about teething troubles, writing in September that 'I thanke God all the rest heare is very well also only Sammys teeth trobles him which makes him a little peevish and nott sleepe soe well a nights'.[66] And she became quite familiar with symptoms that involved dealing with worms in the children: 'Molly was very fevorish the last week but I hope it was nothing but wormes'.[67] For minor bumps and bruises, Mary used Hungary water and 'a bitt of brown paper will cure it agen'.[68] When her daughter Betty had a 'swelled face', for example, Hungary water was used by Mary both morning and evening to achieve 'a perfect cure without doing anything else'.[69] Advice on remedies for very young children was offered by relatives, particularly Ursula Venner, Mary's sister-in-law, who passed on a physician's recommendation in advice regarding Edward soon after he was born, including 'Doctor Gerdnir told me that the oyle of Scorpiones is good to annoynte your little boy's shoulder between the swelling'; oil of scorpions was a panacea for poisons, and recommended for the bite of a mad dog.[70] Ursula expressed her fears about the dangers of teething for young children, and she wrote to Edward about Elizabeth, at six months of age in December 1678, to suggest 'let her gums be rubbed . . . which I hope will be a meanes to break her gummes'.[71] The following month, Ursula added the suggestion of 'the brayne of a hare or the head of a small leek are commonly used to breake the gummes'.[72] The use of a hare's brain derived from classical medicine, and figured in an ointment with honey and butter recommended 'to make Childrens Teeth come without Pain' in the *Queens Closet Opened*.[73] However, Mary appeared not to take up these suggestions but to rely on her own preferred remedies with the children. As we saw in the household accounts, she favoured purging and often purchased rhubarb and syrup of roses. She also used other purging herbs, and while away in London in 1690 she gave instructions for the cook to ensure a good store of 'centrey', writing 'dont forgett to give it the children as I use to doe'.[74] The remedy 'centrey' was probably centaury, a bitter and tonic herb, which would have provided a purging action.[75] Back at Chipley, Mary put rhubarb in her daughter's drink as a purge to treat a 'break out all over her face'.[76] When rhubarb did not appear to help her son Sammy in another complaint, Mary turned to the use of 'glisters', probably clysters or enemas, to empty the bowels.[77] Ursula continued to proffer remedies, and Mary did try at least one recommendation from her sister-in-law, explaining to Edward 'poor Nanny is ill of a violent paine in her head ever since Munday morning and is very fevorrish and sometimes sick at her stomach the last night I gave her a glister which wrought very well and when she went to bead some of my sister's antidote'.[78] But Ursula's antidote did not work and Mary found Nanny was 'not better' in the morning, so she 'sent for Dr Passons ... her to be lett blood 10 ounces'.[79] Thus, Mary would summon a medical practitioner if the remedies that she tried appeared to be unsuccessful and she expressed satisfaction that purging was to be achieved through bloodletting. Newton observes that kitchen physic continued, likely with considerable expenditure of effort into the late seventeenth century, and was not readily replaced by professional medicine.[80] In Mary Clarke's care of the children, it was the need to purge which largely drove her actions and, even when medical practitioner advice was given, she was concerned that medical treatment by others should be similar in approach. Calling for the medical practitioner may have been a response to lack of improvement, but it could also serve to confirm the approach taken by a lay householder in their medical stance. Although Mary did arrange for medicinal herbs to be prepared for the children, most of her remedies were purchased, and the key role of purchased prepared medicines may have been under-represented in household healthcare.

Sending for the medical practitioner

Until recently, historical accounts of the use of medical practitioners for illnesses in children have generally argued that medical practitioners were infrequently called upon to attend children. Porter and Porter give the example of Ralph Josselin, vicar of Earl's Colen in Essex, who hardly ever summoned a practitioner over forty years, even when his children were dying.[81] Mary Lindemann says that consulting someone outside the family was unpredictable, and that some families never did so for a variety of reasons, from fear to geographical location, despite a 'profusion of choices'.[82] Where a medical practitioner was consulted in relation to children, this was more likely to be the apothecary, midwife or surgeon rather than the physician.[83] Indeed, Pollock says of the diary sources 'there does not seem as if much could be done for sick children' and that 'few parents called a doctor'.[84] Newton provides a more recent and substantial survey of children's healthcare and claims that medical advice from professional practitioners was only sought after all efforts in the household had failed.[85] However, within the households considered for this book, there seemed to be varied approaches and medical advice could be sought alongside self-help healthcare, as we have seen above in the context of the Clarke household. Even though the men in these families were regularly away from home, they were actively interested in the details of their children's illnesses and they sought advice on behalf of the family. Mary and Edward Clarke's letters often included mention of requests for help from medical practitioners on behalf of members of the family, including children and servants. Mary frequently sought additional assistance even though she might identify a probable cause for why a condition had worsened. To illustrate, she wrote to Edward about Sammy, 'who has gone backward very much in his going since this cold wether came in and is now much out of order with a surfeit he tooke by overcharging his stomach with too much wigg'.[86] Mary decided in this instance to call on the local apothecary, Mr Smith, and she wrote reassuringly the next day, 'After I had writt he was worse which made me unsatisfied till I had spoke with Mr Smith who I sent for and he brought some things with him to give him and tells me he will do very well and he is much better'.[87] Mary appeared to be fairly sure of the cause of the child's illness, but she still requested the apothecary's advice and medicines to confirm her view and help resolve the problem. Mary also called upon medical practitioners to help if a complaint persisted despite her treatment. She wrote to Edward in October 1694 that 'Molly is very well but extremely costive longer than I give her ruburbe in her beare and she is very apt to break out all over her face'. A few weeks later she worried, 'I cannot get Mollys face well'.[88] Edward then wrote on behalf of Mary to John Locke, seeking advice: 'I must begg alsoe your direction in the following case. Mrs Clarke writes mee that little Molly has had a sharp ugly humour breakeing out all over her face'.[89] Edward's letter to Locke further stated:

> Mrs Clarke hopes by such a good dyett, and such purging and other directions as you shall thinke proper, the child will doe very well again . . . My wife has endeavoured to purge her by an infusion of rubarb, but the child is verie difficult to be purged, and therefore my wife earnestly desires your thoughts and directions upon the whole matter, which shee promises shall bee punctually observed.[90]

So Edward identified the cause of illness according to Mary and also explained her active efforts to treat the child. Rather than relinquishing control, these examples suggest that Mary attempted to maintain her participation in treatment. The Clarke family also refused to accept the advice of another physician who thought that there was 'little to be done' about Sammy's illness, and Edward contacted Locke for a further opinion in 1695.[91] Mary confirmed that she 'would be glad' if Edward could obtain Locke's advice.[92] Thus, Edward acted as a mediator for obtaining a further opinion when both self-help and other medical advice were ineffective. Although the Clarke family relied on Locke for additional medical advice, they were perhaps fortunate in having an individual with medical expertise so closely involved with the family. In other cases it was evident that the apothecary was called upon to provide medical advice and support. Bridget Fortescue maintained close links with a local apothecary based in the town of Barnstaple in North Devon. He was Joseph Baller (1642–1712),[93] and Bridget obtained details of remedies, including recipes for children's ailments. He provided instructions for a purging remedy (Figure 6.2):

Madam

I think the Recipe is much the same and may be made thus. Take sharp pointed dock rootes 4 ounces, Angellica Rootes one ounce Sarsaparilla one ounce, China half an ounce Ivory one ounce steel one ounce and a half harts tongue leaves and baume of each one handfull. boil all in 3 quarts of Water to 2 q[uar]ts adding about the later end of the boiling or just as you take it from the fire half a pint of the white Lisbon wine and cover it close till tis cold then strain and bottle it.[94]

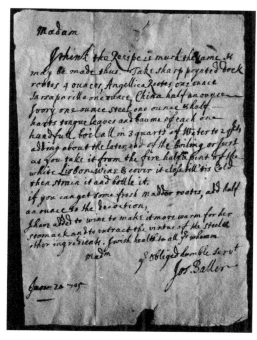

FIGURE 6.2 *Letter from Joseph Baller, apothecary, to Bridget Fortescue, 20 June 1705, Fortescue of Castle Hill papers, 1262M/FC/7, Devon Heritage Centre (courtesy of the Countess of Arran).*

That the recipe was 'much the same' indicates that this recipe had been previously given by the apothecary. The recipe contained imported medicinal ingredients such as sarsaparilla and china root, and Baller continued his letter with suggestions of further additions, and some explanation of the mechanism of action: 'if you can get some fresh madder rootes, add half an ounce to the decoction, I have added to wine to make it more warm for her stomack and to extract the virtue of the steel and other ingredients'.[95] This letter bore many similarities to an undated recipe in the loose collection of Fortescue household recipes which was endorsed 'the Childrens drink by mr Baller' and included china roots, sarsaparilla, ivory and dock steeped in beer.[96] Sarsaparilla and china root were also ingredients of a further undated recipe endorsed 'my one [own] drink from Mr Baller when with child'.[97] These ingredients were perceived as strengthening and tonic items, and Bridget was able to draw on the apothecary's advice without further recourse to a physician when she felt the preparation was needed again.[98] Burnby flags up the role of the apothecary in providing a 'health-centre in miniature' in the early modern period: although studies of apothecaries have tended to focus on their professional development rather than their role in enabling lay people, especially women, not only to obtain medicinal supplies but also to develop confidence in healthcare, a topic that deserves further exploration.[99]

The later seventeenth-century letters and accounts illustrate the extent of concern and effort of parents to obtain appropriate healthcare for their children, whether through self-help or the attention of medical practitioners. This is consistent with the high degree of anxiety noted by Joseph Illick amongst parents in the seventeenth century.[100] Both men and women might be actively involved in care for their children, and Newton shows that there was not always a clear gender division in the roles of parents as carers.[101] For example, John Evelyn described in his diary the illness of his five-year-old son Richard in 1658, and the Evelyn recipe book notes the giving of treatment for the 'chin cough'.[102] As Lisa Smith shows, both men and women could be involved in summoning medical advice, administering remedies and reporting patient progress, although women were more likely to write about children's illnesses than men.[103] In the case of the Clarke family, we have seen that Mary tended to have direct involvement with the children's healthcare and the local apothecary, whilst Edward was more likely to mediate with medical advisers in London. Similarly, in the Fortescue family, Bridget took on the role of actively providing healthcare for the children while liaising directly with the local apothecary, and Hugh helped with advice and medicinal supplies from London.

Making a diagnosis

At the start of this chapter, we saw how Mary Clarke identified the complaint of her daughter, Jenny, and took steps to provide treatment. According to

Locke made it clear that Mary should have asked for learned advice from a physician, and he identified a boundary between lay and learned advice based on who was the 'better judge'. By criticizing Mary's 'guesses', he brought into question both her medical knowledge and her concern for the health of the child. Despite Mary's extensive experience with the care of her children, and her keen efforts to adhere to the medical orthodoxy of purging to maintain and restore health, her knowledge and skill were considered of little consequence in determining the nature of a specific disease and subsequent treatment in this case of rickets.

In relation to healthcare, the credulity of women was further questioned by suggestions that they could not distinguish providers of suitable medical advice, and this kind of criticism is often identified with male authors, from physicians to clergy.[115] Christopher Merret, in *The Accomplisht Physician* (1670), blamed women for spreading details of 'vulgar' physicians, claiming that 'if a man chance to be surprized with sickness, he presently asks his Wife, what Doctor he shall send to, who instantly gives her direction to him, that had her by the Nose last'.[116] Some disapproval sought to distinguish women of different status: for instance, in *The Gentlewoman's Companion*, elderly and uneducated women provided the focus in comments about the 'vulgar errours' of 'some old Dotard of our sex', and gentlewomen were advised to take care not to be 'abused by their credulous and ignorant Nurses'.[117] Nagy suggests that hostility towards women providing medical services came from men within the medical profession.[118] However, some women contributed to establishing and maintaining medical boundaries: for example, Isabella Duke associated women medical practitioners with quacks in her correspondence with John Locke, writing to him of the danger of ruining her health 'by putting my self into the hands of some Quack Doctress'.[119] Thus, although Isabella sought information from Locke about cures for agues to help her friends and neighbours, she also expressed outright criticism of other women who would attempt cures. Women could thus face uncomfortable conflict between expectations of providing elements of healthcare and criticism of their involvement in medical activities.

A focus on medicines

The efforts made by parents to obtain medicines for treating their children could also be criticized. As we saw in Chapter 3, the household accounts did provide detail of purchases of prepared medicines. Although the understanding of purgation as important for maintaining health was widespread, the way in which prepared medicines claiming to be purgatives worked was questioned. In *The Efficacy and Extent of True Purgation* (1696), Everard Maynwaringe, a Helmontian physician, attacked both commercial remedy sellers and learned medical practitioners for their adherence to the long-standing use of 'divers' purgatives for different humours.[120] He fully agreed that, of all 'physical operations', purgation 'is the most general, useful, and advantagious: For this alone, being well and truly performed, seldom fails to give good Relief' and he noted that most people used this sort of remedy 'without the Advice of a Physician'.[121] However, he disparaged both the classical view that purgatives operated selectively, each 'by their different formal Propriety and specific Qualities' attracting a 'different Humor or Matter' and the 'contrary' view that 'Paracelsus, Joubertus, and others, have asserted; Purging Medicines to operate . . . in a hostile Manner . . . drive out noxious Humors'.[122] Instead, he drew on Helmontian ideas of fermentation and claimed that a universal purgative should be used, so that the whole body was involved in 'Consent and Co-operation' in order that 'impure and useless Matter is brought from all Parts, to be discharged'.[123] Thus, he asserted that the use of some purgatives carried a danger that some matter might be left behind and the 'Venom then lies a breeding . . . there comes an after Reckoning to account for'.[124] Having noted that two children died from a 'mercurial powder' given by an 'Empyrick at Oxford', Maynwaringe described the properties of a 'true' purgative as 'wholesom', 'Placid in Operation' and 'applicable to all Cases, requiring Purgative Energy'. Such a medicine could be used at any time of year and by those who were weak.[125] These differences of opinion relating to purging did affect the lay person's views about purging, and were reflected in lay concerns as we will see in discussing Bridget Fortescue's fears in Chapter 7.

Some cure-alls were widely advertised for self-help use as 'universal medicines'. However, universal medicines were not approved by all, and opposition came from a number of authors, some who sought to promote self-help, others who tried to reinstate the medical practitioner. According to The Kitchin-Physician (1680), 'natural, useful and proper medicines' from the 'rich Garden of nature' could be used without the need of translation by learned or 'mean-spirited Physicians' or those with 'pretended Universal Medicines'.[126] The author advised that learned assistance was not necessary 'in common and ordinary distempers which many times the diligent Nurse, or Housewife, by her plain and common Experience in Herbs and Plants' could cure.[127] Even those who defended past Galenic practice of physicians acknowledged that remedies were now the main focus of treatment without which the physician could not cure. James Primrose (c. 1598–1659), a physician in Hull, wrote in support of the Galenic tradition in Popular Errours. Or, the Errours of the People in Physick (1651), and further argued that physicians ought to be more involved in making medicaments, 'for remedies doe cure without a physician, but not a physician without remedies'.[128] He saw remedies as best used to treat individuals on a constitutional basis, castigating women who meddled in physick and surgery by using remedies from books, and he argued that remedies needed to be altered according to the person, place, part affected and other circumstances'.[129] As Galenic, Paracelsian, Helmontian and other physicians argued about the right way to treat illness from a practitioner perspective, medicines were a prime focus of medical debate, and Wear notes that 'method' had become a term of abuse signifying old-fashioned dogma.[130] For example, Maynwaringe criticized the 'vast extent of Physick-Learning' and concluded that 'The Stress of Curing lies mostly; and often wholly upon the Excellency of Medicine' rather than the 'Notions and Theorems' of professors.[131] As Ian Mortimer points out, the seventeenth century saw a shift in the way in which medicines were perceived, so that they became increasingly dominant in the treatment of illness.[132] Perhaps it was not surprising that lay people eagerly focused on collecting medicines in recipe books and spending rose on frequently purchased medicines for household members, since the 'excellency of medicine' had become such a key factor in treating disease. Whether the medicines were recommended by Galenists, Paracelsians or Helmontians, the medicament had become the most significant element of medical treatment.

Setting boundaries on household medicine

How did self-help fare beyond the end of the seventeenth century? Purchases of both medicinal supplies and medical services are said to have further increased in the eighteenth century, in a 'booming health culture'.[133] Yet, Anne Digby writing on medical practitioners and the market from 1720 onwards says, 'well-informed Georgian consumers showed marked scepticism about the remedies proffered by the "medical" profession so that in many cases the household retained sovereignty as the consumer of its own physic'.[134] This perspective acknowledges the role of self-help and points toward the ongoing intermingled nature of self-help and professional services. Michael James provides the example of Lady Hannah East, who used both self-help and professional practitioners, being reluctant at times to administer prescribed medications.[135] Some lay individuals developed extensive household practices and made their own medicines, as evidenced in the diary of Nicholas Blundell (1669–1737) of Little Crosby, a Catholic landowner who became actively involved in all aspects of the health of his family and neighbourhood.[136] He collected recipes and plants, made remedies, applied plasters, dressed wounds and advised others; moreover his activities were assisted by the local apothecary and physician.[137] The extent of self-help in the eighteenth century may have provoked further efforts by physicians to develop the distinction between professional and domestic medicine. The use of the term domestic in a medicinal context appeared widely in the later eighteenth century, particularly with the publication in 1769 of *Domestic Medicine*, by William Buchan (1729–1805).[138] Buchan, a Scottish physician who settled in Sheffield and then London, provided much medical information in his book including advice on preventative measures in healthcare, and it was a runaway success with many reprints.[139] Although Buchan claimed to be laying medicine open in his book, his main justification for this was to enable people to 'ask and follow advice' from the right sort of people, i.e. physicians, instead of taking 'any thing that is recommended to them by their credulous neighbours'.[140] He said of the physician and the quack that the 'line betwixt them is not sufficiently apparent', and argued that the best way to destroy quackery would be to increase knowledge of medicine.[141] Buchan was not keen on the great reliance of people on medicines, and he took the opportunity to argue that the 'generality of people lay too much stress upon medicine, and trust too little to their own endeavours', and by this he meant that they needed 'proper food, fresh air, cleanliness'.[142] Domestic practitioners were further severely criticized in the eighteenth century by James Parkinson (1755–1824), a physician of London's East End. He was convinced that 'many lives are lost by neglecting to apply sufficiently soon for medical aid, and by improper treatment of diseases by domestic practitioners'.[143] In *Medical Admonitions Addressed to Families* (1799), Parkinson argued that the role of the domestic practitioner involved just two things: first, to identify when a medical practitioner should be sought; and second, to carry out without question the directions given by the medical practitioner.[144] Both Buchan and Parkinson emphasized the inability of the lay person to effectively diagnose disease, and domestic medicine was effectively limited to recognizing a need for hygiene, treating minor complaints and carrying out the doctor's bidding.

Conclusion

In this chapter we have seen that named recipients of household healthcare were primarily household members, and little evidence of medical treatment for the poor emerges in the household accounts in the later seventeenth century, despite other detailed assistance based on money, food and clothing. This finding contrasts with the expectations of higher-status households in the earlier seventeenth century regarding their provision of healthcare for the neighbourhood. The development of organized welfare for the poor may have reduced the necessity of direct provision although high-status women might be expected to maintain some involvement. Closer examination of household accounts in relation to children reveals that medicinal items purchased for treating children could differ from one household to another, although most approaches to child health remained concerned with the effectiveness of purging. The emphasis of child-related recipes in household medicinal recipe collections was also on humoral matters, with many recipes for particular child-related complaints such as rickets, worms and convulsions. Fewer recipes were recorded for common problems in childhood, although suggestions were evidently received about self-help remedies that might be used including prepared medicines recommended by physicians. As women gained experience, children's health appeared to be an area of increasing confidence in recognition and assessment of complaints and provision of remedies. Medical practitioners were called on by families, sometimes to confirm a diagnosis and self-help treatment, and at other times to provide further treatment advice. Contacts with medical practitioners were often mediated by male spouses, and

7

'I Troble Noe Body with My Complaints': Chronic Disorders

Chronic disorders could be troublesome, although many seventeenth-century conditions were suffered without particular treatment. Some complaints took a long time to resolve while others were intermittent, and recurred repeatedly over time. Some people avoided dealing with chronic problems because they feared that the treatment would be more painful, especially where surgery was concerned.[1] Chronic complaints provided many opportunities for trying out self-help remedies, and this chapter explores the nature of some chronic complaints and what actions people took, from self-help to negotiations with medical practitioners about their treatment. The chronic problems encountered by Mary Clarke and Bridget Fortescue provide examples of their efforts to manage and resolve ongoing disorders. Mary Clarke's dropsy-like condition worsened as she grew older, but she hoped that symptoms might fade as they had on previous occasions. As her legs and abdomen swelled up, Mary wrote to her husband, Edward, in February 1701: 'the swelling in my legs and Belly have bin more trobelsome to me for some time past then usuall, but I troble noe body with my Complaints being in hopes it will weare off agenn'.[2] The ongoing health problems of Bridget Fortescue were related to the King's evil, or scrofula, from which she had suffered since childhood,[3] resulting in repeated swellings and sores on her neck. Later in life, Bridget wrote to her husband, Hugh, that 'you know I have been trying all my Life long and have gone trew [through] 10 or 12 seferel [several] sortes of methodes' as well as 'treying many medsons my selfe'.[4] She had often sought the advice of medical practitioners and tried self-help remedies in attempts to resolve the complaint. The relationship of self-help to medical practitioners is considered here in letters that detail how treatments were negotiated. Through their letters, we will see how Mary and Bridget attempted to help themselves and the different strategies used in their negotiations with medical advisers. Both women found that their views on suitable therapeutic approaches were challenged, by their husbands as well as by medical practitioners. They sought ways to influence therapeutic determination, from assessment of the nature of their complaints through to choices made about suitable medicines and other treatment. As in the previous chapter about children's complaints, we will see that beliefs about the kinds of medicines given were significant, although the strategies used to ensure preferred choices could differ in these negotiations with medical practitioners.

Although many long-term complaints resulted from untreated problems, some were experienced as part of aging or disability. A humoral framework emphasized the longer-term effects of any illnesses, and conditions such as cancer were perceived as resulting from accumulation of corrupted humours.[5] The term 'chronic' was used in the seventeenth century to refer to slow or lingering complaints in contrast to 'sharpe' diseases, such as plague; the latter was an epidemic disease that still occurred in periodic outbreaks, for example in Norwich, Colchester, Newcastle and London.[6] Dobson notes the association of acute disease with epidemics in the *Bills of Mortality*, providing records of perceived causes of death, and these records distinguished 'chronical diseases' from 'acute and epidemical diseases'.[7] Although acute and infectious disease were predominant causes of mortality in the past, the effects of chronic complaints were also significant in contributing to disabilities and other problems.[8] Untreated conditions could result in ongoing skin complaints, bone changes and loss of teeth from nutritional deficiencies (such as in scurvy and rickets), unresolved ulcers and abscesses (arising from wounds and venereal disease), damaged organs (causing circulatory and respiratory limitations), and loss of use of limbs or senses (due to gangrene resulting in amputations, infections causing loss of hearing or sight).[9] Some chronic complaints were related to environmental conditions, and Cockayne identifies a range of itchy, mouldy, smelly and dirty aspects of early modern England, with consequent efforts to implement public regulations for the avoidance of disease and infestation.[10] Older age may have contributed to poor health through the exacerbation of complaints and weakness, although it is evident that the perception of how 'old' someone was could depend on varied criteria, not only chronological age but also cultural factors.[11] Average life expectancy between 1600 and 1649 averaged 36.4 years, and was lower still for the poor living in towns and cities but, since many deaths occurred in childhood, at least half of those who survived beyond the age of twenty-five could expect to live on to over sixty years of age.[12] Even longer lives were possible by the end of the seventeenth century when average life expectancy rose, for example to 41.8 years in a Devon parish.[13] The effects of aging on the body were generally regarded in humoral terms, as a process of cooling and drying, so that 'cold' illnesses predominated in the older person. These changes could affect cognitive function, sensibility, movement and mood, and could be worse for women who were perceived as constitutionally colder and wetter.[14] Elizabeth Isham recorded details of her mother's illnesses in the 1640s and described how her mother 'would complane of coldnes saying she had truly undergon the infermities of olde age'.[15] However, not all experiences of older age were cast as negative: for instance, John Locke recorded his perceptions of Alice George in March 1681, supposedly 108 years old, noting that 'her hearing is very good', 'memory and understanding perfectly good' and that she 'never took any physic but once about 40 years since'.[16] Although the real age that Alice attained is questionable, Locke was a reliable observer and her condition may not have been untypical for an elderly person.[17] Thus, the range of chronic complaints experienced in the seventeenth century was wide, from irritating minor conditions to severe disabling infirmities, and some maintained good health for many years of their lives. Several recurring concerns in chronic disorders were pain and melancholy, and the household recipe collections provided a range of suggestions for self-help.

Self-help and chronic complaints

Chronic complaints often gave rise to pain, and diaries and autobiographical material suggest that there were varied ways to manage it. Pain could not always be ignored, and patients had a rich vocabulary for different types of pain.[18] Some people believed that pain was inescapable, or even necessary for a cure to proceed.[19] Such chronic suffering was commonly reported as many preferred to refuse surgery and cautery that were perceived as more painful than the condition itself.[20] A seventeenth-century surgeon in London noted that patients with tumours might delay seeking further care for a period of 'some days' to 'many years'.[21] Varied strategies were taken in response to pain, and distraction from it was one possibility if no remedies could help. Reading in the sick chamber was the method used by Lady Hoby when she suffered from severe toothache in March 1600 and obtained 'diverse medesons that did litle profett', claiming that she began to feel better only when her husband read to her.[22] Other remedies for pain could be applied externally, and Olivia Weisser describes how individuals often self-treated swellings and 'bumps' with topical remedies such as plasters, poultices and ointments, attending the surgical practitioner only when such efforts were exhausted.[23] Regarding recipes found for pain in the database for this book, of the 159 recipes that mentioned pain in the title, two-thirds were for external application to various parts of the body. Some internal remedies were also suggested, ranging from syrups and drinks to pills and lozenges. These recipes contained slightly more animal-derived household constituents than the average medicinal recipe, such as eggs, honey and milk, while common plant ingredients ranged from roses to sage and wormwood. Medical practitioners described pain in classical terms, particularly understanding it as a disruption of animal spirits moving to and from parts of the body.[24] Remedies with cold qualities were thus thought to be appropriate since they were thought to suppress the movement of the animal spirits and so reduce pain. Amongst remedies for pain in printed advice books, the use of cooling poppy seeds in various preparations in Nicholas Culpeper's *A Physicall Directory* of 1649 was suggested to 'ease pain' and 'provoke sleep',[25] and opium was recommended by Coelson in *The Poor-Mans Physician* of 1656 for pain in gout and sleeplessness.[26] However, dosage with poppy-based preparations such as opium could be rather uncertain, being known to be dangerous since the time of Galen.[27] Thomas Sydenham (1624–89) developed a form of laudanum, an opiate-containing tincture, and claimed that it provided an advantage in making exact doses possible, although his preparation was not taken up widely until the eighteenth century.[28]

A range of other chronic complaints may have been treated with self-help, according to Margaret Pelling and Richard Smith, particularly problems of old age involving sight, hearing, teeth and persistent conditions which were more likely to have been helped by traditional healers, self-help or use of purchased remedies rather than 'elite practitioners'.[29] Cheerfulness was considered especially important in maintaining good health, and individuals who were suffering from ongoing complaints might complain of their 'low spirits': for example, Mary Clarke wrote of her melancholy and its effects on her health. She complained how 'very often I find a great decay of spirritts . . . and by this meanes keeps me very leane and low sperrited', a condition that she thought was a hindrance to 'gathering strength'.[30] Almost ten years later, Mary's letters during 1704 and 1705 further complained of a 'continuall opreshion on my spirits' and being 'very melloncoly'.[31] Another person who complained of melancholy damaging her health was Hannah Allen of Derbyshire who wrote in the late seventeenth century, after her husband died, that 'my melancholy hath bad effects upon my body'.[32] Melancholy was much debated in the seventeenth century, and extensive discussion of its causes and treatment can be seen in the *Anatomy of Melancholy* by Robert Burton (1577–1640), published in 1621.[33] Recent studies reveal that some identified religious causes and blamed the illness of melancholy on excessive concerns about salvation and redemption.[34] However, many people believed the long-standing explanation that melancholy was connected with an excess of choleric humours or black bile.[35] There were many recipes and self-help remedies for conditions of melancholy or low spirits, and use of alcohol-based preparations to raise the spirits was widespread.[36] Crawford and Gowing record a letter from Anne Dormer (1648?–95) to her sister about her 'restless nights and unquiet days' and her thanks for the sending of wine, saying: 'I allow myself all I can drink of any sort, which never exceeds six spoonfuls, and unless my spirits be very low indeed I cannot prevail with my self to take any for many days'.[37] Margaret Boscawen received a letter from her sister in 1683 with detailed instructions for several remedies, the purpose of the medicines being for treating 'malincoly', through treating the spleen and purging the offending humours:

> Dear Sister ... I send you these medisons for malincoly and the spleen in Johns wort and gill go by ground [ground ivy] together or alone made and taken like ('tea' and 'tae' crossed out) tea, the first and last thing is good, and to purge malincoly, sena steeped in bear or ale half an ounce devided into 4 quart bottels, and let them drinke it for there ordinary drink, for as long time as you see cause, the common stra[w]burys eaten plentiful is good.[38]

Numerous recipes for melancholy based on syrups and distilled cordial waters were found in both the household recipe collections and printed books.[39] Many distilled waters were named after high-status individuals or medical practitioners, such as 'Dr Butler's cordial water against melancholly' in the *Queens Closet Opened*.[40] Margaret Boscawen's 'large book' included 'An excellent syrupe for a week stomacke and for melancholy', 'A cordiall against mallancholy and vapours', and further titles of recipes for melancholy were noted by her from printed texts.[41] The distilled cordial water of 'aqua mirabilis' was described in almost every recipe collection, including the Clarke family recipe collection (see Figure 7.1).

To make aqua mirabilis

> 3 pintes of white wine put into it a pint of Aqua vite, and half a pint of the Juce of sellindine of the Juce of mint and Balm of each a quarter of an ounce, of quiubibbes [cubebs] cardamum Gallingal Mellelot of each a quarter of an ounce, of mace ginger nutmegs and cloves of each a dram, bruse all thes and put them to the wine and sellendine then put all into the Limbeck of glasse and let it steep 24 hours stopping it close with a cloth. You may take of the best half a pinte and as much of the second of the third you may take somwhat more, this small water you may drink of twice or thrice a week it is very good for the stomack, you must put sugar into every glass, you may hang in musk and ambergreice if you please.[42]

Elaine Leong notes the potential of the distilled and cordial waters held in quantity by Elizabeth Freke for treating many kinds of weakness, from the stomach to the heart and head, including aqua mirabilis.[43] Notably these kinds of preparations, such as cordials, were thought of as strengthening and warming. They often contained ingredients that had warming properties, such as aqua vitae and sugar alongside exotic spices. In the Fortescue recipe collection, there was a further cordial item on an undated handwritten note that claimed to be a cure-all for numerous complaints including melancholy. The note did not specify ingredients, but gave indications and use for a cordial powder:

Bannister's powder

The Cordiall powder is a mo[st] [si]ngular medicine to be used in burning and pestilentiall fevers small pox measles, soundings, tremblings of the heart faintness and Melancholy passions it is good for rheume, a weake stomack, windiness of the spleene, and to strengthen all the members and principall parts of the body: the dose is from five graines to twelve and is to be taken with a little wine and sugar but if it may be gotten it were good to mix with it either Cardus Benedictus water dragon Scabies [scabious?] or Angelica water or if need be the iner of a pleasant apple or a pomgranat soe it will be of more levre for the griefes aforesaid; it may be taken twice a day or oftner if the case soe require.[44]

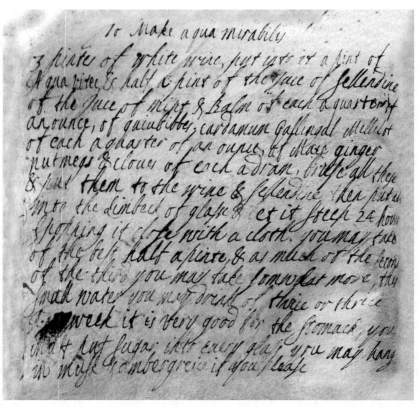

FIGURE 7.1 'To make aqua mirabilis', Elizabeth Clarke Her Booke, 1666, fol. 20r, Sanford Family of Nynehead Papers, DD\SF/3306, Somerset Heritage Centre (courtesy of Somerset Heritage Trust).

This note of Bannister's powder may have referred to one of the costly powders claimed as plague remedies that were advertised by Stephen Bradwell in the early seventeenth century, and derived from his grandfather, John Banister, a well-known Elizabethan practitioner.[45] The cordial in powder form was somewhat atypical in the context of a recipe collection since the notes did not include details of ingredients for making up the preparation. Nevertheless, the claims made for this powder appear to have been of sufficient importance to warrant being copied. Such ready-prepared items would have been most convenient to purchase and transport, ideal for self-help use in many conditions. The use of this cordial powder was recommended with a prepared distilled water which could also have been purchased easily.

Nursing care and housewifery

Alongside the range of self-help medication possibilities, the ill person needed care, and in chronic conditions this might be care that extended over months and years. Pelling's detailed discussion of the terminology of nursing, shows that terms such as 'watching' and 'tending', when used to describe the care of the sick, were becoming obsolete by the end of the seventeenth century.[46] Nursing involved many day-to-day activities which were closely linked to housework, providing for bodily nourishment and hygiene, and these could be time-consuming and repetitive. Outside of the sickroom, nursing also involved obtaining medicines, preparing special foods and dressings, organizing laundry and making the house ready for visitors and medical practitioners. In addition, there were related household management activities including the reallocation of tasks previously done by the sick person, stepping in to make decisions on behalf of the sick person, planning and budgeting for costs and, ultimately, making arrangements for funerals. However, a lack of evidence of day-to-day activities can make it difficult to characterize this type of work further, resulting in the frequent 'invisibility' of nursing.[47] Servants were ubiquitous but largely unseen and unrecognized in the household records for their contribution to nursing care in the household.[48] Servants did appear occasionally in the seventeenth-century household accounts in items related to purchase of medicines and sending for medical assistance, and indeed Bridget Fortescue mentioned servants and healthcare in several of her letters. In a letter to her husband soon after the New Year 1707/8 about preparations for her trip to London to obtain further medical advice, Bridget identified her care needs. She wrote: 'I dout Bety will not be abell to loke [look] to my ealments [ailments] as she shuld and Lily cant dreas [dress] us so that I fear in the condison I am I shall need both'.[49] Thus, Bridget needed both servants to accompany her to London. Servants needed to be able to travel with their employer, even if it meant that they might neglect their own family.

Some elements of nursing care in the home were provided by visiting family members, and this could involve staying on at length in the household.

Edward Clarke's sister, Ursula Venner, came to stay at Chipley when Mary had her 'great illness', after miscarrying in the autumn of 1695.[50] Mary Burgess, a servant in the household, wrote to Edward that 'Mrs Venor gives her service to you shee has bin heer ever since Mrs Clarks great illness and intends to stay if able till you come home'.[51] Mortimer's detailed study of probate accounts and the care of the dying shows that while the demand for paid medical care increased in the seventeenth century relative to paid nursing care, there was an association of fewer payments for nursing care with households where there was a woman such as the deceased's wife or other close female kin. Such findings suggest that sick nursing was an obligation largely carried out by women.[52] Although it is often presumed that nurses and carers were women, some examples show that men could be active in arranging or providing nursing care for others. Ilana Ben-Amos identifies the example of James Fretwell (b. 1699) and his brother, both Lancashire yeomen, who took turns in caring for their father when he became ill, arranging nursing help and numerous different types of treatment.[53] In the context of the dying, Mortimer notes examples of male helpers in attendance of sick individuals who were troubled or distressed and needed to be restrained in bed or some other way, as well as general tending of smallpox victims.[54] Ongoing assistance with nursing care could also be the reason for a request for additional charitable help for the longer term. For instance, a letter was sent to Edward Clarke in 1694 seeking 'favour for my Brother who although he is weak outwardly and helpless as to his limbs yet is not so disabled but constantly can come to church or chappell'.[55] The writer explained that 'my Bros [brother's] freinds are willing to find him a nurse or to allow extraordinary for any theire that shall take the trouble of tending him at night and mornings to help on his cloths'.[56] The emphasis on the brother's ability to attend church may have been given to assure the potential donor of a deserving case for charitable assistance. Whether care originated with male or female relatives, Ben-Amos calculates that care of the elderly by their offspring may not always have been possible since as many as a third of adults who were sixty-five years or over were estimated to have no child remaining alive.[57]

Personal attention to housewifely duties in higher-status households was more likely to require supervision of servants than direct physical involvement in daily tasks. Meldrum describes an 'unravelling of the housewife-servant elision' during the seventeenth century so that by the start of the eighteenth century, the household tasks and managerial status that were previously combined by the housewife had become largely separated, and he highlights the significant level of co-operation that was evident between mistresses and servants.[58] Housewifely tasks seemed to provide a target for some criticism, especially in literature contrasting rural and urban lifestyles. Male authors of the seventeenth century were ready to portray the household activities of 'dull country madams' who spent 'their time in studying receipts' with talk 'of painful childbirth, servants' wages' and 'their husband's good complexion and his leg'.[59] It was not only men who expressed criticisms of housework, as there were some women speaking out against expectations of the housewife, including some aspects of healthcare. Sarah Fyge Egerton (1670–1723) suggested a desire to daringly break free from the old-fashioned 'nice Order' of her sex, and she railed against 'useful Housewifery' and 'Good Cures for Agues' and wished not to be 'chain'd to the nice Order of my Sex'.[60] Lady Damaris Masham (1658–1708), in a letter to John Locke in 1685, referred to the dullness of 'household affairs'.[61] It is evident from other letters to Locke that Lady Masham did involve herself both in the preparing and procuring of medicines, although she referred to them in a joking manner: 'I can but think you would smile to see Cowley and my surfeit waters jumbled together; with Dr More and my gally pots of mithridate and discordium'.[62] Another notable woman of the period, Margaret Cavendish (1623?–73), exclaimed that 'the truth is, I have somewhat Err'd from good Huswifry, to write Nature's Philosophy'.[63] Lady Mary Chudleigh (1656?–1710) made clear that she considered domesticity a temporary state in which women had to wait before joining an elevated world of truth and knowledge where they could 'with enlightened minds' the 'whole of nature know'.[64] She wrote that 'We'll bear our fate, and never once complain . . . The Poor we'll feed, to the Distress'd be kind/And strive to Comfort each afflicted Mind./Visit the Sick, and try their Pains to ease'.[65] Mary's reference to long-suffering lack of complaint conveys her impatient view of the role of a virtuous woman. Yet personal attention to household duties was regarded by some as essential, despite the precious time involved. Maria Thynne (1578–1611) promised her husband: 'I will be inferior to none of my Deverill neighbours in playing the good housewife, though they strive till they stink'.[66] When Mary Evelyn (c. 1635–1709) asked her husband, John Evelyn (1620–1706), for guidance on her role, he responded that she must manage servants, keep accounts and inventories, learn something of still-room and dairy work and 'not despise the knowledge of herbs and their vertues' and, indeed, Mary Evelyn was highly critical of other women who did not fulfil their household duties.[67] She wrote to her son in January 1673/4 that 'all time borrowed from family duties is misspent'.[68] Frances Harris notes however that, earlier in the marriage in 1652, Mary had indicated her reluctance to move back to England from the Continent, 'fearing the care of house keeping will take up the greatest part of my time'.[69] Thus, women were much aware of the labour and time which could be involved in household duties including care of the sick.

Therapeutic choices and determining treatment

For some individuals suffering from chronic complaints, there was a need to call on medical practitioners for ongoing attention, as was the case for

Bridget Fortescue. In letters to her husband Hugh, Bridget described her continuing complaints; swellings in her neck, colicky pains and gripes, a 'looseness' and 'soreness' in the belly, and shivers of an ague-like complaint. In February 1707/8 she reported some improvement in her colicky pains but noted pains elsewhere, 'being free of my colick peanes more then a weke but my bely on the right side is so sore that I can move very litell'.[70] Her main complaint, the King's evil, caused repeated sores and swellings on her neck.[71] The outcome of the visit of a medical practitioner was a proposal to further open the sores and to drain them. She explained what the surgeon, Mr Jenkinson, had said after examining her neck:

> I got him this mor[n]ing to sarch it and he asuars me its in very good order and the bone very safe but he thinkes it will hardly heall without being opened the holl [hole] being small and thee holones [hollowness] being do[w]n ward from the bone and from the holl but he promised me this night to writ and sattesfey you about it [and] thee other sores are as the[y] ware.[72]

Bridget wrote to Hugh several days later to assure him that she was improving, although 'very weke and not quiet free of ye sorenes in my bely yet' so that she could not yet travel,[73] referring to a long-planned but never-achieved journey up to London. Earlier in February 1707/8, Bridget had written of the dangers of a surgical procedure on her neck – 'I know thee plas [place] is more dangerus being all among the cordes and near the bone however I am in the hand of the same god that use to delever and will if he sees fite' – and she asked for Hugh's prayers for the success of the procedure.[74] Hugh must have responded with concern as Bridget sought to downplay the danger and wrote: 'as to the sore I told you I apprehend no danger from and I wod can as wilingly trost Mr Jenkingson as any and if you and the Drs aprove of opening it I sopos it will sone [soon] be holl [whole]'.[75] Bridget called on a number of other medical practitioners, some local and some based in London. Hugh was directly involved in consulting with Doctor Morton in London on behalf of Bridget, and he relayed instructions from the doctor. She expressed great relief when there was agreement amongst the medical practitioners who advised her locally and from afar, 'both thos Dcr hear and with you', saying that 'all agreeing puts me in much hart and hope god has direked that shall be the mines [means] to restore me to parfet helth'.[76]

The procedure of opening the sores did eventually take place in March 1707, and Bridget wrote to Hugh that 'Mr Jenkson has opend the sore to the bottom and finds it very clin [clean] and in good order he shall writ you himselfe tomorrow'.[77] Things did improve slightly soon after and Bridget was able to say: 'I go on with my watters . . . rather better than wores [worse] but wether its the bad wether or the moving of the Humers I cant tell'.[78] Despite her sickly condition throughout this period, Bridget managed the

claimed as a reassurance for her husband, could confirm that she was right in her medical views. When she suffered a fit of colic, suspected to be an ague, she wrote to Hugh that 'I have now both mr Baller and Mr Barber with me and they hope it will [go] of agane you see I take all care of myself'.[96] The apothecary was an ally for Bridget in her efforts to determine the means used in her treatment and he was willing to support her views, though we cannot be sure whether this was entirely in order to maintain her patronage. When Bridget disagreed about the diagnosis of her condition with Doctor Barber, who thought she was suffering from an ague, she found support from the apothecary: 'mr Baller when he came was of Docr Mortons mind that was no Ague what ever it was I bles god I am free of it and have had no returen sines [since] nether of Ague nor colicke'.[97] On various other occasions, Bridget sought the opinion of a number of different medical practitioners but the apothecary provided a constant source of advice, opinion, medicinal knowledge, recipes and reassurance. Apothecaries were lengthily persecuted by physicians with accusations of stealing and adulterating their prescriptions,[98] and this animosity was reinforced because apothecaries were so successful in maintaining links with wealthy lay families through their willingness to provide medical advice.

The relationship between the 'patient' and the 'practitioner' was complex, as can be seen from the above negotiations about therapeutic matters in which Bridget forcefully expressed her therapeutic views based on her own experiences of treating herself and as a household practitioner. Another forceful individual, Mary Clarke, had a somewhat different perspective on appropriate therapeutic strategies, and we turn now to see how she expressed her views.

Therapeutic choices and the lay patient

Mary Clarke thought highly of medical practitioners, especially those in London. For instance, she recommended to her uncle, John Buckland, in 1678, that he take advice in London. She was concerned to hear of his 'distemper', and hoped it would not hinder his 'intentions of a journey to London, to advise with the ablest phisiones heare, which I hope would prove much for your advantage and I am sure to the great sattisfacktions of all your fr[e]inds espeshily myselfe'.[99] As noted above, Mary and Edward Clarke maintained a close relationship with one learned medical practitioner over a lengthy period, John Locke, and the Clarke family sought medical help from him for various individuals, from the children to servants and Mary herself. Locke provided many suggestions, including recommendations based on a range of at least thirty-five native plants along with imported remedies such as Peruvian bark, ginger, rhubarb, jalap, balsam of Peru, gums and spices.[100] Mary's later health problems focused around having painful and swollen legs, and she received instructions on taking medications and diet from Locke. However, it seems that Mary sometimes had trouble in following all of her instructions as Locke subsequently wrote to Edward that it would be inappropriate 'to trouble her with any new rules about her health, fearing that if we multiply them too much we shall have none observed'.[101] After some persuasion, Mary agreed to treatment with her local doctor and carefully followed his directions. Locke wrote later that year: 'I am glad to find you so much resolved (as you have reason) to follow his directions . . . and do tell you but that half your cure depends on the Doctor's prescriptions, the other half is in your own mind. Cheerfulness will have a greater efficacy towards your recovery than anything the apothecaries shops can afford'.[102] Cheerful conversation was regarded as a cure for 'black, dreadful, or despairing thoughts'.[103] Despite her belief in medical practitioners, Mary did sometimes disagree with them, and she reacted defiantly to this advice given by Locke. However, such a disagreement could be quite problematic for the patient in the early modern household when the source of advice was someone of significant status and repute. Within the mountains of correspondence in the archives relating to the Clarke family, there is a letter that appears to be a draft written by Mary in response to Locke's suggestion that 'cheerfulness' could help resolve her complaints:

> Your last very kind Letter I receved and am sorry if you understood mine to be full of reproach, and noe pitty, for your Confinement, and therefore doe take this first opportunity to assure you that if my pitty could have Given any reliefe to infirmityes you would have bin soune innabled to Come to London nay further to Chipley a place which is very unhappy as well as the owner in being so farr from otes [Oates], and my frends theare: wheare I am willing still to flatter my selfe I have soe many ['frends' crossed out] that if the above said remidy would have cured I should not have now neede to Complaine of swelled legs or any other Greevance; which you are soe kind to tell me Cheerefullness is the best remidy.[104]

She first apologized for not expressing concern for Locke's own ill health, but then took up Locke's suggestion regarding 'cheerfulness'. She criticized his 'advice' saying that if it provided a cure then she would have no 'neede to Complaine'. Mary continued, rather caustically:

> I confess the advice is very agreeable to my naturall temper, and if I should tell you wayes and meanes I use to put it in practtiss perhaps you would hardly crediett me and thearefore I will spare you and my selfe to att this time [added 'that act agst'] and only wonder that you that have knowne me and my circomstances from my cradle perhaps better than any frend now in being should not be more surprised that my leggs have boren me up till this time; but I hope God that governs all things for the best will continue mee some time longer for the sake of my children.[105]

In this undated letter, Mary was evidently displeased with the medical advice that she had received from Locke on this occasion, and she expressed surprise that such a suggestion should be made to her. We can see that she struggled to place Locke in a suitable role, in relationship to her as a sick person, whether as a long-standing friend of the family, a distant medical practitioner, or an errant and unsympathetic acquaintance. Mary was expected to show reciprocal concern for his ill health, and was supposed to be grateful for Locke's gift of advice. The Clarkes could not readily dispense with Locke's involvement in family affairs and the letter is undated: it may not have been sent, signifying that Mary herself was in some difficulty about the appropriateness of her response.[106] However, Edward continued to encourage Mary to follow Locke's advice, suggesting that she should come to London to see him.[107] Mary found another way to express her disapproval, as she subsequently wrote to Edward with the view that an 'indiffrent Dr that is near and can see all the changes and alteration that may happen are more safe and benifishiall than these great ones that deales in the dark at a distance'.[108] To emphasize her displeasure, Mary may have used the same words that Locke had sent to her when he criticized her diagnosis of rickets a year before while he was 'in the dark' and 'at a distance'.[109] At that time Mary also expressed the view that safety, as well as efficacy, was connected with close observation of the sick person.[110] She might have been referring indirectly to a lack of visits by Locke, since the family correspondence was regularly punctuated with invitations to him to visit and her protests about his lack of contact. In a later letter, Locke (possibly with some relief) agreed that a local physician would be best for Mary, particularly as 'her life is not to be ventured upon directions at this distance'.[111] Mary did accept treatment from a local medical practitioner, although she continued to provide reports for Edward to pass on to Locke. In May 1697, Mary reported further observations on her own condition, including that her swollen legs were connected with her menstrual cycle:

> I find my leggs more free from swelling this morning then I have this halfe yeare, and thearefore doe hope the diett drinke will doe what was expectted from it without any further troble which I should be very glad of for my owne sattisfacktion as well as every bodye else, but <u>I had forgott to aquaint you with one observation that I have made on my selfe which is that I find my leggs to be more than ordinary swelled once a month just before the time that nature discharges it selfe, which I very much wonder att, haveing them very regularly and enough and much better colered within this halfe year than since I miscarried, all which impute to my diett drinke</u> [Mary's emphasis].[112]

Discussion of monthly courses and miscarriage was not restricted to women, and as Jennifer Evans and Sara Read have identified, male spouses were actively involved in expressing concern and seeking advice and remedies for problems relating to fertility and pregnancy.[113] Mary continued to ponder on her own complaints, and was open to the suggestions of other medical practitioners, receiving enquiries as to her health from another local medical practitioner. She wrote of the visit of Dr Parsons in June 1697 who 'was heare about a fortnight since to inquier how I did and I told him I was very well only the swelling of my leggs continued still'.[114] As a result, she explained, 'we concluded to drink one barrell or 2 more of the diett drink and if that did not remove it, then he sed he thought it would be best to trie something else'.[115] However, although she initially agreed with the medical advice given, Mary then decided to reject this advice and maintain her existing medicines: 'I have great faith in this diett drink and garlick and as long as I am not worss I am loth to begin with Dr Passens'.[116] Thus, Mary constantly reviewed her health status and medicines, and she felt able to reject the attentions of another medical practitioner if she could see no significant change in her condition. Whilst she was treated with great care by her husband and Locke, and Mary appeared to agree with their advice, the extent to which these views corresponded with her own view is not entirely clear. It is noteworthy that Locke's therapeutic methods were much gentler than those of most contemporary physicians,[117] and Mary's letters indicated that she sought stronger remedies at various times. In April 1697, she wrote to Edward to affirm that she was following instructions, but that she thought a purge was needed as 'these things will nott doe of themselfes'.[118] And Mary was conscious of the expenditure involved in medical treatment. Some years later she wrote to Edward: 'As to an account of myself I think I am much the same, the phesicke that I take seemes to help spend so much of my time and your mony but I find very little else comes of it'.[119] Thus, Mary often questioned whether she was receiving the most suitable treatment, either expressing a desire for stronger medicines or pointing out inconsistent and ineffective advice. Mary's compliance with medicines was variable. She disliked the taste of medicines such as Peruvian bark and garlic, although she did find a way to take them, telling Edward, 'my way is now to shove it in a spoonful of sacke, and so swallow it, and drink a spoonfull of sack after it'.[120] Mary had previously discontinued a suggested lay remedy because it was too 'fiddly' to prepare saying 'I am apt to think such little buisnesses will doe me but very little good'.[121] Some remedies were far too unpleasant to take: when Mary was recommended vomits, she chose not to take these, her 'stomacke being so very tender', and preferred to continue with her previous remedies.[122] The ultimate sanction that Mary used was her refusal to take her medicines.

Medical authority

Porter and Porter suggest that the 'hit and miss' of early modern therapeutic treatment meant that medicine was 'open to patient power'.[123] The erratic nature of recovery or other outcomes also meant that success in therapeutic terms was often difficult to identify. Some lifelong complaints resulted in relationships with varied medical practitioners, such as the considerable efforts of Anne Conway to obtain treatment for her migraines, first by William Harvey (1578–1657) and later by the charismatic healer, Valentine Greatrakes (1629–83).[124] The patient of higher status had significant input into determining decisions about their medical care. The changing role of the sick person in contributing to medical decisions was notably raised by N. D. Jewson in the 1970s, suggesting that the sick person had disappeared from the discourse of the eighteenth-century medical arena as the focus of medical treatment moved from the bedside to the hospital and on to the laboratory.[125] These changes occurred in step with the ways in which medical knowledge was produced, and accompanied an increasing separation of patients and practitioners, and the establishment of professional medical authority. Stolberg further discusses the experiences of patients and their perspectives in relation to practitioners, and questions whether the basis of their relationships relied on patronage alone, positing a complex mix of confidence and distrust.[126] One underlying reason for confusion and scepticism may have been the range of differing medical approaches available,[127] so that medical authority could be questioned. Bridget and Mary, in their relationships with spouses, family and medical practitioners, also bear witness to an additional ambiguity in relation to medical authority faced by women in early modern England. This is particularly noted by Alison Wall, in that women might have authority in household matters and yet also be subject to male authority.[128] Both Bridget and Mary had much confidence and strong views about what constituted suitable treatment and accompanying medicines in their individual cases. However, although women of higher status and wealth might have had significant power in the doctor–patient relationship, they also had to negotiate within a patriarchal context.[129] Bridget had considerable belief in her own medical skills and knowledge as a household practitioner, based on her own experience with treating family members and others for agues and other complaints using her mother's remedies. She had sufficient experience to overtly challenge medical practitioners on the nature of the treatment provided. Her understanding was based on a traditional Galenic view of purging, and she did not disagree that purging was needed to remove corruption but she did question how it should be done. Whether a doctor yielded to Bridget's medical argument or whether he decided to concede her viewpoint rather than lose an important patient is not entirely clear, as it is likely that the prospect of loss of her patronage ensured serious consideration and concessions. In the Fortescue recipe collection, an undated recipe for a 'glister' provides some indication of her anxiety and anger. In this recipe, Bridget unexpectedly set out her view of the medical advice given to her by the medical practitioners. The recipe started with a list of ingredients but then changed dramatically in tone as she wrote of the doctors' 'conceits'.[130]

She wrote of her 'sense and feeling' which contrasted with the 'reason' of the medical practitioners and she objected strongly that they could refuse to accept her views, and 'denye the thing In every perticular that I have any powre to command'.[131] Bridget here expressed her conflict with physicians and, despite her successes in negotiating treatment, she identified her lack of 'power to command' in relation to healthcare. In contrast, Mary Clarke largely avoided directly disputing medical authority, rather she responded by questioning inconsistency between doctors and making complaints about the taste of medicines that were administered. Mary might refuse to take remedies, and she also complained if she thought that her medicines were insufficiently strong in their purging effects.

Conclusion

Various aspects of chronic disorders have been considered in this chapter, and self-help possibilities for those who suffered from painful complaints. Melancholy was widely experienced and recipes included cordials, syrups and distilled waters, many of which had cure-all status. In older age and chronic conditions, letters show the concern of husbands for their wives and encouragement to accept medical practitioner treatment, while wives sought to allay concerns about their health. There were differences in perceptions of the treatments proffered by medical practitioners, and Porter and Porter suggest that there was much distrust of doctors in this period,[132] whereas Weisser describes how people shared views, 'creating a patchwork of interpretations of health' based on common understanding of humoral principles.[133] As patients with chronic complaints, both Bridget Fortescue and Mary Clarke stayed close to a humoral understanding in their views of illness, although they differed on the suitability of medicines to achieve these ends, and used varied strategies to negotiate with medical practitioners. The experiences of Bridget and Mary provide us with considerable detail of the thinking behind such negotiations and suggest that the process of determining a therapeutic approach was complex, drawing on experiences including self-help. Bridget accused medical male practitioners of lies and conceits and going against her 'sense', flagging up her lack of 'power to command' despite her experience as a lay household healthcare practitioner. Mary showed that patients could have a number of strategies for ensuring their views were taken into account, including lack of compliance in taking medicines that tasted bad or were deemed insufficiently strong or effective. Medicines played an important role in strategies to maintain therapeutic determination, whether seen from the perspective of the lay household healthcare practitioner or the patient.

cultural and ideological gap emerging between some generations, with differing views of the value of homemade medicines. Mary Clarke expressed criticism of the 'little medicines' proffered by family and friends, preferring purchased medicines and the prescriptions of learned physicians, especially 'troppicall' remedies. Further critical views came not only from medical practitioners but also from women who expressed impatience with time lost to housewifery tasks from intellectual pursuits.

Many resources available in the seventeenth-century household were recognized for their role in medical treatment, but foods and medicines were increasingly differentiated as the century progressed. Foods were understood to have various qualities which enabled their use as medicines, although they could also contribute to corruption and compromise the body in dealing with illness. Thus foods were recast as potential dangers, or irrelevant and ridiculous, in medical terms. The processes involved in making up many medicinal preparations were possible in the kitchen, although recipe collections indicated increasing interest in preparations for internal use rather than plasters and ointments. Some preparations such as distillation involved additional costs and labour, and shortcuts were suggested using prepared ingredients. In terms of resources, there were some influences related to an increasing separation of public and private spaces. The self-sufficiency of larger households was disappearing, as Amanda Vickery points out, and the balance of production and consumption further shifted in the eighteenth century.[1] The emerging middling sort provided an expanded market for prepared medicines, and the home was becoming a more domestic environment associated with femininity,[2] and differences in household healthcare were being further shaped as domestic medicine emerged as clearly separated from professional medicine. Medicine has been problematic in characterizing domestic changes because the home continued to provide a significant space for the practice of healthcare, bringing in a range of advisers and practitioners.[3] Although there were many continuities, some further separation was apparent in terms of resources for preparing medicines; for example, the production of distilled waters became less feasible while these were readily available as commercial preparations. Women appeared to become less unified across different levels of wealth and status despite their supposed common causes of recipe collection and health provision.[4] Writing on aristocratic women in the eighteenth century, Ingrid Tague notes that women of old-fashioned families might include 'potting eels and making medicines' amongst their tasks.[5] The ever-expanding availability of new imported and purified remedies with considerable cure-all claims provided an alternative to the preparation of household remedies and also reflected the increasing claims of medical practitioners who sought to undermine long-standing Galenic theory and practice.

Household healthcare practices in the seventeenth century tell us much about how people thought about health and illness, and these beliefs could be seen in what they purchased or provided for household members in terms of treatment. The beneficiaries of most household medicine purchases in the later seventeenth century were family and household members, and there were few reports of direct medical treatment of the poor. Advice from family members often related to the recommendations of medical practitioners, although not everyone sought advice of this kind. Alongside this was the view of ill health based on diagnosis of individual diseases rather than considering a person's own bodily constitution and humoral status. Tensions between these differing perspectives could be seen in varied styles of household healthcare and self-help, and there were expressions both of resistance to change and desire for new methods and approaches. However, lay attempts to provide a diagnosis, particularly in the case of a newly identified disease such as rickets, could be sharply criticized by the medical practitioner. Professional medical men sought to further delineate boundaries for household healthcare, for example through undermining confidence in diagnosis, to establish medical authority in determining therapeutics in the home, through the promotion of 'domestic medicine'.

Household medicine was a significant element of domestic activity in the seventeenth century, and medicines were both made and purchased to some extent in all of the households considered. Yet healthcare in the household involved much more and, in this study, we have seen the active efforts made by lay individuals to prevent illness through controlling news, obtaining advice on lifestyles, seeking preventative bloodletting and other treatments, as well as providing nursing for effective recovery. Through self-help, many individuals gained confidence and experience which enabled them to identify and treat illnesses, and to further contribute to therapeutic determination. Nevertheless, the focus on household medicine in this study, from medicinal recipes to purchased medicines, is consistent with the increasing emphasis on medicines in household healthcare. Herein lies a double-edged sword since, although the use of medicines enabled self-help, there was increasing dependence on commercially supplied medicine as household resources were becoming less relevant. Ultimately, the reduced role of the household was reflected in the boundaries placed on lay medicine, especially domestic medicine and the activities of women.

In this study I have sought to question assumptions about household healthcare and to expose both the importance of household medicine and complexity of self-help. I hope that this book provides a resource to assist scholars and others in qualifying their perceptions of seventeenth-century self-help and household healthcare. Much more needs to be done, through research on household accounts and medicinal recipes, to develop further understanding of early modern medicine. Household healthcare both mirrored medical developments in wider society, and it also had an internal dynamic which was based on the differing views and experience of key individuals involved, as patients, practitioners, well-wishers or advisers, and other potential beneficiaries. My study has shown not only how self-help contributed to determining therapeutic practices, but also how self-help did not always mean self-sufficiency and independence from medical practitioners. A fundamental issue was the way in which 'medicines' were understood and chosen by individuals, reflecting their varied medical understandings in a landscape of contrasting medical theories and practices. From a wider programme of healthcare concerns and activities, individuals came to focus on the effects of specific medicinal preparations which might be made at home or purchased, thus enabling a self-help culture which continued to flourish in the following century.

1693	Sept 9 Pd ¼ lb coffee 2 s, & a lemmon 6 d	30
1693	Sept 23 Pd 3 drachm's Rubarb	18
1694	Sept 15 Pd ¼ lb Carraway Seeds	2
1695	Pd ¼ ouz of Rhubarb	12
1695	May 11 Pd an ounce of Aniseed 1d, pd ditto of Liquoris 2 d, & 2 brushes 6d	9
1695	Aug Pd 3 quarters of a pint of the oyle of roses	16
1695	Pd ½ lb of rosin 3d, & ½ lb Lapis Calaminaris 7d, & ½ lb Bole armanack 2s	34
1695	Aug 3 Pd 2 brushes 8d, & 2 lb rosin 14d	22
1695	June 20 Pd ¼ lb Caraway comfitts 4d, pr gloves & Maer John	10
1695	Jul 6 Pd 1 ouz Mace 20d, ½ ouz Cynamon 4d, ½ ouz cloves & Mace 7d & 1 lb of Raysins of the sunne 5d	36
1695	Jan 2 Pd ¼ lb cynamon at Wellington	27
1695	Jan 23 Pd ½ pecke mustard seed	9
1696	June 15 Pd powder of wormwood, powder of Rhubarb, powder of Corolina, Burnt Hartshorne of each one drachm	8
1696	Pd bottle of the syrrup of roses	6
1696	Jun 16 Pd 6 th of white lead	30
1696	June 18 Pd bottle of ye syrrup of roses	20
1696	Nov 12 Pd worme powder for ye Children to me Cookersby	6
1696	Dec 5 Pd ¼ lb Caraway seeds Att Taunton	3
1697	Pd ½ oz of nutts & ditto of Cynamon	8
1697	July 10 Pd Annisseeds & liquoris	3
1697	Oct 21 Pd ¼ lb allspice	8
1699	Pd 2 ouz Carraway seeds	2
1699	Nov 4 Pd 2 ouz carraway seeds 2d & oyle 7 Mas Sammys's wig 4d	6
1699	Nov 21 Pd John Gardiner what he had formerly laid out ½ lb Allspice 1s, ¼ lb Carraway seed 3d, ¼ lb ground ginger 1 ½ d	16.5
1700	April 6 Pd worme powder for the children	12
1700	Pd a bottle of oyle	6
1700	May 27 pd Goody Carpenter for Egremony	4

1700	July 15 To a poore woman for popyes	4
1700	July 25 Pd for centrey	6
1700	Jan 8 Att Taunton. Pd ¼ lb allspice & 2 ouz of white browne thread 5d	9
1700	Jan 22 Pd Annyseed & carraway seed 4d & milke 6d	10
1700	March 1 Att Taunton Pd 3 lobster 4 s & 1/4th Carraway seeds 3d & ¼th aniseeds 3d	54
1701	May 3 Pd ¼ th Carraway & ditto of Anniseed Paid Mr Ellons Bill the beginning Aprill 5 viz	5
1701	May 22 Pd 1 lb of figs for my little Mas at Holcombe	4
1701	July 24 Pd 1 lb hopps 13d ¼ th Cynamon 2s ½ th Allspice 10d	47
1701	Aug 9 Pd ¼ th anniseeds	4
1701	Oct 13 Att Taunton & JH & ½ oz of Rhubarb	30
1701	Oct 23 Att Taunton & JS when I went to meett my young Mas etc & ¼ lb All spice 6d, ¼ th ground ginger 2d	6
1701	Pd 2 oz aniseed	2
1701	Pd liquoris	3
1701	Pd 1 oz nutmegs	9
1701	Pd ½ lb carraway comfits 7d & 2 cakes 5d & 2 horses expenses	18
1701	Jan 3 Pd 20 grains pulvis sanctus & 10 grains Scammony in powder & Mas Samel	3
1701	Jan 10 Pd 6lb sugar 3d & ¼ th Allspice	45
1701	Pd 2 bottles anniseed water 1s 2d, & pudding pott	15.5
1702	June 19 Pd Will Jewell what he had laid out at Wells & dreke[?] 2d,¼ th ginger, 2 ½ & wormseed 1d & Mas Sammy	5.5
1702	Aug 1 Mr Crosse Pd ¼ th Allspice 6d, ¼ th ground ginger	8
1702	Pd ½ th carraway seeds, formerly & Joshua Mill	4
1702	Pd brimstone	2.5
1702	Aug 29 Pd ½ lb allspice	12
1702	Oct 10 Pd ½ th Allspice 11d & piece tape	21.5
1702	Oct 24 Pd ½ lb allspice	12
1702	Dec 24 Pd rose water	8

Oil of roses	1	0.75	0.75	16	21.3
Rose water	1	1	1	10	10.0
Rose water (damask)	1	1	1	6	6.0
Sallet oil	2	3	1.5	42	14.0
Syrup	1	0.5	0.5	18	36.0
Purchase by gallon					
Aqua vita	4	5	1.25	240	48.0
Brandy	18	41.25	2.29	2595	62.9

Note that these prices are based on household account entries where both purchase price and quantity were given. Average prices are rounded to 1 decimal place.

Source: Anne Stobart, 'The Making of Domestic Medicine: Gender, Self-Help and Therapeutic Determination in Household Healthcare in South-West England in the Late Seventeenth Century' (PhD thesis, Middlesex University, 2008). Appendix 3.7, 'Purchased Ingredients and Average Prices'.

GLOSSARY

Modern sources used for this glossary include the *Oxford English Dictionary Online*; Allen and Hatfield, *Medicinal Plants in Folk Tradition*; and Grieve, *A Modern Herbal*. Many traded goods can be found online in the 'Dictionary of Traded Goods and Commodities, 1550–1820' by Nancy Cox and Karin Dannehl, http://www.british-history.ac.uk/no-series/traded-goods-dictionary/1550-1820/ (accessed 23 April 2015). Latin plant names in the glossary are based on 'The Plant List', http://www.theplantlist.org/ (accessed 15 May 2015). An edition of Quincy, *Pharmacopoeia Officinalis* (1730) proved helpful in providing both English and Latin indexes.

agrimony (*Agrimonia eupatoria*) a plant of the rose family commonly used as a drink or distilled water.

ague a fever that could have cold, hot and sweating stages.

alembic apparatus for distillation, a still.

alkermes dried bodies of insects on the Mediterranean kermes oak (*Quercus coccifera*) made into a cordial confection.

almond oil pressed oil from bitter or sweet almonds used for skin, lung and children's complaints.

aloe (*Aloe* species) a bitter fleshy plant with purgative action.

alum sulphate of aluminium and potassium, a mineral salt, used in baking, tanning, dyeing and as an astringent medicine to stop bleeding.

amber fossilised resin.

ambergris costly wax-like substance from the intestines of the sperm whale, used in perfumery and medicinal preparations.

angelica (*Angelica archangelica*) tall aromatic member of the carrot family with many uses for seeds, stem and roots.

aniseed (*Pimpinella anisum*) seeds from a plant of the carrot family, used in coughs, colic and childhood ailments.

antimony metal used in many medicinal preparations, toxic and strongly purging.

aqua fortis strong water, alcoholic spirit.

aqua vitae distilled spirits, 'water of life', often flavoured with herbs.

archangel (*Lamium album*) white deadnettle, an astringent herb.

ash (*Fraxinus excelsior*) bark, keys (seed), leaves of the tree all used as bitter and purging remedies.

astringent a substance which is drying, regarded as binding of belly or skin and used as a styptic to stop bleeding.

balm refers to various aromatic plants, possibly lemon balm (*Melissa officinalis*) thought to cure many ills, strengthen the memory and renew youth. Also an abbreviation for balsam.

balm of Gilead costly and fragrant resinous balsam noted for healing ulcers and 'inward decays', sourced from the resin of *Commiphora* species in Arabia.

balsam an aromatic oily or resinous medicinal preparation, usually for

external application, for healing
wounds or soothing pain.

barberry (*Berberis vulgaris*) bitter
bark and acidic red berries widely
used to make a conserve, regarded
as having cooling properties.

Bath water *see* spa water.

bay (*Laurus nobilis*) aromatic leaves
and berries of a Mediterranean tree;
also an expressed oil of bays.

betony (*Stachys officinalis*) a herb of
the mint family with drying
qualities used in a distilled water for
bruises and wounds.

bezoar stone a concretion from the
stomach of an animal such as a
goat, regarded as an antidote.

black alder *see* buckthorn.

blessed thistle (*Centaurea benedicta*)
one of a number of thistles with
leaves and seeds having many
healing properties.

bole armeniac an astringent earth
from Armenia used in diarrhoea
and thought to absorb 'sharp and
acrid humours'.

brimstone sulphur, used in making
gunpowder, dyeing textiles, and for
constipation and skin diseases of
man and animals.

brooklime (*Veronica beccabunga*) a
water-loving plant of the figwort
family used as an antiscorbutic and
diuretic.

broom (*Cytisus scoparius*) a shrubby
plant of the pea family thought to
benefit dropsy, liver and kidneys.

broth liquid or thin soup in which
something is boiled, such as herbs,
grain, meat and vegetables; *see also*
decoction.

buckthorn (*Frangula alnus* or
Rhamnus cathartica) the bark and
berries of native trees which were
used in bitter and purgative
preparations.

bushel a measure of capacity
equivalent to eight gallons used for
fruit and grains.

camphor aromatic resinous substance
produced from Asian trees such as
Camphora officinarum, with a bitter
taste and reputed anti-aphrodisiac
properties.

canary sack fortified white wine
imported from the Canary Islands.

caraway (*Carum carvi*) a plant of the
carrot family whose seeds were
thought to promote digestion, often
made into comfits.

carduus benedictus *see* blessed
thistle.

cassia *see* senna.

cataplasm a poultice or a plaster.

caudle a warm sweetened drink with
ale or wine and spices given to sick
people and women in childbed.

centaury (*Centaurium erythraea*)
bitter-tasting herb of the gentian
family used as a tonic and for
expelling worms.

chamomile (*Chamaemelum nobile*
and others) daisy-like creeping
plants with many uses, including
digestive and nervous complaints.

china root (*Smilax china*) an Asian
shrubby climbing plant, the roots
were introduced into Europe as a
remedy for gout and venereal
disease.

chin-cough complaint of children
involving a violent and convulsive
cough, now called whooping cough.

cinnamon (*Cinnamomum verum*)
dried inner bark of an East Indian
tree or related *Cassia* species.
Fragrant, and considered digestive
and restorative.

citron (*Citrus medica*) large yellow
citrus fruit of Asian origin used to
make a distilled water.

cleavers (*Galium aparine*) scrambling
plant of the bedstraw family used as
a spring tonic and in skin
complaints.

cloves (*Eugenia uniflora*) aromatic
dried flower buds believed to be
good against the plague.

polychrest cure-all remedy suitable for many different complaints.

polypody (*Polypodium vulgare*) a common fern root used in purging drinks.

poppy (*Papaver* species) various plants used for dried seeds and also milky latex with properties of painkilling and inducing sleep.

posset a drink made of milk curdled with ale or wine.

pound approximately 454 g, *see* ounce.

ptisan *see* tisane.

purge a medicine designed to evacuate or remove impurities; or the use of such a medicine.

quart equivalent to two pints.

Queen of Hungary water *see* Hungary water.

quicksilver mercury, or its metal compounds; used originally for skin diseases, and used in the sixteenth century to treat syphilis.

resin viscous, sticky, aromatic substance secreted by certain trees (especially conifers) and used in varnishes, adhesives, medicines and other products.

rheum watery secretions which caused running nose and eyes; usually the common cold.

rhubarb (*Rheum rhaponticum*) costly root imported from China and used as a purgative.

rosa solis (*Drosera rotundifolia*) cordial or liqueur originally made with the juice of the sundew plant to strengthen and nourish the body.

rose various rose species were used including damask rose (*Rosa* x *damascena*), rose preparations included conserve, cordial, honey and syrup.

rosemary (*Rosmarinus officinalis*) large evergreen shrub used in preparation known as Queen of Hungary water for cosmetic and other purposes.

rosin *see* resin.

rue (*Ruta graveolens*) bitter and acrid plant of Southern Europe.

saffron (*Crocus sativus*) dried stigmas used as a cordial and sudorific.

sage (*Salvia officinalis*) a Mediterranean plant with culinary or medicinal uses; or wood sage (*Teucrium scorodonia*), a bitter herb used for skin complaints and fevers.

Saint Johns wort (*Hypericum perforatum*) a herb widely used for wounds, and other complaints from catarrh to bedwetting.

sal prunella salt made from saltpetre and brimstone which was 'diuretic and cooling' and given in fevers and sore throats.

saltpetre nitre, potassium nitrate, which was given to promote the flow of urine and sweat.

sarsaparilla (*Smilax officinalis*) dried roots of a climbing South American plant used as an alterative and tonic and in the treatment of syphilis.

sassafras (*Sassafras albidum*) an aromatic North American tree, providing bark used to treat venereal diseases.

saunders (*Santalum* species) fragrant wood from Asia with red, yellow and white varieties.

savoury (*Satureja montana*) an aromatic herb with culinary uses, similar to garden marjoram.

scrofula swelling and sores of the glands about the neck; probably due to tubercular infection of the neck glands.

scruple apothecary measure of weight equivalent to 1.18 g; three scruples made a dram and each scruple was divided into 20 grains.

scurvygrass (*Cochlearia officinalis*) plant of the cabbage family believed to cut phlegm and possess antiscorbutic properties.

senna (*Senna alexandrina*) dried leaves or seed pods of a type of shrub used as a purgative; imported from Egypt, India and the Mediterranean.

simple a medicine or medicament composed of or concocted from one constituent.

skillet cooking utensil of brass, copper, or other metal, usually having three or four feet and a long handle, used for boiling liquids, stewing meat, etc.

snakeroot root of various North American plants, such as *Aristolochia serpentaria* and *Polygala senega*, thought to be a poison antidote.

soldanella a kind of bindweed (*Calystegia* species) mainly used as a purge.

sorrel *see* dock.

spa water water derived from mineral springs; including Bath water.

Spanish pap *see* panada.

spermaceti a waxy substance found in the head of the sperm whale, used as the basis for ointments.

spirit of wine *see* aqua vitae.

stampe to pound in a mortar; to crush or extract juice.

still *see* alembic.

stone complaint due to hard concretions in the bladder or kidney.

strong water *see* aqua fortis.

succory (*Cichorium intybus*) flowers of the wild succory or chicory were used for inflammation of the eyes; roots and leaves were used as a mild laxative.

surfeit excessive consumption likely to lead to corruption in the body.

tamarisk (*Tamarix gallica*) evergreen shrub introduced from the Mediterranean and locally frequent by the sea.

tartar potassium bitartrate, present in grape juice, deposited in a crude form in the process of fermentation, and used as a purgative.

tent a rolled bandage used to probe and cleanse a wound or keep it open.

theriac compound medicine famed as a poison antidote, also known as 'treacle'.

tisane a nourishing or medicinal drink made with barley.

treacle Venice treacle was an electuary composed of over fifty ingredients made under official supervision; London treacle was made to the formula of the *London Pharmacopoeia*. *See also* theriac.

turmeric (*Curcuma longa*) aromatic root-stock of an East Indian plant used medicinally for flatulent colic: also known as zedoary.

turpentine oily resin from coniferous trees, common turpentine was derived from wild pine (*Pinus sylvestris*).

unguent thick ointment for external application, usually containing fats or oils.

unguentum basilicon ointment containing oils and resins used in wound treatment.

Venice treacle *see* treacle.

verdigris copper acetate, a green crystalline substance used as a medicine for skin and eye conditions.

vervain (*Verbena officinalis*) plant with many folkloric associations, medicinal and ritual uses, having purging and cooling actions.

vinegar dilute acetic acid used to dissolve juices and balsams, regarded as a preservative against pestilence.

violet (*Viola odorata* and other *Viola* species) flowering herb often made into syrup.

vomit a medicine which causes vomiting in order to purge the stomach: an emetic.

wen a lump or swelling on the body.

white archangel (*Lamium album*) a woodland deadnettle plant in the mint family used in treating skin complaints.

wigg a fermented drink of sour milk, buttermilk or whey which might be flavoured with herbs.

wind colic colic due to flatulence.

wormseed (*Erysimum cheiranthoides*) seed of a plant in the cabbage family, and other species, traditionally used to clear the bowel of parasites and worms.

wormwood (*Artemisia absinthium*) a bitter herb of the daisy family used to flavour beer and in medicines for wind and griping pains in the stomach.

yarrow (*Achillea millefolium*) a plant in the daisy family with bitter and anti-inflammatory properties.

13 Michael Hunter and Annabel Gregory (eds), *An Astrological Diary of the Seventeenth Century: Samuel Jeake of Rye 1652–1699* (Oxford: Clarendon Press, 1988), pp. 8, 56.

14 Lowe, *Diary of Roger Lowe*, p. 22.

15 Rosemary O'Day, 'Tudor and Stuart Women: Their Lives through Their Letters', in James Daybell (ed.), *Early Modern Women's Letter-Writing, 1450–1700* (Basingstoke: Palgrave, 2001), p. 129; Sara J. Steen, '"How Subject to Interpretation": Lady Arbella Stuart and the Reading of Illness', in Daybell, *Early Modern Women's Letter-Writing*, p. 123.

16 Whyman, *Sociability and Power*, p. 11.

17 Alison D. Wall, *Two Elizabethan Women: Correspondence of Joan and Maria Thynne, 1575–1611* (Devizes: Wiltshire Record Society, 1983), letter 44, p. 30.

18 Olivia Weisser, 'Grieved and Disordered: Gender and Emotions in Early Modern Patient Narratives', *Journal of Medieval and Early Modern Studies* 42, no. 2 (2013): 247–73. The role of emotions in illness is further explored in Ulinka Rublack, 'Fluxes: The Early Modern Body and the Emotions', *History Workshop Journal* 53, no. 1 (2002): 1–16.

19 Ursula Venner, letter to Mary Clarke, 23 July 1692, DD\SF/3084, SHC.

20 Ursula Venner, letter to Mary Clarke, 25 July 1692, DD\SF/3084, SHC.

21 Robert Burton, *The Anatomy of Melancholy*, vol. 2, introduction by Holbrook Jackson (London: Dent, 1972), pp. 102–3.

22 [Jael Boscawen], letter to Bridget Fortescue, 15 January [1702/3?], 1262M/FC/1, DHC. Jael Boscawen, née Godolphin, was a sister-in-law of Hugh Boscawen, having married his brother Edward Boscawen in 1665, *ODNB*.

23 Ursula Venner, letter to Edward Clarke, 1 January 1678/9, DD\SF/3086, SHC.

24 Elizabeth Clarke Her Booke, 1666, DD\SF/3306, SHC.

25 Posset might be served in a bowl, dish or pot as well as a posset cup, *OED*. Posset 'ale' or posset 'drink' likely referred to the thin clear whey of the curdled posset; see J. K. Crellin, 'Possets', *Notes And Queries* 14, no. 1 (1967): 3.

26 Sarah Hutton and Marjorie Nicolson (eds), *The Conway Letters: The Correspondence of Anne, Viscountess Conway, Henry More, and Their Friends, 1642–1684* (Oxford: Clarendon Press, 1992), letter dated 7 June 1654, p. 307.

27 Ursula Venner, letter to Edward Clarke, 8 November 1695, DD\SF/3084, SHC.

28 Ibid.

29 Mary Clarke, letter to John Spreat, 22 October 1698, BIWLD, 324R; see D. Wake, 'Use of Brown Paper', *Pharmaceutical Journal* 247 (1991): 391.

30 John Quincy, *Pharmacopoeia Officinalis and Extemporanea*, 8th ed. (London: J. Osborn and T. Longman, 1730), p. 76.

31 Mary Clarke, letter to Edward Clarke, 1 May 1697, DD\SF/3833, SHC.

32 John Pechey, *The Compleat Herbal of Physical Plants Containing All Such English and Foreign Herbs, Shrubs and Trees, as Are Used in Physick and Surgery* (London: Printed for Henry Bonwicke, 1694), pp. 344–5.

33 Chapter 3 details purchases of the Clarke household.

34 Elizabeth Isham, 'Book of Rememberance', Perdita Project, University of Warwick, http://web.warwick.ac.uk/english/perdita/Isham/index_bor.htm (accessed 9 April 2015), fol. 13v.

35 Edward Clarke, letter to Edward Clarke Senior, 15 June 1676, DD\SF/3833, SHC.

36 Jane Strachey, letter to Mary Clarke, 7 December 1695, DD\SF/3069, SHC. John Verney (1640–1717) also wrote of the medical services in London, Whyman, *Sociability and Power,* p. 58.

37 Mary's mother, Elizabeth Jepp (née Buckland), was described as a cousin of John Locke in correspondence, although no substantiating evidence for this relationship has been found; John Locke, *The Correspondence of John Locke,* 8 vols, ed. E. S. De Beer (Oxford: Clarendon Press, 1976–89), vol. I, flyleaf and p. xxiii.

38 *ODNB.*

39 Edward Clarke, letter to John Locke, 14 February 1681/2, in Bridget Clarke, 'The Life and Correspondence of Edward Clarke of Chipley, 1650–1710' (unpublished typescript, 4 vols, 1997), p. 111.

40 John Locke, letter to Edward Clarke, 22 March 1685/6, ibid., p. 123.

41 John Spreatt, letter to John Locke, 23 March 1689/90, ibid., p. 159.

42 Edward Clarke, letter to Mary Clarke, 9 November 1695, DD\SF/3069, SHC.

43 Mary Clarke, letter to Edward Clarke, 6 May 1704, DD\SF/3833, SHC.

44 Ursula Venner, letter to Edward Clarke, 14 June 1676, DD\SF/3084, SHC.

45 Ursula Venner, letter to Edward Clarke, 1 January 1676/7, DD\SF/3084, SHC.

46 Ursula Venner, letter to Edward Clarke, 17 April 1678, DD\SF/3086, SHC.

47 Ursula Venner, letter to Edward Clarke, 22 May 1678, DD\SF/3086, SHC.

48 Ursula Venner, letter to Edward Clarke, 1 June 1678, DD\SF/3086, SHC.

49 Anne Summers, 'Nurses and Ancillaries in the Christian Era', in Irvine Loudon (ed.), *Western Medicine: An Illustrated History* (Oxford: Oxford University Press, 1997), p. 192.

50 Ursula Venner, letters to Edward Clarke, 15 April 1678, 11 May 1678, 2 November 1678, DD\SF/3086, SHC; Clarke, 'Life and Correspondence', pp. 65, 94.

51 Ursula Venner, letter to Edward Clarke, 19 June 1676, ibid., p. 85. A 'sennight' is a week (*OED*).

52 Edward Clarke of Chipley's will, which was not proved until 1679, included Edward Clarke as son and heir, and £20 for a ring to Mary Clarke 'as a token of my affection' and also 'To my daughter Ursula Venner, of whose care and kindness in my present weakness, I am very sensible, £100 and to her son Gustavus Venner, £100'. Frederick A. Crisp (ed.), *Abstracts of Somersetshire Wills,* p. 33.

53 Ursula Venner, letter to Edward Clarke, 1 January 1676/7, DD\SF/3084, SHC.

54 Ursula Venner, letter to Edward Clarke, 16 June 1678, DD\SF/3086, SHC.

55 Ursula Venner, letter to Edward Clarke, 28 August 1678, DD\SF/3086, SHC.

56 Ursula Venner, letter to Edward Clarke, 4 July 1679, DD\SF/3086, SHC.

57 Ursula Venner, letters to Edward Clarke, 11 May 1678, 22 May 1678, DD\SF/3086, SHC.

58 Whyman, *Sociability and Power*, p. 127; Bridget Hill, *Women Alone: Spinsters in England, 1660–1850* (New Haven: Yale University Press, 2001), pp. 68, 173.

59 Mary Clarke, letter to Edward Clarke, 6 March 1696/7, DD\SF/3833, SHC.

60 Mary Clarke, letter to Edward Clarke, [1696?], BIWLD, 278R.

61 Quoted in Porter and Porter, *Patient's Progress,* p. 41.

62 Mary Clarke, letter to Edward Clarke, 17 June 1696, DD\SF/3069, SHC.

63 Ursula Venner, letter to Edward Clarke, 19 June 1676, DD\SF/3084, SHC.

64 Ursula Venner, letter to Edward Clarke, 29 May 1678, DD\SF/3086, SHC.

65 Ursula Venner, letter to Edward Clarke, 14 January 1678/9, DD\SF/3086, SHC.

66 Ursula Venner, letters to Edward Clarke, 27 April 1678, 11 May 1678, DD\SF/3086, SHC.

67 Ursula Venner, letter to Edward Clarke, 18 May 1678, DD\SF/3086, SHC.

68 Mary Clarke, letters to Edward Clarke, 2 February 1694/5, DD\SF/3833; 6 February 1694/5, DD\SF/3069, SHC.

69 Ursula Venner, letter to Edward Clarke, 3 May 1700, DD\SF/3086, SHC.

70 Ursula Venner, letter to Edward Clarke, 8 July 1676, DD\SF/3084, SHC.

71 Mr Dyke, letter to Edward Clarke, 28 September 1700, DD\SF/3069, SHC.

72 Weisser, 'Grieved and Disordered', pp. 258–60.

73 'I prey God blesse the meanes for his recovery', Ursula Venner, letter to Edward Clarke, 15 April 1678, DD\SF/3086, SHC.

74 Mary Clarke, letter to John Spreat, 23 November 1704, DD\SF/2813–2821, SHC.

75 Ibid.

76 Hunter and Gregory, *Astrological Diary of the Seventeenth Century*, p. 57.

77 Bridget Fortescue, letter to Hugh Fortescue, 8 February 1707/8, 1262M/FC/9, DHC.

78 Bridget Fortescue, letter to Hugh Fortescue, 6 February 1707/8, 1262M/FC/9, DHC.

79 Bridget Fortescue, letter to Hugh Fortescue, 8 February 1707/8, 1262M/FC/9, DHC.

80 Ibid.

81 John Buckland, letter to Edward Clarke, 13 May 1676, in Clarke, 'Life and Correspondence', p. 63.

82 Bridget Fortescue, letters to Hugh Fortescue, 6 and 8 February 1707/8, 1262M/FC/9, DHC.

83 Bridget Fortescue, letter to Hugh Fortescue, 6 February 1707/8, 1262M/FC/9, DHC.

84 Bridget Fortescue, letter to Hugh Fortescue, 29 February 1707/8, 1262M/FC/9, DHC.

85   Bridget Fortescue, letter to Hugh Fortescue, 5 March 1707/8, 1262M/FC/9, DHC.

86   [Jael Boscawen], letter to Bridget Fortescue, 26 July [1702], 1262M/FC/1, DHC.

87   [Jael Boscawen], letter to Bridget Fortescue, 2 September [1702], 1262M/FC/1, DHC.

88   Bridget Fortescue, letter to Aunt B. [Jael Boscawen], undated draft, 1262M/FC/1, DHC.

89   T. Jenkinson, letter to Hugh Fortescue, 7 March 1707/8, 1262M/FC/10, DHC.

90   T. Jenkinson, letter to Hugh Fortescue, 9 March 1707/8, 1262M/FC/10, DHC.

91   George Short, letter to Mary Clarke, 13 December 1686, DD\SF/2742 Part 1, SHC.

92   Michael Stolberg, *Experiencing Illness and the Sick Body in Early Modern Europe* (Basingstoke: Palgrave Macmillan, 2011), p. 60.

93   Adam Eyre, 'A Dyurnall', in H. J. Morehouse (ed.), *Yorkshire Diaries and Autobiographies in the Seventeenth and Eighteenth Centuries* (Durham: Surtees Society and Andrews and Co., 1875), p. 39.

94   Dorothy H. Woodforde, *Woodforde Papers and Diaries* (London: Peter Davies, 1932), entries for 21 September 1686 and 24 May 1687.

95   Lady Russell, letter to Dr Fitzwilliam, 17 July 1685, Robert W. Uphaus and Gretchen M. Foster (eds), *The Other Eighteenth Century. English Women of Letters 1660–1800* (East Lansing: East Lansing Colleagues Press, 1991), p. 190.

96   Hannah Newton, *The Sick Child in Early Modern England, 1580–1720* (Oxford: Oxford University Press, 2012), p. 70.

97   Clarke, 'Life and Correspondence', p. 190. This was Edward, the eldest boy, born 29 January 1680/1.

98   Lucinda M. Beier, 'Seventeenth-Century English Surgery: The Casebook of Joseph Binns', in Christopher Lawrence (ed.), *Medical Theory, Surgical Practice: Studies in the History of Surgery* (London: Routledge, 1992), p. 56.

99   Sidney Lee, *The Autobiography of Edward, Lord Herbert of Cherbury* (London: George Routledge, 1886), p. 29.

100 Wendy Churchill, *Female Patients in Early Modern Britain: Gender, Diagnosis and Treatment* (Farnham: Ashgate, 2012), p. 75.

101 Peter H. Niebyl, 'Galen, Van Helmont, and Bloodletting', in Allen G. Debus (ed.), *Science, Medicine and Society in the Renaissance: Essays to Honour Walter Pagel* (London: Heinemann, 1972), pp. 13–52.

102 Wear, *Knowledge and Practice*, p. 379.

103 E. Copeman, 'On Bloodletting', *British Medical Journal*, no. 13 (December 1879): 932–3.

104 Hutton and Nicolson, *The Conway Letters,* p. 394.

2 Medicines or Remedies

1   Alexander Read, *Most Excellent and Approved Medicines and Remedies for Most Diseases and Maladies Incident to Man's Body* (London: Printed by J. C. for George Latham, 1651), sig. A2, A4.

2   See, for example, Kenelm Digby, *The Closet of Sir Kenelm Digby Knight Opened*, ed. Anne MacDonell (London: Philip Lee Warner, 1910). The culture of secrets is explored in: William Eamon, *Science and the Secrets of Nature: Books of Secrets in Medieval and Early Modern Culture* (Princeton: Princeton University Press, 1994); Allison Kavey, *Books of Secrets: Natural Philosophy in England, 1550–1660* (Urbana: University of Illinois Press, 2007); Elaine Leong and Alisha Rankin (eds), *Secrets and Knowledge in Medicine and Science, 1500–1800* (Farnham; Burlington, VT: Ashgate, 2011); William R. Newman and Anthony Grafton, *Secrets of Nature: Astrology and Alchemy in Early Modern Europe* (Cambridge, MA: MIT Press, 2001).

3   Harold Love, 'Oral and Scribal Texts in Early Modern England', in John Barnard, D. F. McKenzie and Maureen Bell (eds), *The Cambridge History of the Book in Britain Volume 4: 1557–1695* (Cambridge: Cambridge University Press, 2002), p. 105; for instance, Lady Frances Catchmay desired her son to 'lett every one of his Brothers and Sisters to have true Coppyes' of her recipe book, 'A Booke of Medicens, c. 1625', Western MS184A Wellcome Library, flyleaf.

4   Harold Love, *Scribal Publication in Seventeenth-Century England* (Oxford: Clarendon, 1993), pp. 54–8.

5   Elaine Leong, 'Collecting Knowledge for the Family: Recipes, Gender and Practical Knowledge in the Early Modern English Household', *Centaurus 55*, no. 2 (2013), pp. 90–3.

6   For example, 'An approved water for to cure a consumption', a recipe written on the inside front cover of the Clifford household account book, Stewards Accounts, 1692–1702, Clifford Family Archive (CFA).

7   More recipe collections are now becoming available in digital form online, aided by the efforts of the Early Modern Recipe Online Collective (EMROC), http://emroc.hypotheses.org (accessed 5 November 2015). Edited and published seventeenth-century manuscript recipe books in part or full include Susanne Avery, *A Plain Plantain: Country Wines, Dishes and Herbal Cures from a Seventeenth Century Household M.S. Receipt Book, Susannah Avery (Fl. 1688)*, ed. Russell G. Alexander (Ditchling, Sussex: St Dominic's Press, 1922); Leonard Guthrie, 'The Lady Sedley's Receipt Book, 1686, and Other Seventeenth-Century Receipt Books', *Proceedings of the Royal Society of Medicine* VI (1913): 150–69; Archdale Palmer, *The Recipe Book, 1659–1672, of Archdale Palmer, Gent.*, ed. Grant Uden (Wymondham: Sycamore Press, 1985); David Potter, 'The Household Receipt Book of Ann, Lady Fanshawe', *Petits Propos Culinaires* 80 (2006): 19–32; George Saintsbury, *Receipt Book of Mrs Ann Blencowe, A. D. 1694* (London: Adelphi, 1922); David E. Schoonover, *Lady Borlase's Receiptes Booke* (Iowa City: University of Iowa Press, 1998); Hilary Spurling, *Elinor Fettiplace's Receipt Book: Elizabethan Country House Cooking* (Harmondsworth: Penguin, 1986); Christina Stapley, *The Receipt Book of Lady Anne Blencowe* (Basingstoke: Heartsease, 2004); B. Stitt, 'Diana

Astry's Recipe Book c. 1700', *Bedfordshire Historical Record Society* 37 (1957): 83–168; George Weddell, *Arcana Fairfaxiana Manuscripta* (Newcastle-on-Tyne: Mawson, Swan and Morgan, 1890).

8   Some of these attributions may reflect archival practices and assumptions rather than original compilers.

9   Elaine Leong and Sara Pennell, 'Recipe Collections and the Currency of Medical Knowledge in the Early Modern "Medical Marketplace"', in Jenner and Wallis, *Medicine and the Market*, pp. 134–5; Leong, 'Collecting Knowledge for the Family', p. 96. Studies of recipe books have also focused on the potential to portray women's lives and networks, see Janet Theophano, *Eat My Words: Reading Women's Lives through the Cookbooks They Wrote* (New York: Palgrave Books, 2002), pp. 2–6.

10 Marcy L. North, *The Anonymous Renaissance: Cultures of Discretion in Tudor-Stuart England* (Chicago: University of Chicago Press, 2003), p. 213.

11 Elaine Hobby, 'A Woman's Best Setting Out Is Silence: The Writings of Hannah Woolley', in G. MacLean (ed.), *Culture and Society in the Stuart Restoration: Literature, Drama, History* (Cambridge: Cambridge University Press, 1995), pp. 179–200: Hunter, 'Sisters of the Royal Society'; Michael Hunter, 'The Reluctant Philanthropist: Robert Boyle and the "Communication of Secrets and Receits in Physick"', in Grell and Cunningham, *Religio Medici*, pp. 247–72; Jennifer Stine, 'Opening Closets: The Discovery of Household Medicine in Early Modern England' (PhD thesis, University of Stanford, 1996), pp. 210–14.

12 Mary E. Fissell, 'Making Meaning from the Margins: The New Cultural History of Medicine', in F. Huisman and J. Warner (eds), *Locating Medical History: The Stories and Their Meaning* (Baltimore: Johns Hopkins University Press, 2004), pp. 364–89; Marti Makinen, 'Efficacy Phrases in Early Modern English Medical Recipes', in Irma Taavitsainen and Päivi Pahta (eds), *Medical Writing in Early Modern English* (Cambridge: Cambridge University Press, 2011), p. 159.

13 The household recipe collections included recipes collected by Margaret Boscawen and Bridget Fortescue (1262M/FC/6–8, DHC); Recipe Book Compiled by Lady Rachel Fane, c. 1630 (U269/F38/2, Kent History and Library Centre); Clifford family recipe volumes (CFA, 1689, 1690, 1691–1752); Maddam Alice Cole Her Receipt Booke (DD\SF/3310, SHC); Elizabeth Clarke Her Booke, 1666 (DD\SF/3306, SHC); Pharmacopilium (Handwritten Book of Recipes, Medical, Herbal and for Wine-Making, Devon and Exeter Institution); Elinor Fettiplace, *The Complete Receipt Book of Lady Elinor Fettiplace*, 3 vols. (Bristol: Stuart Press, 1999).

14 Culinary and cosmetic recipes were excluded from further analysis unless they specifically referred to health concerns. For more on cosmetics in early modern times, see Farah Karim-Cooper, *Cosmetics in Shakespearean and Renaissance Drama* (Edinburgh: Edinburgh University Press, 2006); Sally Pointer, *The Artifice of Beauty: A History and Practical Guide to Perfumes and Cosmetics* (Stroud: Sutton, 2005); Edith Snook, *Women, Beauty and Power in Early Modern England* (Basingstoke: Palgrave Macmillan, 2011).

15 Over one-third of recipes had attributions in Leong and Pennell, 'Recipe Collections', p. 138; David B. Goldstein, *Eating and Ethics in Shakespeare's England* (Cambridge: Cambridge University Press, 2013), p. 151.

77 The Right Honorable the Lady Cliffords Booke of Receipts, 1689, CFA, pp. 145, 149; 'Small Book', 1262M/FC/8, DHC, fol. 11; 'Plant Notebook', 1262M/FC/7, DHC, fol. 3.

78 Goldstein, *Eating and Ethics*, n. 70, p. 245.

79 Cavallo and Storey, *Healthy Living*, p. 2.

80 Anne Stobart, '"Lett Her Refrain from All Hott Spices": Medicinal Recipes and Advice in the Treatment of the King's Evil in Seventeenth-Century South-West England', in Michelle DiMeo and Sara Pennell (eds), *Reading and Writing Recipe Books, 1550–1800* (Manchester: Manchester University Press, 2013), pp. 212–14. Diet and health is further discussed in Chapter 5.

81 For a description of the origins of thought around bloodletting, see Shigehisa Kuriyama, *The Expressiveness of the Body and the Divergence of Greek and Chinese Medicine* (New York: Zone Books, 2002), pp. 206–17. See also examples of bloodletting towards the end of Chapter 1.

82 *Natura Exenterata*, pp. 67, 196, 221, 248, 279, 365; Boyle, *Medicinal Experiments*, pp. 13, 15; 'Loose Items', 1262M/FC/8, DHC, items 1, 4, 12, 40; Maddam Alice Cole Her Receipt Booke, DD\SF/3310, SHC, fol. 14; Elizabeth Clarke Her Booke, 1666, DD\SF/3306, SHC, p. 79.

83 On the persistence of magical beliefs, see Keith Thomas, *Religion and the Decline of Magic: Studies in Popular Beliefs in Sixteenth and Seventeenth Century England* (London: Weidenfield and Nicholson, 1971), p. 14.

84 Charles Webster, *From Paracelsus to Newton: Magic and the Making of Modern Science* (Cambridge: Cambridge University Press, 1982); see Chapter 4 for discussion of magical ingredients.

85 Helen Smith, *'Grossly Material Things': Women and Book Production in Early Modern England* (Oxford: Oxford University Press, 2012), pp. 212–13.

86 'Collection of Cookery Receipts by Martha Hodges, Robert Foster and Others', Western MS2844, Wellcome Library, inside cover.

87 'Large Booke', 1262M/FC/6, DHC, fol. 28r.

88 Joanna Stephens famously sold her secret recipe for treating the stone in the eighteenth century to the government; see A. Viseltear, 'Joanna Stephens and Eighteenth Century Lithontriptics: A Misplaced Chapter in the History of Therapeutics', *Bulletin of the History of Medicine* 42 (1968): 199–220.

89 Lady Clinton, letter to Margaret Boscawen, 16 April 1683, 1262M/FC/1, DHC.

90 Isabella was sister to Sir Walter Yonge, a friend of Edward Clarke and John Locke. Isabella Duke, letter to John Locke, 21 October 1686, Locke, *Correspondence*, letter 873, vol. III, p. 57.

91 Ibid.

92 Isabella Duke, letters to John Locke, 14 March 1687 and 7 May 1687, Locke, *Correspondence*, letters 918, 1018, vol. III, pp. 153, 382.

93 Locke also criticized Mary Clarke for attempting medical diagnosis; see Chapter 6.

94 Discussion of gifts as bribes can be found in Felicity Heal, *The Power of Gifts: Gift-Exchange in Early Modern England* (Oxford: Oxford University Press, 2014), pp. 180–206.

95   This was likely a tubercular complaint; see Stobart, 'Lett Her Refrain from All Hott Spices', p. 205.

96   Elizabeth Penhallow, letter to Elizabeth Harvey, 25 October 1679, 1262M/FC/7, DHC. It has not been possible to identify who Elizabeth Penhallow was, although Penhallow was a common name in Cornwall. White archangel was white deadnettle (*Lamium album*), OED.

97   Diet drinks were herb-flavoured 'physical ales'; see C. Anne Wilson, *Food and Drink in Britain: From the Stone Age to Recent Times* (London: Constable, 1973), p. 388.

98   'Loose Items', 1262M/FC/8, DHC, items 113, 118, 119.

99   Ibid., item 113.

100   Theophano, *Eat My Words*, p. 102; Felicity Heal, 'Food Gifts, the Household and the Politics of Exchange in Early Modern England', *Past and Present* 199 (2008): 46. Ilana K. Ben-Amos has drawn attention to the decline in personal obligation in transition to modern society; see Ilana K. Ben-Amos, 'Gifts and Favors: Informal Support in Early Modern England', *Journal of Modern History* 72, no. 2 (2000): 295–9.

101   Heal, 'Food Gifts', pp. 48, 62.

102   Heal, *The Power of Gifts*, p. 38.

103   Ibid., p. 17.

104   Mary Clarke, letter to Edward Clarke, 26 October 1696, in Clarke, 'Life and Correspondence', p. 328.

105   Read, *Most Excellent and Approved Medicines*, sig. A4.

Section Two

3 Early Modern Spending on Healthcare

1   Spicksley, *Business and Household Accounts*, p. xxv; Jeannie Dalporto (ed.), *Essential Works for the Study of Early Modern Women: Part 3. Volume 5. Women in Service in Early Modern England* (Aldershot: Ashgate, 2008), introduction, p. xviii; Rebecca E. Connor, *Women, Accounting and Narrative: Keeping Books in Eighteenth-Century England* (London: Routledge, 2004), p. 19; Victoria E. Burke, ' "The Art of Numbering Well": Late-Seventeenth-Century Arithmetic Manuscripts Compiled by Quaker Girls', in James Daybell and Peter Hinds (eds), *Material Readings of Early Modern Culture: Texts and Social Practices, 1580–1730* (Basingstoke: Palgrave Macmillan, 2012), p. 248.

2   On the economy of households, and the persistence of traditional ways, see Jane Humphries, 'Household Economy', in R. Floud and P. Johnson (eds), *The Cambridge Economic History of Modern Britain* (Cambridge: Cambridge University Press, 2004), pp. 238–67.

3   Alice Clark, 'A Note by Alice Clark', in Norman Penney (ed.), *The Household Account Book of Sarah Fell of Swarthmoor Hall* (Cambridge: Cambridge University Press, 1920), p. xxvii.

4   In the first half of the seventeenth century, Alice Le Strange distinguished foods
    and medicines in her kitchen accounts and general disbursements; see Whittle
    and Griffiths, *Consumption and Gender*, p. 105.

5   Of the few items where a woman's medical status was defined in a payment
    record, she was most likely to be described as a midwife or wet nurse.

6   Beverly Lemire, *The Business of Everyday Life: Gender, Practice and Social
    Politics in England, c. 1600–1900* (Manchester: Manchester University Press,
    2005), p. 195; on gifts, see also Ben-Amos, 'Gifts and Favors', p. 313; David
    Cheal, ' "Showing You Love Them": Gift Giving and the Dialectic of Intimacy',
    in Aafke E. Komter (ed.), *The Gift: An Interdisciplinary Perspective*
    (Amsterdam: Amsterdam University Press, 1996), pp. 95–106.

7   Medicinal plants from the garden and the countryside are further considered in
    Chapter 4.

8   Margaret Spencer Account Book, 1610–1613, MS Add 62092, British Library,
    fols 18v, 19v.

9   Clarke, 'Life and Correspondence', p. 110.

10 Gray, *Devon Household Accounts*, p. 160.

11 Ibid., pp. 153, 156.

12 Leong, 'Making Medicines', p. 164.

13 Gray, *Devon Household Accounts*, p. 46. Scurvygrass was also purchased for
    the household of the Earl of Bedford, in April 1653, 'Paid to John Morrice for
    scurvygrass, or gittings, to put in the children's ale, 4d'; see Gladys S. Thomson,
    Life in a Noble Household, 1641–1700 (London: Jonathan Cape, 1937), p. 77.

14 Gray, *Devon Household Accounts*, pp. 115, 171.

15 Brushfield, 'Financial Diary', p. 187.

16 A payment of £5 was recorded to 'Doctor Villven' on 10 October 1640 and 'to
    Mr Bidgood his apothecary then' for £2, Gray, *Devon Household Accounts*,
    p. 177.

17 Brushfield, 'Financial Diary', p. 227.

18 Ibid., p. 209.

19 Ibid., p. 191.

20 Ibid., p. 219.

21 Ibid., p. 222.

22 Ibid., p. 228.

23 L. M. Munby (ed.), *Early Stuart Household Accounts* (Hitchin: Hertfordshire
    Record Society, 1986), p. 172.

24 Whittle and Griffiths, *Consumption and Gender*, p. 109. See also note 37
    regarding mithridate.

25 Spicksley, *Business and Household Accounts of Joyce Jeffreys*, pp. 48, 60, 155,
    171, 180, 183.

26 Personal Accounts of Elizabeth Wentworth, 1655–1708, MS Egerton 2609,
    British Library.

27 Ibid., pp. 40–47.

28 Account Book of Household Expenses at Chipley, 1685–1702, DD\SF/3304 Part 1, SHC, fol. 3.

29 Natasha Glaisyer, *The Culture of Commerce in England, 1660–1720* (Woodbridge: Royal Historical Society and Boydell Press, 2006), p. 150.

30 Account Book of Household Expenses at Chipley, 1685–1702, DD\SF/3304 Part 1, SHC, fol. 93.

31 A range of apothecary jars can be seen in Briony Hudson, *English Delftware Drug Jars: The Collection of the Museum of the Pharmaceutical Society of Great Britain* (London: Pharmaceutical Press, 2006).

32 Account Book of Household Expenses at Chipley, 1685–1702, DD\SF/3304 Part 1, SHC, fols. 4–6, 13, 14, 41, 43, 47, 49, 60, 67, 74, 96, 102.

33 Ibid., fol. 37.

34 Ibid., fol. 99.

35 Ibid., fol. 87.

36 Stewards Accounts, 1692–1702, CFA, fols 23r, 31r.

37 Albert Watson, *Theriac and Mithridatium: A Study in Therapeutics* (London: Wellcome Historical Medical Library, 1966).

38 Stewards Accounts, 1692–1702, CFA, fols 8v, 17r, 31r, 134r, 137r, 142r, 145r, 151r.

39 Ibid., fols 17r, 108r.

40 Mazzards were a particular variety of red cherry grown in North Devon; see Michael Gee, *Mazzards: The Revival of the Curious North Devon Cherry* (Exeter: Mint Press, 2004).

41 Bridget Fortescue, letter to Hugh Fortescue, 15 February 1707/8, 1262M/FC/9, DHC.

42 Household Account Book, 1699–1704, 1262M/FC/18, DHC, fol. 31v.

43 Ibid., fols. 21r–25r.

44 Ibid., fols. 23r, 26r, 29r.

45 Nicholas Culpeper, *A Physicall Directory* (London: Peter Cole, 1649), p. 256. Care of the breasts and belly involved generous use of 'oils and liniments'; see Jacques Gélis, *History of Childbirth: Fertility, Pregnancy and Birth in Early Modern Europe*, trans. Rosemary Morris (Cambridge: Polity Press, 1991), p. 79.

46 Household Account Book, 1699–1704, 1262M/FC/18, DHC, fol. 32r.

47 Ibid., fols. 4r, 15r, 26r.

48 Culpeper, *Pharmacopoeia Officinalis*, pp. 528–9. See also 'Butter and Cheese Making' in G. E. Fussell, *The English Dairy Farmer, 1500–1900* (London: Frank Cass, 1966), Chapter 5.

49 A. Strodes Expences, 1679 to 1718, D/BUL/F3, Dorset History Centre, fol. 12r.

50 Ibid., fol. 13r. There were links between sellers of spirits and medicinal items in descriptions such as 'brandy merchant and druggist'; see J. A. Chartres, 'Spirits in the North-East? Gin and Other Vices in the Long Eighteenth Century', in Helen Berry and Jeremy Gregory (eds), *Creating and Consuming Culture in North-East England, 1660–1830* (Aldershot: Ashgate, 2003), p. 151.

43 Eileen White and Layinka Swinburne, 'Two Seventeenth Century Grocers in York: The Inventories of Richard Jaques (1655) and Suckling Spendlove (1690)', *York Historian* 19 (2002): 23–47.

44 Cardanus Riders, *Riders (1679) British Merlin: Bedeckt with Many Delightful Varieties, and Useful Verities ... With Notes of Husbandry, Physick, Fairs and Marts* (London: Tho. Newcomb for the Company of Stationers, 1679), sig. B5.

45 Account Book of Household Expenses at Chipley, 1685–1702, DD\SF/3304 Part 1, SHC, fol. 4.

46 Ibid., fol. 89.

47 Ibid., fol. 88.

48 Ibid., fol. 35.

49 Herbert, *Female Alliances*, p. 108.

50 Stewards Accounts, 1692–1702, CFA, fols 14v, 34r.

51 Ibid., fol. 43r. Broom buds were considered a delicacy to stimulate and correct appetite, Grieve, *Modern Herbal*, p. 126.

52 A. Strodes Expences, 1679 to 1718, D/BUL/F3, Dorset History Centre, fols 14r, 20r, 48v.

53 Ibid., fols 29v, 30r, 61r.

54 Ibid., fol. 24r.

55 Markham, *English House-Wife*, pp. 62–5.

56 Ibid., pp. 62–3.

57 Ibid., p. 64.

58 *Natura Exenterata*, p. 393.

59 On early modern gardens, see also Rebecca Bushnell, *Green Desire: Imagining Early Modern English Gardens* (Ithaca, NY: Cornell University Press, 2003); Jill Francis, 'John Parkinson: Gardener and Apothecary of London', in Francia and Stobart (eds), *Critical Approaches,* pp. 229–46; Jennifer Munroe, '"My Innocent Diversion of Gardening": Mary Somerset's Plants', *Renaissance Studies* 25, no. 1 (2011): 111–23; Carole Rawcliffe, '"Delectable Sightes and Fragrant Smelles": Gardens and Health in Late Medieval and Early Modern England', *Garden History* 36, no. 1 (2008): 3–21; C. Anne Wilson, *The Country House Kitchen Garden 1600–1950: How Produce Was Grown and How It Was Used* (Stroud: Sutton, 1998).

60 Stephen Blake, *The Compleat Gardeners Practice, Directing the Exact Way of Gardening, in Three Parts. The Garden of Pleasure, Physical Garden, Kitchen Garden* (London: Printed for Thomas Pierrepoint, 1664), preface.

61 Malcolm Thick, 'Garden Seeds in England before the Late Eighteenth Century: I. Seed Growing', *Agricultural History Review* 38 (1990): 59.

62 *Natura Exenterata*, p. 278.

63 'Plant Notebook', 1655–1702, 1262M/FC/7, DHC. This twelve-leaf booklet contains handwriting and shorthand notes which are similar to those in Margaret Boscawen's 'large book'.

64 Ibid. Of twenty-eight references to plants, nineteen can be matched to Nicholas Culpeper, *English Physitian Enlarged* (London: Peter Cole, 1653) or further editions up to 1666. After 1666, the numerous pagination errors in this book were corrected.

65 'Plant Notebook', 1262M/FC/7, DHC, fols. 4r and 4v.

66 'Large Book', 1262M/FC/6, DHC, fol. 46v.

67 Water agrimony is described as hemp agrimony or as bur marigold by different sources; see Grigson, *Englishman's Flora*, p. 375.

68 Grieve, *A Modern Herbal*, pp. 14–15.

69 Culpeper, *English Physitian Enlarged*, pp. 6, 7.

70 'Plant Notebook', 1262M/FC/7, DHC, fols 3v, 11r.

71 Culpeper, *English Physitian Enlarged*, pp. 10, 11.

72 Black alder referred to alder buckthorn (*Rhamnus frangula*); Grieve, *A Modern Herbal*, p. 135.

73 Ibid., pp. 682, 701.

74 Quincy, *Pharmacopoeia Officinalis*, p. 195; a detailed explanation of the cultivation of the damask rose can be found in Tobyn et al., *Western Herbal Tradition,* pp. 253–70.

75 Leong, 'Medical Remedy Collections', pp. 98–103.

76 Household Account Book of Robert Eyre and Wife, 1640–1645, C. G. Lewin Collection, NRA20976. My thanks to Chris Lewin for providing this information.

77 Penney, *Household Account Book of Sarah Fell*, pp. 27, 61, 75, 93, 383, 395.

78 Ibid., pp. 327, 367, 375.

79 Account Book of Household Expenses at Chipley, 1685–1702, DD\SF/3304 Part 1, SHC, fol. 61.

80 'To Make Paracelsus playster Good for many Diseases', The Right Honorable the Lady Cliffords Booke of Receipts, 1689, CFA, p. 160; *Natura Exenterata*, p. 296; Lower, *Dr Lowers and Several Other Eminent Physicians Receipts,* p. 42.

81 Quincy, *Pharmacopoeia Officinalis*, p. 112.

82 Elizabeth Clarke Her Booke, 1666, DD\SF/3306, SHC, fol. 79r. A 'bollster' was probably a pad or cushion for insertion into the wound, *OED*.

83 Mary Clarke, letter to Edward Clarke, 24 August 1695, BIWLD, 214R.

84 Edward Clarke, letter to Mary Clarke, 31 August 1695, DD\SF/3069, SHC.

85 Account Book of Household Expenses at Chipley, 1685–1702, DD\SF/3304 Part 1, SHC, fol. 67.

86 Burnt hartshorn appeared in at least seven recipes particularly for diarrhoea and worms in children in Lower, *Dr. Lowers and Several Other Eminent Physicians Receipts*, pp. 5, 50, 66, 74, 91, 94, 98.

87 Inserted sheet, Elizabeth Clarke Her Booke, 1666, DD\SF/3306, SHC, between fols 86 and 87.

5 'Butter for to Make the Ointment'

1   Household Account Book, 1699–1704, 1262M/FC/18, DHC, fol. 4r.

2   Andrew Boorde, *A Compendyous Regyment or a Dyetary of Helth* (London: Wyllyam Powell, 1547), chapter xviii. Note that 'meate' refers to all food not just animal protein.

3   Albala, *Eating Right in the Renaissance*, p. 242.

4   William Bullein, *Bulleins Bulwarke of Defence against All Sicknesse, Soarenesse, and Woundes That Doe Dayly Assaulte Mankinde* (London: Thomas Marshe, 1579), fol. 1.

5   *OED*.

6   O'Hara-May, 'Foods or Medicines?', p. 62.

7   *OED*; Burnett, *Liquid Pleasures*, pp. 93–4.

8   Sidney M. Mintz, *Sweetness and Power: The Place of Sugar in Modern History* (New York: Viking, 1985); Kim F. Hall, 'Culinary Spaces, Colonial Spaces: The Gendering of Sugar in the Seventeenth Century', in Valerie Traub, M. Lindsay Kaplan and Dympna Callaghan (eds), *Feminist Readings of Early Modern Culture* (Cambridge: Cambridge University Press, 1996), pp. 168–90.

9   Wear, *Knowledge and Practice,* pp. 37–40, 166, 167; Gentilcore, 'Body and Soul', p. 146.

10 John Wilkins, 'Galen's Simple Medicines: Problems in Ancient Herbal Medicine', in Francia and Stobart (eds), *Critical Approaches*, p. 178.

11 O'Hara-May, 'Foods or Medicines?', p. 67; Huggett, *The Mirror of Health*, p. 3.

12 Ibid., p. 2.

13 O'Hara-May, 'Foods or Medicines?', p. 67.

14 John Archer, *Every Man His Own Doctor* (London, Printed for the author, 1673), pp. 3–4.

15 Ibid., p. 3.

16 Steven Shapin, '"You Are What You Eat": Historical Changes in Ideas About Food and Identity', *Historical Research* 87, no. 237 (2014): 379–80; see also Paul Lloyd, *Food and Identity in England, 1540–1640: Eating to Impress* (London: Bloomsbury, 2015).

17 Adam Fox, 'Food, Drink and Social Distinction in Early Modern England', in Steve Hindle, Alexandra Shepard and John Walter (eds), *Remaking English Society* (Woodbridge: Boydell Press, 2013), pp. 178, 182.

18 J. C. Drummond and Anne Wilbraham, *The Englishman's Food: A History of Five Centuries of English Diet*, rev. ed. (Oxford: Alden Press, 1957), p. 158.

19 Cited in Gilly Lehmann, *The British Housewife: Cookery-Books, Cooking and Society in Eighteenth-Century Britain* (Totnes: Prospect Books, 2002), p. 29.

20 Huggett, *The Mirror of Health*, pp. 4–6.

21 Albala, *Eating Right in the Renaissance,* pp. 177–80, 241–3.

22 Diary of Lewis Tremayne, Tremayne Family of Heligan, St Ewe, Cornwall Record Office, DDT1296; Riders, *Riders (1679) British Merlin*, sig. B5.

Proverbs also provided advice on diet, see Fox, *Oral and Literate Culture*, pp. 157–8.

23 Shigehisa Kuriyama, 'The Forgotten Fear of Excrement', *Journal of Medieval and Early Modern Studies* 38, no. 3 (2008): 423–4.

24 Wear, *Knowledge and Practice*, p. 156.

25 Further details of preventative healthcare according to the non-naturals are provided in Cavallo and Storey, *Healthy Living*.

26 Dobson, *Contours of Death and Disease*, p. 31. On ideas about hygiene, see also Emily Cockayne, *Hubbub: Filth, Noise and Stench in England, 1600–1770* (New Haven: Yale University Press, 2007); Lisa T. Sarasohn, '"That Nauseous Venemous Insect": Bedbugs in Early Modern England', *Eighteenth-Century Studies* 46, no. 4 (2013): 513–30.

27 Sandra Cavallo, 'Invisible Beds: Health and the Material Culture of Sleep', in Anne Gerritsen and Giorgio Riello (eds), *Writing Material Culture History* (London: Bloomsbury, 2015), p. 146.

28 Ginnie Smith, 'Prescribing the Rules of Health: Self-Help and Advice in the Late Eighteenth Century', in Roy Porter (ed.), *Patients and Practitioners: Lay Perceptions of Medicine in Pre-Industrial Society* (Cambridge: Cambridge University Press, 1985), pp. 258, 259.

29 Wear, *Knowledge and Practice*, p. 401.

30 Burton, *Anatomy of Melancholy*, introduction, p. 16.

31 Thomas Muffet, *Healths Improvement* (London: Printed by Tho. Newcomb for Samuel Thomson, 1655), p. 287. This book was posthumously printed.

32 Nicholas Culpeper, *Health for the Rich and Poor, by Dyet, without Physick* (London: Printed by Peter Cole, 1656).

33 Thomas Cock, *Kitchin-Physick: Or, Advice to the Poor* (London: D. Newman, 1676), title page.

34 T. K., *The Kitchin-Physician: Or, a Guide for Good-Housewives in Maintaining Their Families in Health* (London: Samuel Lee, 1680), pp. 71–2.

35 Archer, *Every Man His Own Doctor*, p. 149.

36 Muffet, *Healths Improvement*, p. 33.

37 Quincy, *Pharmacopoeia Officinalis*, pp. 79, 103, 166.

38 Ibid., p. 147.

39 Ibid., p. 226.

40 Ibid., pp. 78, 80.

41 Mintz, *Sweetness and Power*, p. 104.

42 Quincy, *Pharmacopoeia Officinalis*, p. 247.

43 Ibid., pp. 247–8.

44 Ibid., p. 125.

45 Ibid., p. 227.

46 'Large Book', 1262M/FC/6, DHC, fols 19r, 19v.

47 Quincy, *Pharmacopoeia Officinalis*, p. 227.

133 Quincy, *Pharmacopoeia Officinalis*, p. 369.

134 Wear, *Knowledge and Practice*, p. 55.

135 Merret, *The Accomplisht Physician*, p. 57.

136 Ibid.

137 In late seventeenth-century London, over 50 per cent of households in Cheapside, a wealthy area, had no servants, and 88 per cent of families in Tower Hill lacked servants; Mark Merry and Philip Baker, '"For the House Her Self and One Servant": Family and Household in Late Seventeenth-Century London', *London Journal* 34, no. 3 (2009): 217.

138 Receipts of All Kinds, 1691–1752, CFA, p. 24.

Section Three

6 Therapeutics in the Family

1 Mary Clarke, letter to Edward Clarke, 10 April 1697, DD\SF/3833, SHC. Jane [Jenny] was born 9 February 1693/4 and was their tenth child, Clarke, 'Life and Correspondence', p. 213.

2 See Elaine Hobby, 'Early Modern Midwifery Manuals and Herbal Practice', in Francia and Stobart (eds), *Critical Approaches*, pp. 67–85; Hilary Marland (ed.), *The Art of Midwifery: Early Modern Midwives in Europe* (London: Routledge, 1994); Adrian Wilson, *The Making of Man-Midwifery: Childbirth in England, 1660–1770* (London: University College of London Press, 1995).

3 Entries relating to wet nursing and midwifery were not included in this analysis.

4 Some other payments were associated with specific animals, including physic for dogs and horses, but these are not included in this analysis.

5 Dorothy Marshall, *The English Domestic Servant in History* (London: Historical Association, 1949), p. 24.

6 Gray, *Devon Household Accounts*, pp. 121, 124, 160.

7 Richard Allestree, *The Ladies Calling in Two Parts* (Oxford: Printed at the Theater, 1673), Section II 'Of Wives', p. 207. See also Tim Meldrum, *Domestic Service and Gender 1660–1750: Life and Work in the London Household* (Harlow: Longman, 2000), pp. 90–1.

8 Clarke, 'Life and Correspondence', pp. 159, 190.

9 Mary Clarke, letter to Edward Clarke, [February 1696/7?], BIWLD, 288R. Isaac was also responsible for some household repairs, Clarke, 'Life and Correspondence', p. 355.

10 Mary Clarke, letter to Edward Clarke, 18 May 1697, BIWLD, 297R.

11 Mary Clarke, letter to Edward Clarke, 30 January 1696/7, BIWLD, 285R.

12 Mary Clarke, letter to Edward Clarke, 29 May 1697, BIWLD, 298R.

13 Humphrey may have been the gardener's boy; Clarke, 'Life and Correspondence', p. 226.

14 Mary Clarke, letter to Edward Clarke, 24 May 1697, BIWLD, 310R.

15 Mary Clarke, letter to John Spreat, 6 March 1704/5, BIWLD, 461R.

16 Leong, 'Making Medicines', p. 166.

17 Ann Kussmaul, *Servants in Husbandry in Early Modern England* (Cambridge: Cambridge University Press, 1981), p. 32; Brodie Waddell, *God, Duty and Community in English Economic Life, 1660–1720* (Woodbridge: Boydell Press, 2012), p. 103.

18 W. M., *Queens Closet Opened*, preface to the reader.

19 Beier, *Sufferers and Healers*, p. 215.

20 Timothy Rogers, *The Character of a Good Woman* (London: Printed for J. Harris, 1697), p. 42.

21 Ibid., p. 43.

22 Waddell, *God, Duty and Community*, pp. 45, 107; Owen, *English Philanthropy*, p. 3.

23 Steve Hindle, *On the Parish? The Micro-Politics of Poor Relief in Rural England 1550–1750* (Oxford: Oxford University Press, 2004), pp. 233, 266.

24 Jonathan Reinarz and Leonard Schwarz (eds), *Medicine and the Workhouse* (Rochester, NY: University of Rochester Press, 2013), p. 7.

25 See Mark R. Cohen, 'Introduction: Poverty and Charity in Past Times', *Journal of Interdisciplinary History* 35, no. 3 (2004): 347; Ole P. Grell, 'The Protestant Imperative of Christian Care and Neighbourly Love', in Grell and Cunningham, *Health Care and Poor Relief*, pp. 43–65.

26 Account Book of Household Expenses at Chipley, 1685–1702, DD\SF/3304 Part 1, SHC, fol. 98.

27 Mary Clarke, letter to Edward Clarke, [December 1699?], BIWLD, 358R.

28 Mary Clarke, letter to Edward Clarke, 20 December 1702, BIWLD, 431R.

29 Stewards Accounts, 1692–1702, CFA, fol. 80r.

30 A. Strodes Expences, 1679 to 1718, D/BUL/F3, Dorset History Centre, fols 18r, 22r, 25v, 26v, 32r.

31 Ibid., fols 40v, 62r, 66v.

32 Household Account Book, 1699–1704, 1262M/FC/18, DHC, fol. 2r and passim, payments on at least seventy occasions.

33 Bridget Fortescue, letter to Hugh Fortescue, 29 February 1707/8, 1262M/FC/9, DHC.

34 For more on the introduction of Peruvian bark, see T. W. Keeble, 'A Cure for the Ague: The Contribution of Robert Talbor (1624–81)', *Journal of the Royal Society of Medicine* 90 (1997): 285–90.

35 Snakeroot is not listed by Allen and Hatfield, *Medicinal Plants in Folk Tradition*. Grigson, *The Englishman's Flora*, lists twenty-six different local plant names including the word 'snake', although no indigenous plant was called 'snakeroot'. Bistort (*Polygonum bistorta*) was known as 'snake weed' in parts of Somerset and elsewhere as 'adderwort' or 'snakeweed', and was regarded as very astringent and suitable for 'all kind of Fluxes'. An import

from America was 'Virginian snakeroot' (*Aristolochia serpentaria* or *Polygala senega*); Quincy, *Pharmacopoeia Officinalis*, pp. 106, 183.

36 Bridget Fortescue, letter to Hugh Fortescue, 7 March 1707/8, 1262M/FC/9, DHC. Vickers powder, of unspecified composition, may have been that which was advertised for sale in William Vickers, *A Brief Account of a Specifick Remedy for Curing the King's Evil, Confirmed by Seventy Nine Extraordinary Cures, since October, 1706*, 2nd ed. (London, 1709).

37 Bridget Fortescue, letter to Hugh Fortescue, 7 March 1707/8, 1262M/FC/9, DHC.

38 Anne Digby, *Making a Medical Living: Doctors and Patients in the English Market for Medicine, 1720–1911* (Cambridge: Cambridge University Press, 1994), p. 243.

39 Joan Kent, 'The Rural "Middling Sort" in Early Modern England, circa 1640–1740: Some Economic, Political and Socio-Cultural Characteristics', *Rural History* 10 (1999): 33–6.

40 Allestree, *The Ladies Calling*, p. 55.

41 Ibid., pp. 55–6.

42 Fletcher, *Gender, Sex and Subordination*, p. 237.

43 Account Book of Household Expenses at Chipley, 1685–1702, DD\SF/3304 Part 1, SHC, fols 3v, 7r, 9r, 13r, 14r, 15r, 43r.

44 Elizabeth Clarke Her Booke, 1666, DD\SF/3306, SHC, p. 92.

45 Grieve, *A Modern Herbal*, p. 690; Quincy, *Pharmacopoeia Officinalis*, p. 403. The purchases shown were recorded 15–18 June 1996, Account Book of Household Expenses at Chipley, 1685–1702, DD\SF/3304 Part 1, SHC, fol. 67r.

46 Ibid., fol. 29r.

47 Ibid., fols 48r, 67r, 70r, 86v, 101r.

48 Ibid., fol. 99r.

49 Household Account Book, 1699–1704, 1262M/FC/18, DHC, fol. 4; 'Large Book', 1262M/FC/6, DHC, fol. 30r.

50 'A glister to kill the worms' and 'For convultion fitts', 'Large Book', 1262M/FC/6, DHC, fols 30r, 45v; 'Lady Overes advice to prevent fitts in children', 'Small Book', 1262M/FC/8, DHC, fol. 11r.

51 Newton, *The Sick Child*, pp. 16, 105–8.

52 This finding is in agreement with the survey of Newton, *The Sick Child*, p. 46, Figure 3.

53 For more on epilepsy, see Owsei Temkin, *The Falling Sickness: A History of Epilepsy from the Greeks to the Beginnings of Modern Neurology*, 2nd ed. (Baltimore, MD: Johns Hopkins University Press, 1971).

54 Elizabeth Clarke Her Booke, 1666, DD\SF/3306, SHC, p. 76; W. M., *Queens Closet Opened*, p. 91; 'Large Book', 1262M/FC/6, fol. 2r.

55 W. M., *Queens Closet Opened*, p. 52. The recipe appears in the 'Large Book', 1262M/FC/6, fol. 33r.

56 Ibid., fols 35r, 36r. Other titles selected by Margaret are discussed in Chapter 2.

57 *Natura Exenterata*, p. 75.

58 Newton, *The Sick Child*, pp. 78–89.

59 Fettiplace, *Complete Receipt Book*, p. 3; *Natura Exenterata*, p. 137; 'Large Book', 1262M/FC/8, DHC, fol. 31r; Grey, *A Choice Manuall*, p. 50.

60 There were 191 deaths from this complaint between 1655 and 1658. In the same period there were 1,598 deaths listed under rickets. Valerie A. Fildes, '"The English Disease": Infantile Rickets and Scurvy in Pre-Industrial England', in John Cule and Terry Turner (eds), *Child Care through the Centuries: An Historical Survey from Papers Given at the Tenth British Congress on the History of Medicine at Clyne Castle, Swansea, 6–8th April 1984* (Cardiff: STS Publishing for the British Society for the History of Medicine, 1984), p. 124.

61 Lady Clinton, letter to Bridget Fortescue, 26 December 1693, 1262M/FC/1, DHC.

62 J. P. Griffin, 'Venetian Treacle and the Foundation of Medicines Regulation', *British Journal of Clinical Pharmacology* 58, no. 3 (2004): 318.

63 Mary Clarke, letter to Edward Clarke, 9 January 1694/5, DD\SF/3069, SHC.

64 Mary Clarke, letter to John Spreat, 22 October 1698, BIWLD, 324R.

65 Mary Clarke, letter to Edward Clarke, 21 November 1690, BIWLD, 176R.

66 Mary Clarke, letter to Edward Clarke, 15 September 1694 in Clarke, 'Life and Correspondence', p. 224.

67 Mary Clarke, letter to John Spreat, 17 June 1699, BIWLD, 347R.

68 Mary Clarke, letter to John Spreat, 22 October 1698, BIWLD, 324R; on brown paper see note 29 in Chapter 1.

69 Mary Clarke, letter to Edward Clarke, 4 May 1700, in Clarke, 'Life and Correspondence', p. 460.

70 Ursula Venner, letter to Edward Clarke, 24 June 1676, DD\SF/3084, SHC. Edward was the firstborn of the Clarke children, born 6 May 1676 and died 27 June 1676, Clarke, 'Life and Correspondence', pp. 63, 65; Topsell, *Historie of Foure-Footed Beastes*, p. 185.

71 Ursula Venner, letters to Edward Clarke, 12 December 1678, DD\SF/3086, SHC. The second child, Elizabeth ('Betty'), was born 13 July 1678; Clarke, 'Life and Correspondence', p. 80.

72 Ursula Venner, letter to Edward Clarke, 8 January 1678/9, DD\SF/3086, SHC.

73 W. M., *Queens Closet Opened*, p. 47; on Galen and teething see Frederic Still, *The History of Paediatrics* (London: Dawsons, 1965), p. 46.

74 Mary Clarke, letter to John Spreat, 19 June 1690 in Clarke, 'Life and Correspondence', p. 167.

75 Grieve, *A Modern Herbal*, p. 182; Quincy, *Pharmacopoeia Officinalis*, p. 115.

76 The use of rhubarb 'for a child's face which breaks out with a Watery Humour' is suggested in a recipe in Lower, *Dr Lowers and Several Other Eminent Physicians Receipts*, p. 86.

77 Mary Clarke, letters to Edward Clarke, 22 October 1694, 13 December 1695, in Clarke, 'Life and Correspondence', p. 265; glisters or 'clysters' (*OED*).

78   Mary Clarke, letter to Edward Clarke, 1 May 1700, in Clarke, 'Life and Correspondence', p. 459.

79   Ibid.

80   Newton, *The Sick Child*, pp. 105, 110.

81   Porter and Porter, *Patient's Progress*, p. 70.

82   Mary Lindemann, *Medicine and Society in Early Modern Europe* (Cambridge: Cambridge University Press, 1999), p. 206.

83   Valerie A. Fildes, 'Infant Care in Tudor and Stuart England', *Midwife, Health Visitor, Community Nurse* 22, no. 3 (1986): 79.

84   Linda A. Pollock, *Forgotten Children: Parent–Child Relations from 1500 to 1900* (Cambridge; New York: Cambridge University Press, 1983), p. 131.

85   Newton, *The Sick Child*, p. 109.

86   Mary Clarke, letter to Edward Clarke, 26 January 1694/5, BIWLD, 203R.

87   Mary Clarke, letter to Edward Clarke, 27 January 1694/5, BIWLD, 204R.

88   Mary Clarke, letters to Edward Clarke, 22 October 1694 and 10 November 1694, in Clarke, 'Life and Correspondence', pp. 226, 228.

89   Edward Clarke, letter to John Locke, 27 November 1694, in Clarke, 'Life and Correspondence', p. 230.

90   Ibid., p. 230.

91   Samuel was about three or four years old at this time. Edward Clarke, letter to Mary Clarke, 10 December 1695, DD\SF/3069, SHC.

92   Mary Clarke, letter to Edward Clarke, 13 December 1695, BIWLD, 223R.

93   'Will of Joseph Baller, Apothecary of Barnstaple, Devon, 2 July 1712', National Archives, Kew, PROB 11/527/302.

94   Joseph Baller, letter to Madam Fortescue, 20 June 1705, 1262M/FC/7, DHC.

95   Ibid. Numerous preparations involving steel or iron filings were in favour by the end of the seventeenth century; see Quincy, *Pharmacopoeia Officinalis*, pp. 263–71.

96   'Loose Items', 1262M/FC/8, DHC, item 132.

97   Ibid., item 133. The ingredients of this recipe are similar to diet drinks in *Natura Exenterata*, p. 295.

98   Although sarsaparilla was going out of favour, being criticized for cost and lack of efficacy; Quincy, *Pharmacopoeia Officinalis*, p. 110.

99   Burnby, *Study of the English Apothecary*, p. 116. An exception which considers apothecaries and social networks is Penelope J. Corfield, 'From Poison Peddlers to Civic Worthies: The Reputation of Apothecaries in Georgian England', *Social History of Medicine* 22, no. 1 (2009): 1–21.

100 Joseph E. Illick, 'Child-Rearing in Seventeenth-Century England and America', in Lloyd de Mause (ed.), *The History of Childhood: The Evolution of Parent–Child Relationships as a Factor in History* (London: Souvenir Press, 1974), p. 312.

101 Newton, *The Sick Child*, p. 4.

102 Ibid., pp. 16, 25. Chin-cough is whooping cough, *OED*.

103 Smith, 'Relative Duties of a Man', p. 242, says 31.3 per cent of women's letters concerned children, compared with only 8.1 per cent of men's. Smith notes, however, that a man was more likely to write about his wife's illness (21.3 per cent) than a woman to write about her husband's ill health (6 per cent).

104 Beier, *Sufferers and Healers*, p. 257.

105 Mary Clarke, letter to Edward Clarke, 15 September 1694, in Clarke, 'Life and Correspondence', p. 224.

106 Mary Clarke, letter to Edward Clarke, 19 September 1694, in Clarke, 'Life and Correspondence', p. 225.

107 For an excellent discussion of the development of an ontological approach, see Jacalyn Duffin, *Lovers and Livers: Disease Concepts in History* (Toronto: University of Toronto Press, 2002).

108 Still, *History of Paediatrics*, p. 199.

109 Layinka M. Swinburne, 'Rickets and the Fairfax Family Receipt Books', *Journal of the Royal Society of Medicine* 99, no. 8 (2006): 391–95.

110 Elizabeth Clarke Her Booke, 1666, DD\SF/3306, SHC, fol. 92.

111 Newton, *The Sick Child*, p. 38.

112 Fildes, 'The English Disease', pp. 124–5.

113 Valerie A. Fildes, *Wet Nursing: A History from Antiquity to the Present* (Oxford: Basil Blackwell, 1988), pp. 93–9.

114 John Locke, letter to Mary Clarke, 22 March 1695/6 in Clarke, 'Life and Correspondence', p. 247.

115 Whaley, *Women and the Practice of Medical Care*, pp. 56–9.

116 Merret, *Accomplisht Physician*, p. 11.

117 *The Gentlewoman's Companion* (London: Printed by A. Maxwell for Dorman Nowman, 1673), pp. 165–7. As Elaine Hobby has argued, this publication may have been attributed to Hannah Wolley, but was based on an earlier publication *The Ladies Delight*, and not actually written by her; Hobby, 'A Woman's Best Setting Out', p. 181.

118 Nagy, *Popular Medicine*, p. 71.

119 Isabella Duke, letter to John Locke, in Locke, *Correspondence*, 14 March 1687, no. 918, vol. III, p. 153.

120 Maynwaringe, *Efficacy and Extent of True Purgation*, p. 5.

121 Ibid., p. 1.

122 Ibid., p. 5.

123 Ibid., p. 6.

124 Ibid., p. 11.

125 Ibid., pp. 19, 28.

126 T. K., *The Kitchin-Physician*, title page, sig. A2r.

127 Ibid., sig. A2v.

128 James Primrose, *Popular Errours. Or, the Errours of the People in Physick*, translated by Robert Wittie (London: Printed by W. Wilson for Nicholas Bourne, 1651), pp. 40–1.

129 Ibid., pp. 19–21.

130 Wear, *Knowledge and Practice*, p. 37.

131 Maynwaringe, *Efficacy and Extent of True Purgation*, pp. 31, 33.

132 Mortimer, *Dying and the Doctors*, pp. 208–9.

133 Roy Porter, 'Consumption: Disease of the Consumer Society', in John Brewer and Roy Porter (eds), *Consumption and the World of Goods* (London: Routledge, 1993), p. 69.

134 Digby, *Making a Medical Living*, p. 42.

135 Michael J. James, 'Health Care in the Georgian Household of Sir William and Lady Hannah East', *Historical Research* 82, no. 218 (2009): 705–6.

136 Margaret Blundell, *Blundell's Diary and Letter Book, 1702–1728* (Liverpool: Liverpool University Press, 1952), pp. 60, 67, 68. For another active lay practitioner in the eighteenth century, see Jonathan Barry, *The Diary of William Dyer: Bristol in 1762* (Bristol: Bristol Record Society, 2012).

137 Blundell, *Blundell's Diary*, pp. 63, 65, 71, 90, 91, 238.

138 William Buchan, *Domestic Medicine: Or, the Family Physician* (Edinburgh: Printed for Balfour, Auld and Smellie, 1769).

139 Richard B. Sher, 'William Buchan's *Domestic Medicine*: Laying Book History Open', in Peter Isaac and Barry Mackay (eds), *The Human Face of the Book Trade: Print Culture and Its Creators* (Winchester: Oak Knoll Press, 1999), pp. 47, 48, 55; see also C. E. Rosenberg, 'Medical Text and Social Context: Explaining William Buchan's *Domestic Medicine*', in C. E. Rosenberg (ed.), *Explaining Epidemic and Other States in the History of Medicine* (Cambridge: Cambridge University Press, 1992), pp. 32–56; John B. Blake, 'From Buchan to Fishbein: The Literature of Domestic Medicine', in Guenter B. Risse, Ronald L. Numbers and Judith W. Leavitt (eds), *Medicine without Doctors: Home Health Care in American History* (New York: Science History Publications, 1977), pp. 11–30.

140 Buchan, *Domestic Medicine*, p. xxiii.

141 Ibid., pp. xx, xxiv.

142 Ibid., pp. ix, xxxi; Roy Porter, 'Spreading Medical Enlightenment: The Popularization of Medicine in Georgian England', in Roy Porter (ed.), *The Popularisation of Medicine, 1650–1850* (London: Routledge, 1992), pp. 218, 220.

143 Porter, 'Spreading Medical Enlightenment', p. 225; James Parkinson, *Medical Admonitions Addressed to Families, Respecting the Practice of Domestic Medicine, and the Preservation of Health*, 3rd ed. (London: Printed for C. Dilly et al., 1799), vol. 1, p. iii.

144 Ibid., vol. 1, p. 8.

7 'I Troble Noe Body with My Complaints'

1   Churchill, *Female Patients*, p. 128.

2   Mary Clarke, letter to Edward Clarke, 21 February 1701/2, DD\SF/3833, SHC.

3   Stobart, 'Lett Her Refrain from All Hott Spices', p. 205.

4   Bridget Fortescue, letter to Hugh Fortescue, 6 February 1707/8, 1262M/FC/9, DHC.

5   Michael Stolberg, 'Metaphors and Images of Cancer in Early Modern Europe', *Bulletin of the History of Medicine* 88, no. 1 (2014): 48–74; Alanna Skuse, 'Wombs, Worms and Wolves: Constructing Cancer in Early Modern England', *Social History of Medicine* 27, no. 4 (2014): 636–7.

6   *OED*. Modern definitions portray chronic illness as lasting longer than three months. On plague, see Peter J. Bowden (ed.), *Economic Change: Prices, Wages, Profits and Rents: 1500–1750* (Cambridge: Cambridge University Press, 1990), p. 53; Charles Creighton, *A History of Epidemics in Britain*, Vol. 1, 2nd ed. (London: Frank Cass, 1965), Chapters X and XII; Paul Slack, *The Impact of Plague in Tudor and Stuart England* (London: Routledge and Kegan Paul, 1985).

7   Dobson, *Contours of Death and Disease*, p. 19; for more on mortality and causes, see E. A. Wrigley and R. S. Schofield, *The Population History of England 1541–1871: A Reconstruction* (Cambridge: Cambridge University Press, 1981), pp. 667–70.

8   Carsten Timmerman, 'Chronic Illness and Disease History', in Mark Jackson (ed.), *The Oxford Handbook of the History of Medicine* (Oxford: Oxford University Press, 2011), p. 394. On the complex causes of disability and miraculous cures, see David Turner, *Disability in Eighteenth-Century England: Imagining Physical Impairment* (London: Routledge, 2012).

9   There is a list of ongoing medical complaints in Porter and Porter, *Patient's Progress*, p. 7.

10 Cockayne, *Hubbub: Filth, Noise and Stench*, pp. 55–6.

11 Aki C. L. Beam, '"Should I as yet Call You Old?": Testing the Boundaries of Female Old Age in Early Modern England', in Erin Campbell (ed.), *Growing Old in Early Modern Europe: Cultural Representations* (Aldershot: Ashgate, 2006), p. 11; Anne Kugler, '"I Feel Myself Decay Apace": Old Age in the Diary of Lady Sarah Cowper (1644–1720)', in Lynn Botelho and Pat Thane (eds), *Women and Ageing in British Society since 1500* (Harlow: Longman, 2001), pp. 66–88; Helen Yallop, *Age and Identity in Eighteenth-Century England* (London: Pickering and Chatto, 2013), p. 141.

12 Wear, *Knowledge and Practice,* p. 12; E. A. Wrigley, 'Mortality In Pre-Industrial England: The Example of Colyton, Devon, over Three Centuries', in D. V. Glass and R. Revelle (eds), *Population and Social Change* (London: Edward Arnold, 1972), pp. 243, 252–3.

13 Ibid., p. 271.

14 Lynn Botelho, 'Old Age and Menopause in Rural Women in Early Modern Suffolk', in Botelho and Thane (eds), *Women and Ageing in British Society since 1500,* pp. 43–63; Daniel Schäfer, *Old Age and Disease in Early Modern*

Medicine, translated by Patrick Baker (London: Pickering and Chatto, 2011), pp. 26, 33; Michael Stolberg, 'A Woman's Hell? Medical Perceptions of Menopause in Early Modern Europe', *Bulletin of the History of Medicine* 73 (1999): 409.

15 Elizabeth Isham, 'Book of Rememberance', fol. 17v, University of Warwick, available at http://web.warwick.ac.uk/english/perdita/Isham/index_bor.htm (accessed 10 May 2015).

16 Peter Laslett, *The World We Have Lost* (London: Routledge, 1965), pp. 109–10.

17 Peter Laslett, *A Fresh Map of Life: The Emergence of the Third Age* (Cambridge, MA: Harvard University Press, 1991), p. 108.

18 Stolberg, *Experiencing Illness*, pp. 28–9.

19 See Joanna Bourke, *The Story of Pain: From Prayer to Painkillers* (Oxford: Oxford University Press, 2014), pp. 273–8.

20 Roselyne Rey, *The History of Pain*, translated by L. E. Wallace, J. A. Cadden and S. W. Cadden (Cambridge, MA: Harvard University Press, 1995), p. 63.

21 Philip K. Wilson, *Surgery, Skin and Syphilis: Daniel Turner's London (1667–1741)* (Amsterdam: Rodopi, 1999), p. 37.

22 Andrew Cambers, *Godly Reading: Print, Manuscript and Puritanism in England, 1580–1720* (Cambridge: Cambridge University Press, 2012), pp. 65–6.

23 Olivia Weisser, 'Boils, Pushes and Wheals: Reading Bumps on the Body in Early Modern England', *Social History of Medicine* 22 (2009): 325–6.

24 Katherine A. Walker, 'Pain and Surgery in England, circa 1620–circa 1740', *Medical History* 59, no. 2 (2015): 260.

25 Culpeper, *A Physicall Directory*, p. 64.

26 Coelson, *The Poor-Mans Physician*, pp. 94, 144.

27 Culpeper, *English Physitian Enlarged*, p. 199.

28 Rey, *History of Pain*, pp. 64, 83; Thomas Dormandy, *The Worst of Evils: The Fight against Pain* (New Haven: Yale University Press, 2006), pp. 130–2.

29 Margaret Pelling and Richard M. Smith (eds), *Life, Death and the Elderly: Historical Perspectives* (London: Routledge, 1991), introduction, p. 8.

30 Mary Clarke, letter to Edward Clarke, 15 April 1695, BIWLD, 212R.

31 Mary Clarke, letters to John Spreat, 20 November 1704 and 29 March 1705, BIWLD, 458R and 464R.

32 Cited in Crawford and Gowing (eds), *Women's Worlds*, p. 269.

33 Burton, *Anatomy of Melancholy*. See also Clark Lawlor, *From Melancholia to Prozac: A History of Depression* (Oxford: Oxford University Press, 2012).

34 David Walker, Anita O'Connell and Michelle Faubert, *Depression and Melancholy, 1660–1800* (London: Pickering and Chatto, 2012), p. xxv.

35 Coelson, *The Poor-Mans Physician*, p. 1; see also Noga Arikha, *Passions and Tempers: A History of the Humours* (New York: Ecco, 2007), especially Chapters 4 and 5.

36 Marika Keblusek, 'Wine for Comfort: Drinking and the Royalist Exile Experience, 1642–1660', in Adam Smyth (ed.), *A Pleasing Sinne: Drink and Conviviality in Seventeenth-Century England* (Woodbridge, Suffolk: Boydell and Brewer, 2004), p. 57. Some people thought that alcohol might cause melancholy – see Jeremy Schmidt, *Melancholy and the Care of the Soul: Religion, Moral Philosophy and Madness in Early Modern England* (Aldershot: Ashgate, 2007), p. 175.

37 Anne Dormer, letter to her sister Lady Elizabeth, 24 Aug. [1687], cited in Crawford and Gowing, *Women's Worlds*, p. 36.

38 Lady Clinton, letter to Margaret Boscawen, 28 April 1683, 1262M/FC/1, DHC.

39 Pechey, *Compleat Herbal*, p. 14 et seq., Culpeper, *English Physitian*, p. 5 et seq.

40 W. M., *Queens Closet Opened*, p. 293.

41 'Large Book', 1262M/FC/6, DHC, fols 31r, 33r, 37r. The cordial recipe came from Read, *Most Excellent and Approved Medicines*, p. 49.

42 Elizabeth Clarke Her Booke, 1666, DD\SF/3306, SHC, fol. 20r.

43 Leong, 'Making Medicines', pp. 153, 157.

44 'Loose Items', 1262M/FC/8, DHC, item 56 endorsed 'Bannister's powder' (undated).

45 Creighton, *History of Epidemics in Britain*, p. 516.

46 Pelling, 'Nurses and Nursekeepers', pp. 184–6.

47 Davies, 'Rewriting Nursing History', p. 25.

48 Meldrum, *Domestic Service*, p. 141.

49 Bridget Fortescue, letter to Hugh Fortescue, 6 February 1707/8, 1262M/FC/9, DHC.

50 Clarke, 'Life and Correspondence', pp. 256–7.

51 Mary Burgess, letter to Edward Clarke, 16 September 1695, BIWLD, 219R.

52 Mortimer, *Dying and the Doctors*, pp. 182–5.

53 Ben-Amos, 'Gifts and Favors', p. 304.

54 Mortimer, *Dying and the Doctors*, pp. 151–2.

55 Mary Burgess, letter to Edward Clarke, 22 October 1694, DD\SF/3833, SHC.

56 Ibid.

57 Ilana K. Ben-Amos, *Human Bonding: Parents and Their Offspring in Early Modern England* (Oxford: University of Oxford, 1997), p. 12.

58 Meldrum, *Domestic Service*, pp. 179, 181.

59 Quoted in Stine, 'Opening Closets', p. 72.

60 Sarah Egerton, 'The Liberty', in Robert W. Uphaus and Gretchen M. Foster (eds), *The Other Eighteenth Century. English Women of Letters 1660–1800* (East Lansing: East Lansing Colleagues Press, 1991), p. 140.

61 Lady Masham, letter to John Locke, 14 November [1685], in Locke, *Correspondence*, vol. II, p. 757. John Locke lived with Lady Masham and her husband at Oates for many years; see Goldie, *John Locke and the Mashams*.

62 Ibid., p. 25.

63 Quoted in Archer, 'Women and Alchemy', Chapter 5, p. 5.

64 Mary Chudleigh, *The Poems and Prose of Mary, Lady Chudleigh*, p. 39.

65 Ibid.

66 Cited in Bernard Capp, *When Gossips Meet: Women, Family and Neighbourhood in Early Modern England* (Oxford: Oxford University Press, 2003), p. 380.

67 Frances Harris, *Transformations of Love: The Friendship of John Evelyn and Margaret Godolphin* (Oxford: Oxford University Press, 2003), pp. 71, 252.

68 Harris, 'Living in the Neighbourhood of Science', p. 199.

69 Ibid., p. 200.

70 Bridget Fortescue, letter to Hugh Fortescue, 29 February 1707/8, 1262M/FC/9, DHC.

71 Stobart, 'Lett Her Refrain from All Hott Spices', p. 204.

72 Bridget Fortescue, letter to Hugh Fortescue, 24 February 1707/8, 1262M/FC/9, DHC.

73 Bridget Fortescue, letter to Hugh Fortescue, 27 February 1707/8, 1262M/FC/9, DHC.

74 Bridget Fortescue, letter to Hugh Fortescue, 8 February [1707/8], 1262M/FC/9, DHC.

75 Bridget Fortescue, letter to Hugh Fortescue, 27 February 1707/8, 1262M/FC/9, DHC.

76 Bridget Fortescue, letter to Hugh Fortescue, 24 February 1707/8, 1262M/FC/9, DHC.

77 Bridget Fortescue, letter to Hugh Fortescue, 7 March 1707/8, 1262M/FC/9, DHC.

78 Bridget Fortescue, letter to Hugh Fortescue, 9 March 1707/8, 1262M/FC/9, DHC.

79 Bridget Fortescue, letter to Hugh Fortescue, 10 February [1707/8], 1262M/FC/9, DHC.

80 Ibid.

81 Ibid.

82 Ibid.

83 Bridget Fortescue, letter to Hugh Fortescue, 17 February [1707/8], 1262M/FC/9, DHC.

84 Ibid.

85 Bridget Fortescue, letter to Hugh Fortescue, 6 February 1707/8, 1262M/FC/9, DHC.

86 A 'tent' referred to a kind of bandage which could be used to keep a wound open (*OED*).

87 Burton, *Anatomy of Melancholy*, introduction, p. 212.

88 Read, *Most Excellent and Approved Medicines*, p. 144.

89 Hannah Newton, '"Nature Concocts & Expels": The Agents and Processes of Recovery from Disease in Early Modern England', *Social History of Medicine* 28, no. 3 (2015): 465–86.

90 Wear, *Knowledge and Practice*, p. 378.

91 Bridget Fortescue, letter to Hugh Fortescue, 24 February 1707/8, 1262M/FC/9, DHC. See Chapter 6, note 35, for discussion of the identity of Bridget's snakeroot.

92 Ibid.

93 Ibid.

94 Bridget Fortescue, letter to Hugh Fortescue, 29 February 1707/8, 1262M/FC/9, DHC.

95 Ibid.

96 Bridget Fortescue, letter to Hugh Fortescue, [28?] February 1707/8, 1262M/FC/9, DHC.

97 Bridget Fortescue, letter to Hugh Fortescue, 29 February 1707/8, 1262M/FC/9, DHC.

98 Wear, *Knowledge and Practice*, p. 464.

99 Mary Clarke, letter to John Buckland, [?] May 1678, BIWLD, 150R.

100 Stannard, 'Materia Medica', 204–7.

101 John Locke, letter to Edward Clarke, 13 January 1695/96, in Clarke, 'Life and Correspondence', p. 271.

102 John Locke, letter to Mary Clarke, 19 September 1696, in Clarke, 'Life and Correspondence', p. 314.

103 William Chilcot, *A Practical Treatise Concerning Evil Thoughts: Wherein Are Some Things More Especially Useful for Melancholy Persons* (Exeter: Printed for Samuel Darker, for Charles Yeo, John Pearce, and Philip Bishop, 1698), p. 254. Cheerfulness is also explored in Helen Yallop, *Age and Identity in Eighteenth-Century England*, especially Chap. 4.

104 Mary Clarke, draft letter to John Locke, [1696?], DD\SF/3304 Part 2, SHC.

105 Ibid.

106 The letter from Mary does not appear in Locke, *Correspondence*.

107 Edward Clarke, letter to Mary Clarke, 31 October 1696, in Clarke, 'Life and Correspondence', p. 331.

108 Mary Clarke, letter to Edward Clarke, 27 February 1696/7, in Clarke, 'Life and Correspondence', p. 359.

109 John Locke, letter to Mary Clarke, 22 March 1695/6, in Clarke, 'Life and Correspondence', p. 247; see note 114 in Chapter 6.

110 Observation of the patient was a perspective which Locke shared with Thomas Sydenham; see Kenneth Dewhurst, *John Locke, 1632–1704,*

Lessius, Leonard. *Hygiasticon: Or, the Right Course of Preserving Life and Health Unto Extream Old Age*. Cambridge: Printed by Roger Daniel, 1634.

Locke, John. *The Correspondence of John Locke*. 8 vols. Edited by E. S. De Beer. Oxford: Clarendon Press, 1976–89.

Lowe, Roger. *The Diary of Roger Lowe, 1663–1674*. Edited by W. L. Sachse. New Haven, CT: Yale University Press, 1938.

Lower, Richard. *Dr Lowers and Several Other Eminent Physicians Receipts Containing the Best and Safest Method for Curing Most Diseases in Humane Bodies*. London: John Nutt, 1700.

M., W. *The Queens Closet Opened*. London: Printed for Nath. Brooke, 1655.

Mace, Thomas. *Riddles, Mervels and Rarities*. Cambridge: Printed for the author, 1698.

Markham, Gervase. *The English House-Wife*. London: Printed by Nicholas Okes for John Harison, 1631.

Marriott, J. *The English Mountebank: Or, a Physical Dispensatory*. London: Printed for George Horton, 1652.

Maynwaringe, Everard. *The Efficacy and Extent of True Purgation*. London: Printed for D. Browne; and R. Clavel, 1696.

Merret, Christopher. *The Accomplisht Physician, the Honest Apothecary, and the Skilful Chyrurgeon*. London: W. Thackeray, 1670.

Moore, Philip. *The Hope of Health Wherin Is Conteined a Goodlie Regimente of Life: As Medicine, Good Diet and the Goodlie Vertues of Sonderie Herbes*. London: Imprinted by Ihon Kyngston, 1564.

Muffet, Thomas. *Healths Improvement*. London: Tho. Newcomb for Samuel Thomson, 1655.

Natura Exenterata, or Nature Unbowelled by the Most Exquisite Anatomizers of Her. London: Printed for H. Twiford, G. Bedell and N. Ekins, 1655.

Palmer, Archdale. *The Recipe Book, 1659–1672, of Archdale Palmer, Gent*. Edited by Grant Uden. Wymondham: Sycamore Press, 1985.

Parkinson, James. *Medical Admonitions Addressed to Families, Respecting the Practice of Domestic Medicine, and the Preservation of Health*. 3rd ed. London: Printed for C. Dilly *et al.*, 1799.

Partridge, John. *The Widowes Treasure*. London: Printed by Edward Alde, for Edward White, 1588.

Partridge, John. *The Treasurie of Commodious Conceits*. London: Richard Jones, 1591.

Pechey, John. *The Compleat Herbal of Physical Plants Containing All Such English and Foreign Herbs, Shrubs and Trees, as Are Used in Physick and Surgery*. London: Printed for Henry Bonwicke, 1694.

Penney, Norman, ed. *The Household Account Book of Sarah Fell of Swarthmoor Hall*. Cambridge: Cambridge University Press, 1920.

Plat, Hugh. *The Jewell House of Art and Nature*. London: Bernard Alsop, 1653.

Poynter, F. N. L., ed. *The Journal of James Yonge [1647–1721]: Plymouth Surgeon*. London: Longmans, 1963.

Primrose, James. *Popular Errours. Or, the Errours of the People in Physick*. Translated by Robert Wittie. London: Printed by W. Wilson for Nicholas Bourne, 1651.

Quincy, John. *Pharmacopoeia Officinalis and Extemporanea*. 8th ed. London: J. Osborn and T. Longman, 1730.

Read, Alexander. *Most Excellent and Approved Medicines and Remedies for Most Diseases and Maladies Incident to Man's Body*. London: Printed by J. C. for George Latham, 1651.

Riders, Cardanus. *Riders (1679) British Merlin: Bedeckt with Many Delightful Varieties, and Useful Verities . . . With Notes of Husbandry, Physick, Fairs and Marts*. London: Printed by Tho. Newcomb for the Company of Stationers, 1679.

Rogers, Timothy. *The Character of a Good Woman*. London: Printed for J. Harris, 1697.

Rugg, Thomas. *Diurnal of Thomas Rugg 1659–1661*. Edited by W. L. Sachse. London: Royal Historical Society, 1961.

Shirley, John. *The Accomplished Ladies Rich Closet of Rarities*. London: Printed by W. and F. Wilde for N. Boddington and J. Blare, 1691.

Sowerby, Leonard. *The Ladies Dispensatory: Containing the Natures, Vertues and Qualities of All Herbs, and Simples Useful in Physick*. London: Printed for R. Ibbetson, 1652.

Topsell, Edward. *The Historie of Foure-Footed Beastes*. London: William Iaggard, 1607.

Tryon, Thomas. *Healths Grand Preservative: Or the Womens Best Doctor*. London: Printed for the Author, 1682.

Turner, William. *A New Herball by William Turner. Part 1*. 1551 ed. Edited by T. L. Chapman, George Tweddle and Marilyn N. Tweddle. Cambridge: Cambridge University Press, 1995.

Vickers, William. *A Brief Account of a Specifick Remedy for Curing the King's Evil, Confirmed by Seventy Nine Extraordinary Cures, since October, 1706*. 2nd ed. London, 1709.

Vivian, J. L. *The Visitations of Cornwall, Comprising the Heralds' Visitations of 1530, 1573, & 1620 with Additions*. Exeter: William Pollard, 1887.

Vivian, J. L. *The Visitations of the County of Devon Comprising the Heralds' Visitations of 1531, 1564 and 1620*. Exeter: Henry S. Eland, 1895.

Wall, Alison D. *Two Elizabethan Women: Correspondence of Joan and Maria Thynne, 1575–1611*. Devizes: Wiltshire Record Society, 1983.

Weatherill, Lorna. *The Account Book of Richard Latham, 1724–1767*. Oxford: Published for the British Academy by Oxford University Press, 1990.

Weddell, George. *Arcana Fairfaxiana Manuscripta*. Newcastle-on-Tyne: Mawson, Swan and Morgan, 1890.

Wolley, Hannah. *The Accomplish'd Ladies Delight in Preserving, Physick, Beautifying, and Cookery*. London: Benjamin Harris, 1685.

Woodall, John. *The Surgeon's Mate. A Complete Facsimile of the Book Published in 1617*. Edited by John Kirkup. Bath: Kingsmead, 1978

Woodforde, Dorothy H. *Woodforde Papers and Diaries*. London: Peter Davies, 1932.

Secondary sources

Albala, Ken. *Eating Right in the Renaissance*. Berkeley: University of California Press, 2002.

Albala, Ken. 'To Your Health: Wine as Food and Medicine in Mid-Sixteenth-Century Italy'. In *Alcohol: A Social and Cultural History*, edited by Mack P. Holt, 11–24. Oxford: Berg, 2006.

Albala, Ken. 'Food for Healing: Convalescent Cookery in the Early Modern Era'. *Studies in History and Philosophy of Biological and Biomedical Sciences* 43 (2012): 323–8.

Allen, David E. and Gabrielle Hatfield. *Medicinal Plants in Folk Tradition: An Ethnobotany of Britain and Ireland*. Portland, OR: Timber Press, 2004.

Arber, Agnes. *Herbals: Their Origin and Evolution: A Chapter in the History of Botany 1470–1670*. London: Cambridge University Press, 1953.

Archer, Jayne E. E. 'Women and Alchemy in Early Modern England'. PhD thesis, Cambridge University, 2000.

Archer, Jayne E. E. 'Women and Chymistry in Early Modern England: The Manuscript Receipt Book (c. 1616) of Sarah Wigges'. In *Gender and Scientific Discourse in Early Modern Culture*, edited by Kathleen P. Long, 192–216. Farnham: Ashgate, 2013.

Arikha, Noga. *Passions and Tempers: A History of the Humours*. New York: Ecco, 2007.

Arnold, Ken. *Cabinets for the Curious: Looking Back at Early English Museums*. Farnham: Ashgate, 2006.

Ashworth, William. *Customs and Excise: Trade, Production and Consumption in England, 1640–1845*. Oxford: Oxford University Press, 2003.

Aspin, Richard. 'Illustrations from the Wellcome Library: Who Was Elizabeth Okeover?'. *Medical History* 44 (2000): 531–40.

Aspin, Richard. 'Testamentary Records of the Sixteenth to Eighteenth Centuries as a Source for the History of Herbal Medicine in England'. In *Critical Approaches to the History of Western Herbal Medicine: From Classical Antiquity to the Early Modern Period*, edited by Susan Francia and Anne Stobart, 149–65. London: Bloomsbury, 2014.

Austin, Anne. *The History of the Clinton Barony, 1299–1999*. Exeter: Short Run Press and Lord Clinton, 1999.

Barker, Hannah and Elaine Chalus, eds. *Gender in Eighteenth-Century England: Roles, Representations and Responsibilities*. Harlow: Longman, 1997.

Barry, Jonathan. 'Literacy and Literature in Popular Culture: Reading and Writing in Historical Perspective'. In *Popular Culture in England c. 1500–1850*, edited by Tim Harris, 64–94. London: Macmillan, 1995.

Barry, Jonathan. *The Diary of William Dyer: Bristol in 1762*. Bristol: Bristol Record Society, 2012.

Barry, Jonathan and Colin Jones, eds. *Medicine and Charity before the Welfare State*. London: Routledge, 1991.

Bayer, Penny. 'From Kitchen Hearth to Learned Paracelsianism: Women's Alchemical Activities in the Renaissance'. In *Mystical Metal of Gold: Essays on Alchemy and Renaissance Culture*, edited by Stanton Linden, 1–28. Brooklyn, NY: AMS Press, 2005.

Beam, Aki C. L. '"Should I as yet Call You Old?": Testing the Boundaries of Female Old Age in Early Modern England'. In *Growing Old in Early Modern Europe: Cultural Representations*, edited by Erin Campbell, 95–116. Aldershot: Ashgate, 2006.

Beier, Lucinda M. *Sufferers and Healers: The Experience of Illness in Seventeenth Century England*. London: Routledge and Kegan Paul, 1987.

Beier, Lucinda M. 'Seventeenth-Century English Surgery: The Casebook of Joseph Binns'. In *Medical Theory, Surgical Practice: Studies in the History of Surgery*, edited by Christopher Lawrence, 48–84. London: Routledge, 1992.

Ben-Amos, Ilana K. *Human Bonding: Parents and Their Offspring in Early Modern England*. Oxford: University of Oxford, 1997.

Ben-Amos, Ilana K. 'Gifts and Favors: Informal Support in Early Modern England'. *Journal of Modern History* 72, no. 2 (2000): 295–338.

Berry, Helen. 'The Pleasures of Austerity'. *Journal for Eighteenth-Century Studies* 37, no. 2 (2014): 261–77.

Best, Michael R. *Gervase Markham: The English House-wife*. Kingston: McGill-Queen's University Press, 1986.

Blake, John B. 'From Buchan to Fishbein: The Literature of Domestic Medicine'. In *Medicine without Doctors: Home Health Care in American History*, edited by Guenter B. Risse, Ronald L. Numbers and Judith W. Leavitt, 11–30. New York: Science History Publications, 1977.

Borsay, Peter. *The English Urban Renaissance: Culture and Society in the Provincial Town 1660–1770*. Oxford: Clarendon Press, 1989.

Botelho, Lynn. 'Old Age and Menopause in Rural Women in Early Modern Suffolk'. In *Women and Ageing in British Society since 1500*, edited by Lynn Botelho and Pat Thane, 43–63. Harlow: Longman, 2001.

Bourke, Joanna. *The Story of Pain: From Prayer to Painkillers*. Oxford: Oxford University Press, 2014.

Brushfield, T. N. 'The Financial Diary of a Citizen of Exeter, 1631–1643'. *Devonshire Transactions* XXXIII (1901): 187–269.

Burke, Peter. *Popular Culture in Early Modern Europe*. London: Temple Smith, 1978.

Burke, Victoria E. '"The Art of Numbering Well": Late-Seventeenth-Century Arithmetic Manuscripts Compiled by Quaker Girls'. In *Material Readings of Early Modern Culture: Texts and Social Practices, 1580–1730*, edited by James Daybell and Peter Hinds, 246–65. Basingstoke: Palgrave Macmillan, 2012.

Burnby, Juanita. *A Study of the English Apothecary from 1660 to 1760*. London: Wellcome Institute for the History of Medicine, 1983.

Burnby, Juanita. 'The Herb Women of the London Markets'. *Pharmaceutical Historian* 13, no. 1 (1983): 5–6.

Burnett, John. *Liquid Pleasures: A Social History of Drinks in Modern Britain*. London: Routledge, 1999.

Burnham, John C. *What Is Medical History?* Cambridge: Polity, 2005.

Bushnell, Rebecca. *Green Desire: Imagining Early Modern English Gardens*. Ithaca, NY: Cornell University Press, 2003.

Cabré, Montserrat. 'Women or Healers? Household Practices and the Categories of Health Care in Late Medieval Iberia'. *Bulletin of the History of Medicine* 82 (2008): 18–51.

Cambers, Andrew. *Godly Reading: Print, Manuscript and Puritanism in England, 1580–1720*. Cambridge: Cambridge University Press, 2012.

Cameron, M. L. 'The Sources of Medical Knowledge in Anglo-Saxon England'. *Anglo-Saxon England* 11 (2008): 135–55.

Campbell, Mildred. *The English Yeoman under Elizabeth and the Early Stuarts*. New York: Augustus M. Kelley, 1942.

Capp, Bernard. *When Gossips Meet: Women, Family and Neighbourhood in Early Modern England*. Oxford: Oxford University Press, 2003.

Cavallo, Sandra. 'Invisible Beds: Health and the Material Culture of Sleep'. In *Writing Material Culture History*, edited by Anne Gerritsen and Giorgio Riello, 143–9. London: Bloomsbury, 2015.

Cavallo, Sandra and Tessa Storey. *Healthy Living in Late Renaissance Italy.* Oxford: Oxford University Press, 2013.

Chamberland, Celeste. 'Partners and Practitioners: Women and the Management of Surgical Households in London, 1570–1640'. *Social History of Medicine* 24, no. 3 (2011): 554–69.

Chartres, J. A. *Internal Trade in England 1500–1700.* London: Macmillan, 1977.

Chartres, J. A. 'Spirits in the North-East? Gin and Other Vices in the Long Eighteenth Century'. In *Creating and Consuming Culture in North-East England, 1660–1830*, edited by Helen Berry and Jeremy Gregory, 37–56. Aldershot: Ashgate, 2003.

Cheal, David. '"Showing You Love Them": Gift Giving and the Dialectic of Intimacy'. In *The Gift: An Interdisciplinary Perspective*, edited by Aafke E. Komter, 95–106. Amsterdam: Amsterdam University Press, 1996.

Churchill, Wendy. *Female Patients in Early Modern Britain: Gender, Diagnosis and Treatment.* Farnham: Ashgate, 2012.

Clarke, Bridget. 'The Life and Correspondence of Edward Clarke of Chipley, 1650–1710'. Unpublished typescript. 4 vols, 1997.

Clericuzio, Antonio. 'From Van Helmont to Boyle: A Study in the Transmission of Helmontian Chemical and Medical Theories in Seventeenth-Century England'. *British Journal for the History of Science* 26 (1993): 303–34.

Clericuzio, Antonio. 'Chemical and Mechanical Theories of Digestion in Early Modern Medicine'. *Studies in History and Philosophy of Biological and Biomedical Sciences* 43, no. 2 (2012): 329–37.

Cliffe, J. T. *The Puritan Gentry: The Great Puritan Families of Early Stuart England.* London: Routledge, 1984.

Clifford, Hugh. *The House of Clifford from before the Conquest.* Chichester: Phillimore, 1987.

Cockayne, Emily. *Hubbub: Filth, Noise and Stench in England, 1600–1770.* New Haven, CT: Yale University Press, 2007.

Cohen, Mark R. 'Introduction: Poverty and Charity in Past Times'. *Journal of Interdisciplinary History* 35, no. 3 (2004): 347–60.

Coley, Noel. '"Cures without Care": "Chymical Physicians" and Mineral Waters in Seventeenth-Century English Medicine'. *Medical History* 23 (1979): 191–214.

Connor, Rebecca E. *Women, Accounting and Narrative: Keeping Books in Eighteenth-Century England.* London: Routledge, 2004.

Cook, Harold. 'The New Philosophy and Medicine in Seventeenth-Century England'. In *Reappraisals of the Scientific Revolution*, edited by David C. Lindberg and Robert S. Westman, 397–436. Cambridge: Cambridge University Press, 1990.

Cook, Harold. 'Markets and Cultures: Medical Specifics and the Reconfiguration of the Body in Early Modern Europe'. *Transactions of the Royal Historical Society* 21 (2011): 123–45.

Cooper, Alix. 'Home and Household as Sites for Early Modern Science'. In *The Cambridge History of Early Modern Science*, edited by Katharine Park and Lorraine Daston, 226–37. New York: Cambridge University Press, 2006.

Cooper, Sheila. 'Kinship and Welfare in Early Modern England: Sometimes Charity Begins at Home'. In *Medicine, Charity and Mutual Aid: The Consumption of Health and Welfare in Britain, c. 1550–1950*, edited by Anne Borsay and Peter Shapely, 55–69. Aldershot: Ashgate, 2007.

Cooter, Roger and Claudia Stein. *Writing History in the Age of Biomedicine*. New Haven and London: Yale University Press, 2013.

Copeman, E. 'On Bloodletting'. *British Medical Journal*, no. 13 (December 1879): 932–3.

Corfield, Penelope J. 'From Poison Peddlers to Civic Worthies: The Reputation of Apothecaries in Georgian England'. *Social History of Medicine* 22, no. 1 (2009): 1–21.

Cox, Nancy. *The Complete Tradesman: A Study of Retailing, 1550–1820*. Aldershot: Ashgate, 2000.

Cox, Nancy. '"A Flesh Pott, or a Brasse Potte or a Pott to Boile In": Changes in Metal and Fuel Technology in the Early Modern Period and the Implications for Cooking'. In *Gender and Material Culture in Historical Perspective*, edited by Moira Donald and Linda Hurcombe, 143–57. Basingstoke: Palgrave Macmillan, 2000.

Crawford, Patricia and Laura Gowing, eds. *Women's Worlds in Seventeenth-Century England*. London: Routledge, 2000.

Creighton, Charles. *A History of Epidemics in Britain*. Vol. 1. 2nd ed. London: Frank Cass, 1965.

Crellin, J. K. 'Possets'. *Notes and Queries* 14, no. 1 (1967): 2–4.

Crisp, Frederick A. 'Strode Family'. *Fragmenta Genealogica* 8 (1902): 97–118.

Dalporto, Jeannie, ed. *Essential Works for the Study of Early Modern Women: Part 3. Volume 5. Women in Service in Early Modern England*. Aldershot: Ashgate, 2008.

Dannehl, Karin. '"To Families Furnishing Kitchens": Domestic Utensils and Their Use in the Eighteenth-Century Home'. In *Buying for the Home: Shopping for the Domestic from the Seventeenth Century to the Present*, edited by David Hussey and Margaret Ponsonby, 27–46. Burlington, VT: Ashgate, 2008.

Davidoff, Leonore and Catherine Hall. *Family Fortunes: Men and Women of the English Middle Class, 1780–1850*. London: Routledge, 1987.

Davies, Celia. 'Rewriting Nursing History-Again?'. *Nursing History Review* 15 (2007): 11–27.

De Grazia, Victoria and Ellen Furlough, eds. *The Sex of Things: Gender and Consumption in Historical Perspective*. Berkeley: University of California Press, 1996.

De Renzi, Silvia. 'Old and New Models of the Body'. In *The Healing Arts, Health, Disease and Society in Europe 1500–1800*, edited by Peter Elmer, 166–95. Manchester: Open University, 2004.

De Vries, Jan. 'Between Purchasing Power and the World of Goods: Understanding the Household Economy in Early Modern Europe'. In *Women's Work: The English Experience, 1650–1914*, edited by Pamela Sharpe, 209–38. London: Arnold, 1998.

Debus, Allen. *The English Paracelsians*. London: Oldbourne, 1965.

Dewhurst, Kenneth. *John Locke, 1632–1704, Physician and Philosopher: A Medical Biography with an Edition of the Medical Notes in His Journals*. London: Wellcome Historical Medical Library, 1963.

Digby, Anne. *Making a Medical Living: Doctors and Patients in the English Market for Medicine, 1720–1911*. Cambridge: Cambridge University Press, 1994.

Dobson, Mary. *Contours of Death and Disease in Early Modern England*. Cambridge: Cambridge University Press, 1997.

Dormandy, Thomas. *The Worst of Evils: The Fight against Pain*. New Haven: Yale University Press, 2006.

Dowd, Michelle M. *Women's Work in Early Modern English Literature and Culture*. New York: Palgrave Macmillan, 2009.

Dowell, Stephen. *A History of Taxation and Taxes in England from the Earliest Times to the Present Day*. Vol. II. London: Longmans, Green and Co., 1884.

Drummond, J. C. and Anne Wilbraham. *The Englishman's Food: A History of Five Centuries of English Diet*. Revised ed. Oxford: Alden Press, 1957.

Duffin, Jacalyn. *Lovers and Livers: Disease Concepts in History*. Toronto: University of Toronto Press, 2002.

Durant, David N. *Life in the Country House: A Historical Dictionary*. London: John Murray, 1996.

Eamon, William. *Science and the Secrets of Nature: Books of Secrets in Medieval and Early Modern Culture*. Princeton: Princeton University Press, 1994.

Earle, Peter. *The Making of the English Middle Class: Business, Society and Family Life in London, 1660–1730*. London: Methuen, 1989.

Elmer, Peter. *The Miraculous Conformist: Valentine Greatrakes, the Body Politic, and the Politics of Healing in Restoration Britain*. Oxford: Oxford University Press, 2013.

Evans, Jennifer. 'Female Barrenness, Bodily Access and Aromatic Treatments in Seventeenth-Century England'. *Historical Research* 87, no. 237 (2014): 423–43.

Evans, Jennifer and Sara Read. '"Before Midnight She Had Miscarried": Women, Men and Miscarriage in Early Modern England'. *Journal of Family History* 40, no. 1 (2015): 3–23.

Fildes, Valerie A. '"The English Disease": Infantile Rickets and Scurvy in Pre-Industrial England'. In *Child Care through the Centuries: An Historical Survey from Papers Given at the Tenth British Congress on the History of Medicine at Clyne Castle, Swansea, 6–8th April 1984*, edited by John Cule and Terry Turner, 121–34. Cardiff: STS Publishing for the British Society for the History of Medicine, 1984.

Fildes, Valerie A. 'Infant Care in Tudor and Stuart England'. *Midwife, Health Visitor, Community Nurse* 22, no. 3 (1986): 79–84.

Fildes, Valerie A. *Wet Nursing: A History from Antiquity to the Present*. Oxford: Basil Blackwell, 1988.

Fissell, Mary E. *Patients, Power and the Poor in Eighteenth Century Bristol*. Cambridge: Cambridge University Press, 1991.

Fissell, Mary E. 'Making Meaning from the Margins: The New Cultural History of Medicine'. In *Locating Medical History: The Stories and Their Meaning*, edited by F. Huisman and J. Warner, 364–89. Baltimore: Johns Hopkins University Press, 2004.

Fissell, Mary E. 'The Marketplace of Print'. In *Medicine and the Market in England and Its Colonies, c. 1450–c. 1850*, edited by Mark S. R. Jenner and Patrick Wallis, 108–32. Basingstoke: Palgrave Macmillan, 2007.

Flather, Amanda J. 'Gender, Space, and Place: The Experience of Service in the Early Modern English Household c. 1580–1720'. *Home Cultures* 8, no. 2 (2011): 171–88.

Fletcher, Anthony. *Gender, Sex and Subordination in England 1500–1800*. New Haven, CT: Yale University Press, 1995.

Flower-Smith, R. P. 'Landowners on the Devon and Somerset Border, 1660–1715'. PhD thesis, University of Exeter, 1996.

Fontaine, Laurence. *History of Pedlars in Europe*. Translated by Vicki Whittaker. Durham, NC: Duke University Press, 1996.

Forbes, R. J. *A Short History of the Art of Distillation from the Beginnings up to the Death of Cellier Blumenthal*. Leiden: E. J. Brill, 1970.

Foust, Clifford M. *Rhubarb: The Wondrous Drug*. Princeton, NJ: Princeton University Press, 1992.

Fox, Adam. *Oral and Literate Culture in England, 1500–1700*. Oxford: Oxford University Press, 2000.

Fox, Adam. 'Food, Drink and Social Distinction in Early Modern England'. In *Remaking English Society*, edited by Steve Hindle, Alexandra Shepard and John Walter, 165–87. Woodbridge: Boydell Press, 2013.

Foyster, Elizabeth. *Marital Violence: An English Family History, 1660–1857*. Cambridge: Cambridge University Press, 2005.

Francis, Jill. 'John Parkinson: Gardener and Apothecary of London'. In *Critical Approaches to the History of Western Herbal Medicine: From Classical Antiquity to the Early Modern Period*, edited by Susan Francia and Anne Stobart, 229–46. London: Bloomsbury, 2014.

Furdell, Elizabeth L. *The Royal Doctors, 1485–1714: Medical Personnel at the Tudor and Stuart Courts*. Rochester, NY: University of Rochester Press, 2002.

Fussell, G. E. *The English Dairy Farmer, 1500–1900*. London: Frank Cass, 1966.

Gauci, Perry. *Emporium of the World: The Merchants of London 1660–1800*. London: Hambledon Continuum, 2007.

Gee, Michael. *Mazzards: The Revival of the Curious North Devon Cherry*. Exeter: Mint Press, 2004.

Gélis, Jacques. *History of Childbirth: Fertility, Pregnancy and Birth in Early Modern Europe*. Translated by Rosemary Morris. Cambridge: Polity Press, 1991.

Gentilcore, David. 'Was There a "Popular Medicine" in Early Modern Europe?' *Folklore* 115, no. 2 (2004): 151–66.

Gentilcore, David. 'Body and Soul, or Living Physically in the Kitchen'. In *A Cultural History of Food in the Early Modern Age*, edited by Beat Kümin, 143–63. London: Bloomsbury, 2013.

Getz, Faye. *Medicine in the English Middle Ages*. Princeton, NJ: Princeton University Press, 1998.

Gibbs, F.W. 'The History of the Manufacture of Soap'. *Annals of Science* 4 (1939): 169–90.

Girouard, Mark. *Life in the English Country House: A Social and Architectural History*. New Haven, CT: Yale University Press, 1978.

Glaisyer, Natasha. *The Culture of Commerce in England, 1660–1720*. Woodbridge: Royal Historical Society and Boydell Press, 2006.

Glaisyer, Natasha and Sara Pennell, eds. *Didactic Literature in England, 1500–1800: Experience Constructed*. Aldershot: Ashgate, 2003.

Goldie, Mark. *John Locke and the Mashams at Oates*. Essex: Parish of High Laver, 2004.

Goldstein, David B. *Eating and Ethics in Shakespeare's England*. Cambridge: Cambridge University Press, 2013.

Green, Monica. *Making Women's Medicine Masculine: The Rise of Male Authority in Pre-Modern Gynaecology*. Oxford: Oxford University Press, 2008.

Grell, Ole P. 'The Protestant Imperative of Christian Care and Neighbourly Love'. In *Health Care and Poor Relief in Protestant Europe, 1500–1700*, edited by Ole P. Grell and Andrew Cunningham, 43–65. London: Routledge, 1997.

Grell, Ole P. and Andrew Cunningham, eds. *Religio Medici: Medicine and Religion in Seventeenth-Century England*. Aldershot: Ashgate, 1996.

Grieve, M. *A Modern Herbal*. 1931 ed. London: Penguin, 1980.

Griffin, J. P. 'Venetian Treacle and the Foundation of Medicines Regulation'. *British Journal of Clinical Pharmacology* 58, no. 3 (2004): 317–25.

Grigson, Geoffrey. *The Englishman's Flora*. Oxford: Helicon, 1996.

Guerrini, Anita. *Obesity and Depression in the Enlightenment: The Life and Times of George Cheyne*. Norman, OK: University of Oklahoma Press, 2000.

Guthrie, Leonard. 'The Lady Sedley's Receipt Book, 1686, and Other Seventeenth-Century Receipt Books'. *Proceedings of the Royal Society of Medicine* VI (1913): 150–69.

Gwynn, Lucy. 'The Architecture of the English Domestic Library, 1600–1700'. *Library and Information History* 26, no. 1 (2010): 56–69.

Hall, Kim F. 'Culinary Spaces, Colonial Spaces: The Gendering of Sugar in the Seventeenth Century'. In *Feminist Readings of Early Modern Culture*, edited by Valerie Traub, M. Lindsay Kaplan and Dympna Callaghan, 168–90. Cambridge: Cambridge University Press, 1996.

Hannay, Margaret P. '"How I These Studies Prize": The Countess of Pembroke and Elizabethan Science'. In *Women, Science and Medicine 1500–1700: Mothers and Sisters of the Royal Society*, edited by Lynette Hunter and Sarah Hutton, 108–21. Stroud: Sutton Publishing, 1997.

Hardman, C. B. 'The Book as Domestic Gift: Bodleian Ms Don. C. 24'. In *Women and Writing, c. 1340–c. 1650: The Domestication of Print Culture*, edited by Anne Lawrence-Mathers and Philippa Hardman, 162–76. York: York Medieval Press, 2010.

Harkness, Deborah E. *The Jewel House: Elizabethan London and the Scientific Revolution*. New Haven: Yale University Press, 2007.

Harley, David. 'Spiritual Physic, Providence and English Medicine, 1560–1640'. In *Medicine and the Reformation*, edited by Ole P. Grell and Andrew Cunningham, 101–17. London and New York: Routledge, 1993.

Harris, Frances. 'Living in the Neighbourhood of Science: Mary Evelyn, Margaret Cavendish and the Greshamites'. In *Women, Science and Medicine 1500–1700: Mothers and Sisters of the Royal Society*, edited by Lynette Hunter and Sarah Hutton, 198–217. Stroud: Sutton, 1997.

Harris, Frances. *Transformations of Love: The Friendship of John Evelyn and Margaret Godolphin*. Oxford: Oxford University Press, 2003.

Harris, Tim. *Restoration: Charles II and His Kingdoms, 1660–1685*. London: Penguin, 2005.

Hartmann, Cyril H. *Clifford of the Cabal: A Life of Thomas, First Lord Clifford of Chudleigh, Lord High Treasurer of England (1630–1675)*. London: William Heinemann, 1937.

Haycock, David B. *'A Thing Ridiculous'? Chemical Medicines and the Prolongation of Human Life in Seventeenth-Century England*. London: London School of Economics, 2006.

Haycock, David B. and Patrick Wallis. *Quackery and Commerce in Seventeenth-Century London: The Proprietary Medicine Business of Anthony Daffy*.

London: Wellcome Trust Centre for the History of Medicine at UCL,
2005.

Heal, Felicity. 'Food Gifts, the Household and the Politics of Exchange in Early
Modern England'. *Past and Present* 199 (2008): 41–70.

Heal, Felicity. *The Power of Gifts: Gift-Exchange in Early Modern England*.
Oxford: Oxford University Press, 2014.

Healey, Jonathan. 'Poverty in an Industrializing Town: Deserving Hardship in Bolton,
1674–99'. *Social History* 35, no. 2 (2010): 125–47.

Healy, Margaret. 'Popular Medicine'. In *The Ashgate Research Companion to
Popular Culture in Early Modern England*, edited by Abigail Shinn, Matthew
Dimmock and Andrew Hadfield, 309–22. Farnham: Ashgate, 2014.

Hecht, J. Jean. *The Domestic Servant Class in Eighteenth-Century England*.
London: Routledge and Kegan Paul, 1956.

Henderson, Paula. *The Tudor House and Garden: Architecture and Landscape in
the Sixteenth and Early Seventeenth Centuries*. New Haven, CT: Yale University
Press, 2005.

Herbert, Amanda E. *Female Alliances: Gender, Identity, and Friendship in Early
Modern Britain*. New Haven: Yale University Press, 2014.

Hill, Bridget. *Women Alone: Spinsters in England, 1660–1850*. New Haven, CT:
Yale University Press, 2001.

Hill, Christopher. *Change and Continuity in Seventeenth-Century England*.
London: Weidenfeld and Nicolson, 1974.

Hindle, Steve. *On the Parish? The Micro-Politics of Poor Relief in Rural England
1550–1750*. Oxford: Oxford University Press, 2004.

Hobby, Elaine. 'A Woman's Best Setting Out Is Silence: The Writings of Hannah
Woolley'. In *Culture and Society in the Stuart Restoration: Literature, Drama,
History*, edited by G. MacLean, 179–200. Cambridge: Cambridge University
Press, 1995.

Hobby, Elaine. 'Early Modern Midwifery Manuals and Herbal Practice'. In *Critical
Approaches to the History of Western Herbal Medicine: From Classical
Antiquity to the Early Modern Period*, edited by Susan Francia and Anne
Stobart, 67–85. London: Bloomsbury, 2014.

Horden, Peregrine. 'Household Care and Informal Networks: Comparisons and
Continuities from Antiquity to the Present'. In *The Locus of Care: Families,
Communities, Institutions, and the Provision of Welfare since Antiquity*, edited
by Peregrine Horden and Richard Smith, 21–67. London: Routledge, 1998.

Hoskins, W. G. *Two Thousand Years in Exeter*. 2nd ed. Chichester: Phillimore, 1963.

Hudson, Briony. *English Delftware Drug Jars: The Collection of the Museum of
the Pharmaceutical Society of Great Britain*. London: Pharmaceutical Press,
2006.

Hudson, Briony. 'A Georgian First Aid Cabinet: Unpacking an Early 19th Century
Medicine Chest'. *Pharmaceutical Historian* 36, no. 3 (2006): 37–43.

Huggett, Jane. *The Mirror of Health: Food, Diet and Medical Theory 1450–1660*.
Bristol: Stuart Press, 1995.

Humphries, Jane. 'Household Economy'. In *The Cambridge Economic History of
Modern Britain*, edited by R. Floud and P. Johnson, 238–67. Cambridge:
Cambridge University Press, 2003–4.

Hunt, S. R. 'Seventeenth Century Manorial Medicine'. *Pharmaceutical Journal* 229
(1982): 758–60.

Nagy, Doreen E. *Popular Medicine in Seventeenth-Century England*. Bowling
    Green, OH: Bowling Green State University Popular Press, 1988.
Newman, William R. and Anthony Grafton. *Secrets of Nature: Astrology and
    Alchemy in Early Modern Europe*. Cambridge, MA: MIT Press, 2001.
Newton, Hannah. *The Sick Child in Early Modern England, 1580–1720*. Oxford:
    Oxford University Press, 2012.
Newton, Hannah. '"Nature Concocts & Expels": The Agents and Processes of
    Recovery from Disease in Early Modern England'. *Social History of Medicine*
    28, no. 3 (2015): 465–86.
Niebyl, Peter H. 'Galen, Van Helmont, and Bloodletting'. In *Science, Medicine and
    Society in the Renaissance: Essays to Honour Walter Pagel*, edited by Allen G.
    Debus, 13–52. London: Heinemann, 1972.
Noble, Louise. *Medicinal Cannibalism in Early Modern English Literature and
    Culture*. New York: Palgrave Macmillan, 2011.
North, Christine. 'Fustian, Figs and Frankincense: Jacobean Shop Inventories
    for Cornwall'. *Journal of the Royal Institution of Cornwall* II, 2.2 (1995):
    32–77.
North, Marcy L. *The Anonymous Renaissance: Cultures of Discretion in Tudor-
    Stuart England*. Chicago: University of Chicago Press, 2003.
O'Day, Rosemary. *The Family and Family Relationships, 1500–1900: England,
    France and the United States of America*. Basingstoke: Macmillan, 1994.
O'Day, Rosemary. 'Tudor and Stuart Women: Their Lives through Their Letters'. In
    Early Modern Women's Letter-Writing, 1450–1700, edited by James Daybell,
    127–42. Basingstoke: Palgrave, 2001.
O'Hara-May, Jane. 'Foods or Medicines? A Study in the Relationship between
    Foodstuffs and Materia Medica from the Sixteenth to the Nineteenth Century'.
    Transactions of the British Society for the History of Pharmacy 1, no. 1 (1970):
    61–97.
Overton, Mark. 'Prices from Probate Inventories'. In *When Death Do Us Part:
    Understanding the Probate Records of Early Modern England*, edited by T.
    Arkell, N. Evans and N. Goose, 120–43. Oxford: Leopard's Head Press, 2000.
Overton, Mark, Jane Whittle, Darron Dean and Andrew Hann. *Production and
    Consumption in English Households, 1600–1750*. Abingdon: Routledge, 2004.
Owen, David. *English Philanthropy, 1660–1960*. Cambridge, MA: Bellknapp Press,
    1965.
Park, Katharine. 'Country Medicine in the City Marketplace: Snakehandlers as
    Itinerant Healers'. *Renaissance Studies* 15, no. 2 (2001): 104–20.
Pelling, Margaret. *The Common Lot: Sickness, Medical Occupation and the Urban
    Poor in Early Modern England*. London: Longman, 1998.
Pelling, Margaret. 'Nurses and Nursekeepers: Problems of Identification in the
    Early Modern Period'. In *The Common Lot: Sickness, Medical Occupation and
    the Urban Poor in Early Modern England*, edited by Margaret Pelling, 179–202.
    London: Longman, 1998.
Pelling, Margaret. *Medical Conflicts in Early Modern London: Patronage, Physicians
    and Irregular Practitioners, 1550–1640*. Oxford: Oxford University Press, 2003.
Pelling, Margaret and Richard M. Smith, eds. *Life, Death and the Elderly:
    Historical Perspectives*. London: Routledge, 1991.
Pennell, Sara. 'The Material Culture of Food in Early Modern England, Circa
    1650–1750'. PhD thesis, University of Oxford, 1997.

Pennell, Sara. 'Consumption and Consumerism in Early Modern England'. *The Historical Journal* 42 (1999): 549–64.

Pennell, Sara. '"All but the Kitchen Sink": Household Sales and the Circulation of Second-Hand Goods in Early Modern England'. In *Modernity and the Second-Hand Trade: European Consumption Cultures and Practices, 1700–1900*, edited by Jon Stobart and Ilja Van Damme, 37–56. Basingstoke: Palgrave, 2010.

Pennell, Sara. '"For a Crack or Flaw Despis'd": Thinking About Ceramic Durability and the "Everyday" in Late Seventeenth- and Early Eighteenth-Century England'. In *Everyday Objects: Medieval and Early Modern Material Culture and Its Meanings*, edited by Tara Hamling and Catherine Richardson, 27–40. Farnham: Ashgate, 2010.

Pennell, Sara. 'Material Culture in Seventeenth-Century "Britain": The Matter of Domestic Consumption'. In *The History of Consumption*, edited by Frank Trentmann, 64–84. Oxford: Oxford University Press, 2012.

Pirohakul, Teerapa and Patrick Wallis. *Medical Revolutions? The Growth of Medicine in England, 1660–1800*. London: London School of Economics and Political Science, 2014.

Pointer, Sally. *The Artifice of Beauty: A History and Practical Guide to Perfumes and Cosmetics*. Stroud: Sutton, 2005.

Pollard, Tanya. 'Spelling the Body'. In *Environment and Embodiment in Early Modern England*, edited by Garett Jr Sullivan and Mary F. Wilson, 171–86. Basingstoke: Palgrave Macmillan, 2007.

Pollock, Linda A. *Forgotten Children: Parent–Child Relations from 1500 to 1900*. New York: Cambridge University Press, 1983.

Pollock, Linda A. *With Faith and Physic: The Life of a Tudor Gentlewoman, Lady Grace Mildmay, 1552–1620*. London: Collins and Brown, 1993.

Ponting, Kenneth G. *The Woollen Industry of South-West England*. Bath: Adams and Dart, 1971.

Porter, Dorothy and Roy Porter. *Patient's Progress: Doctors and Doctoring in Eighteenth-Century England*. Cambridge: Polity in association with Blackwell, 1989.

Porter, Roy. *Disease, Medicine and Society in England, 1550–1860*. Basingstoke: Macmillan, 1987.

Porter, Roy. 'Spreading Medical Enlightenment: The Popularization of Medicine in Georgian England'. In *The Popularisation of Medicine, 1650–1850*, edited by Roy Porter, 215–31. London: Routledge, 1992.

Porter, Roy. 'Consumption: Disease of the Consumer Society'. In *Consumption and the World of Goods*, edited by John Brewer and Roy Porter, 58–81. London: Routledge, 1993.

Porter, Roy. *Quacks, Fakers and Charlatans in Medicine*. Stroud: Tempus, 2003.

Porter, Roy and Dorothy Porter. 'The Rise of the English Drugs Industry: The Role of Thomas Corbyn'. *Medical History* 33 (1989): 277–95.

Potter, David. 'The Household Receipt Book of Ann, Lady Fanshawe'. *Petits Propos Culinaires* 80 (2006): 19–32.

Poynter, F. N. L. 'Nicholas Culpeper and His Books'. *Journal of the History of Medicine and Allied Sciences* 17 (1962): 152–67.

Purkiss, Diane. *The English Civil War: A People's History*. London: Harper Perennial, 2007.

Ramsey, Matthew. 'The Popularization of Medicine in Georgian England'. In *The Popularisation of Medicine in France, 1650–1900*, edited by Roy Porter, 97–133. London: Routledge, 1992.

Rawcliffe, Carole. *Medicine and Society in Later Medieval England*. Stroud: Allan Sutton, 1995.

Rawcliffe, Carole. '"Delectable Sightes and Fragrant Smelles": Gardens and Health in Late Medieval and Early Modern England'. *Garden History* 36, no. 1 (2008): 3–21.

Read, Sara. *Menstruation and the Female Body in Early Modern England*. Basingstoke: Palgrave Macmillan, 2013.

Reinarz, Jonathan and Leonard Schwarz, eds. *Medicine and the Workhouse*. Rochester: University of Rochester Press, 2013.

Rey, Roselyne. *The History of Pain*. Translated by L. E. Wallace, J. A. Cadden and S. W. Cadden. Cambridge, MA: Harvard University Press, 1995.

Robertson, Una A. *The Illustrated History of the Housewife, 1650–1950*. Stroud: Sutton Publishing, 1997.

Rohde, Eleanor S. *The Old English Herbals*. New York: Dover, 1971.

Romanell, Patrick. *John Locke and Medicine: A New Key to Locke*. Buffalo, NY: Prometheus, 1984.

Rose, Francis. *The Wild Flower Key. A Guide to Plant Identification in the Field, With and Without Flowers*. London: Warne, 1981.

Rosenberg, C. E. 'Medical Text and Social Context: Explaining William Buchan's *Domestic Medicine*'. In *Explaining Epidemic and Other States in the History of Medicine*, edited by C. E. Rosenberg, 32–56. Cambridge: Cambridge University Press, 1992.

Rublack, Ulinka. 'Fluxes: The Early Modern Body and the Emotions'. *History Workshop Journal* 53, no. 1 (2002): 1–16.

Saintsbury, George. *Receipt Book of Mrs Ann Blencowe, A. D. 1694*. London: Adelphi, 1922.

Sambrook, P. A. and P. C. D. Brears. *The Country House Kitchen, 1650–1900: Skills and Equipment for Food Provisioning*. Stroud: Sutton Publishing in association with the National Trust, 1996.

Sarasohn, Lisa T. '"That Nauseous Venemous Insect": Bedbugs in Early Modern England'. *Eighteenth-Century Studies* 46, no. 4 (2013): 513–30.

Sarti, Raffaella. *Europe at Home: Family and Material Culture, 1500–1800*. New Haven: Yale University Press, 2002.

Sawyer, Ronald C. 'Patients, Healers and Disease in the Southeast Midlands, 1597–1634'. PhD diss., University of Wisconsin, 1986.

Scammell, Lorna. 'Was the North-East Different from Other Areas? The Property of Everyday Consumption in the Late Seventeenth and Early Eighteenth Centuries'. In *Creating and Consuming Culture in North-East England, 1660–1830*, edited by Helen Berry and Jeremy Gregory, 11–23. Aldershot: Ashgate, 2004.

Schäfer, Daniel. *Old Age and Disease in Early Modern Medicine*. Translated by Patrick Baker. London: Pickering and Chatto, 2011.

Schaffer, Simon. 'Piety, Physic and Prodigious Abstinence'. In *Religio Medici: Medicine and Religion in Seventeenth-Century England*, edited by Ole P. Grell and Andrew Cunningham, 171–203. Aldershot: Scolar Press/Ashgate Pub. Co., 1996.

Schmidt, Jeremy. *Melancholy and the Care of the Soul: Religion, Moral Philosophy and Madness in Early Modern England*. Aldershot: Ashgate, 2007.

Schoonover, David E. *Lady Borlase's Receiptes Booke*. Iowa City: University of Iowa Press, 1998.

Shammas, Carole. *The Pre-Industrial Consumer in England and America*. Oxford: Clarendon Press, 1990.

Shapin, Steven. *A Social History of Truth: Civility and Science in Seventeenth Century England*. Chicago: Chicago University Press, 1994.

Shapin, Steven. '"You Are What You Eat": Historical Changes in Ideas About Food and Identity'. *Historical Research* 87, no. 237 (2014): 377–92.

Shapiro, Barbara J. *A Culture of Fact: England 1550–1720*. Ithaca: Cornell University Press, 2000.

Sharp, Sharon A. 'Folk Medicine Practices: Women as Keepers and Carriers of Knowledge'. *Women's Studies International* 9, no. 3 (1986): 243–49.

Shepard, Alexandra and Garthine Walker. 'Gender, Change and Periodisation'. *Gender and History* 20, no. 3 (2008): 453–62.

Sher, Richard B. 'William Buchan's *Domestic Medicine*: Laying Book History Open'. In *The Human Face of the Book Trade: Print Culture and Its Creators*, edited by Peter Isaac and Barry Mackay, 45–64. Winchester: Oak Knoll Press, 1999.

Siena, Kevin P. *Venereal Disease, Hospitals and the Urban Poor: London's 'Foul Wards', 1600–1800*. Rochester: University of Rochester Press, 2004.

Simonton, Deborah. *Women in European Culture and Society: Gender, Skill and Identity from 1700*. Abingdon: Routledge, 2011.

Siraisi, Nancy G. *Medieval and Early Renaissance Medicine: An Introduction to Knowledge and Practice*. Chicago: University of Chicago Press, 1990.

Skuse, Alanna. 'Wombs, Worms and Wolves: Constructing Cancer in Early Modern England'. *Social History of Medicine* 27, no. 4 (2014): 632–48.

Slack, Paul. 'Mirrors of Health and Treasures of Poor Men: The Uses of Vernacular Literature of Tudor England'. In *Health, Medicine and Mortality*, edited by C. Webster, 237–73. Cambridge: Cambridge University Press, 1979.

Slack, Paul. *The Impact of Plague in Tudor and Stuart England*. London: Routledge and Kegan Paul, 1985.

Slack, Paul. 'Hospitals, Workhouses and the Relief of the Poor in Early Modern London'. In *Health Care and Poor Relief in Protestant Europe, 1500–1700*, edited by Ole P. Grell and Andrew Cunningham, 234–51. London: Routledge, 1997.

Smith, Ginnie. 'Prescribing the Rules of Health: Self-Help and Advice in the Late Eighteenth Century'. In *Patients and Practitioners: Lay Perceptions of Medicine in Pre-Industrial Society*, edited by Roy Porter, 249–82. Cambridge: Cambridge University Press, 1985.

Smith, Helen. *'Grossly Material Things': Women and Book Production in Early Modern England*. Oxford: Oxford University Press, 2012.

Smith, Lisa W. 'Reassessing the Role of the Family: Women's Medical Care in Eighteenth-Century England'. *Social History of Medicine* 16, no. 3 (2003): 327–42.

Smith, Lisa W. 'The Relative Duties of a Man: Domestic Medicine in England and France, ca. 1685–1740'. *Journal of Family History* 31, no. 3 (2006): 237–56.

Snodgrass, Mary E. *Encyclopedia of Kitchen History*. New York: Fitzroy Dearborn, 2004.

Woolf, D. R. 'The "Common Voice": History, Folklore and Oral Tradition in Early Modern England'. *Past and Present* 120 (1988): 26–52.

Wrigley, E. A. 'Mortality in Pre-Industrial England: The Example of Colyton, Devon, over Three Centuries'. In *Population and Social Change*, edited by D. V. Glass and R. Revelle, 243–73. London: Edward Arnold, 1972.

Wrigley, E. A. and R. S. Schofield. *The Population History of England 1541–1871: A Reconstruction*. Cambridge: Cambridge University Press, 1981.

Yallop, Helen. *Age and Identity in Eighteenth-Century England*. London: Pickering and Chatto, 2013.

Yeo, I. Burney. *Food in Health and Disease*. London: Cassell, 1896.

Young, Anne M. *Antique Medicine Chests, or Glyster, Blister and Purge*. London: Vernier Press, 1994.

running costs 71
stills 119
Fortescue, Hugh 7, 9, 24–5, 131–2, 142
Foyster, Elizabeth 5
Freke, Elizabeth 1, 75, 115, 155
Freke, John 97–8
Fretwell, James 158
fruits, dried 92
fruits, exotic 92, 107

Galen 2, 27, 81, 104–5
Galenic tradition 146
gardens 45, 83, 88–9, 91, 95
Gascoign's powder 73
Gater, Sarah 34
gathering 79, 87–9
gender roles 2, 28, 169
gentian 63
Gentleman's Magazine 72
Gentlewoman's Companion, The 145
George, Alice 153
Gerard, John 34, 82, 89, 113
gifting 53, 97–8, 170
gillyflowers 65
ginger 85, 92
glysters 121, 139
God 16, 21, 23, 30
Goldstein, David 49
gonorrhoea 5
gout 19, 51, 109, 154
Gowing, Laura 2
Gray, Todd 57
Greatrakes, Valentine 167
Green, Monica 6
Grey, Elizabeth, *A Choice Manuall of Rare Conceits* 34, 37, 39
groundsel 44–5
gruel 109
guaiacum 60
Guibert, Philbert, *The Charitable Physician with the Charitable Apothecary* 75, **76**, 115

Hamilton, Duke and Duchess of 34
hare's brain 138
Harington, Sir John 106
Harley, Lady Brilliana 21–2
Harris, Frances 159
Hartman, George 114

hartshorn 86, 94, 134
hart's tongue (*Asplenium scolopendrium*) 95, 96, **96**, 136
Harvey, Gideon 86
Harvey, William 167
Hatfield, Gabrielle 81
Haycock, David 99
Hayne, John 7, 59–60, 70, 85
health regimens 106, 111
health promotion 11
Hecht, John 70–1
Helmontian concepts 66, 146
Helmontian physicians 27, 99
Henrietta Maria, Queen 35
herbals 34, 82, 88–9
Herbert, Amanda 2, 74, 88
Herbert, Edward 74, 82
Herbert, George 95
herb gatherers 59
herbs 83, 88–9, 95
herb women 75, 88
Hippocrates 27
historical writers 1
Hobby, Elaine 35
Hoby, Lady 153
honey 65, 108, 138
Hooke, Robert 14
Horden, Peregrine 1
Houghton, John 61, 74
household accounts 7, 55, 57–77
  Alice Le Strange 3, 60
  analysis 5–6, 57–8
  Clarke household 57, 58, 61, 62, 67, 68, 68–70, 77, 93–4, 128–30, 131, 133–4, **134**, 177–83
  Clifford household 57, 63, 67, 68, 68–70, 77, 128, 131
  compilers 57
  detail 57
  Eyre household 92
  Fortescue household 57, 64, 67–8, 68–70, 77, 103, 115–16, 119, 128, 131–2, 134–5
  healthcare expenditure 70–2, 76–7, 170
  ingredient purchases 92–4
  Latham household 72
  medical services spending 66–70, 76–7

medicinal plant purchases 87–8
medicinal purchases, early
    seventeenth-century 58–60
medicinal purchases, later
    seventeenth-century 61–7, 177–83
named beneficiaries 127, 128–30,
    129
and the poor 131–3
running costs 70
Strode household 64–6, 68, 68–70,
    77, 128, 131
household archives 31
household, definition 3–4
household healthcare
    changes in 172–5
    definition 4
household management 21–2
household medicine
    boundaries of 147–8
    definition 4
humoral perspective 16, 27, 30, 36, 49,
    104–5, 109, 110, 121, 137, 152,
    161–2, 168
Hungary water 17–18, 63, 98, 120,
    138
hygiene 148
hyssop 44–5

Illick, Joseph 142
illness
    causes of 2
    experience of 14
    information about 11, 13–15
    recording 14
    withholding information about
        24–5
information 11, 13–15
    sharing 50, 50–1, 52, 53–4, 172–3
    withholding 13, 15–16, 24–5
ingredients 79–101
    added costs 85, 86
    analysis 79–80
    animal 79–80
    for children's ailments 136–7, 137
    Clarke household account 93–4,
        177–83
    cost concerns 73–4
    exotic plants 95–7
    food items 108

household items 82–3, 84, 85, 86, 91
    imported 87
    magical 80
    measures 94
    medicinal plants 79, 80, 81, 81–2, 86,
        87–90, 97–9, 101, 136–7, 137, 170
    mineral 80, 86
    native plants 95–7, 96, 99, 101
    preferences 90–4, 91
    preparation 80
    prices 55, 85–6, 101
    quality concerns 74–5
    spices 85, 86
ingredient sources 79–80, 82–3, 84,
    85–7, 90, 101
    cultivated 45
    household items 44–5, 82–3
    imported 87
    London 86–7
    purchased 45, 46–7, 48
    source species 80
    suppliers 82–3
    women and 85
ipecacuanha 98
Isham, Elizabeth 18, 153
ivy 16

James, Michael 147
Jeake, Samuel 14, 23, 73
Jefferies, Joyce 60
Jepp, Samuel 8
Jesuit's (Peruvian) bark 19, 50, 98, 162
Johnson, Thomas 75
Josselin, Ralph 14, 118, 139

King, Gregory 74
King, Steven 5, 75
King's evil 97, 112, 151–2, 160–3
kitchen physic 103–4
kitchen resources 55–6, 113–18, 121–2,
    173
    equipment 56, 121–2
Kitchin-Physician, The 146
knowledge 2–3, 11
    classical 81
    of medicinal plants 81–2, 88–9
    sharing 13–28, 19, 172–3
    tacit 32
Kuriyama, Shigehisa 106

Ladies Dispensatory, The 82
Ladies Library, The 133
Lancashire 5
lapis calaminaris 93
Laroche, Rebecca 34
Latham, Richard 72
Lawson, William 120
lead 86
lemons 61, 64, 92, 107
Leong, Elaine 1, 30, 35, 48, 90–1, 115, 155
Lessius, Leonard 111
Le Strange, Alice 3, 60
letters 11, 27–8, 127
    advantages 14
    interpretation 14–15
    knowledge sharing 13–28
    to the medical practitioner 18–20
    on nursing care 20–2
    on preventative care 15–16, 26–7
    on recovery 22–3
    self-help treatment advice 16–18
    of support 25–6
    on treatments 23–4
    withholding information 24–5
life expectancy 152
lignum vitae 60
Lindemann, Mary 139
liquorice 92
liverwort 136
Locke, John 8, 19, 27, 50, 58, 67, 77, 94, 140–1, 144–5, 145, 153, 163–6
London 4, 8, 19, 24–5, 86–7, 132, 142, 152, 163
London Dispensatory, (Culpeper) 37
London Pharmacopoeia 3
Lowe, Roger 14
Lower, Richard 35

mace 85, 92
Mace, Thomas 99–101
magical ingredients 80
mallow 95, 96
Markham, Gervase, *The English House-Wife* 34, 88–9, 112
Martin, Lynn 65
Martyn, William 8
Masham, Lady Damaris 159

May, George 99
May butter 64
Maynwaringe, Everard 113, 145–6, 147
mazzards 64
meat 109
Medical Admonitions Addressed to Families (Parkinson) 148
medical advice books 33–5
medical authority 166–8
    boundaries of 121
    and therapeutic determination 171–2
medical debts 72
medical education 48–9
medical practitioners
    access to 19–20
    and chronic complaints 163–6
    contacts with 148–9, 170–1, 174
    healthcare for children 139–42, **141**
    hostility towards women 145
    and letters 18–20, 28
    medical authority 166–8, 171–2
    and pain 153–4
    relationship with patron 26
    religious beliefs 44
    scepticism towards 147, 149
    spending patterns 68–70
medical services
    access 4–5, 19–20
    continuum of 5
    payment 58
    spending on 3, 66–70
medicinal preparations *116*, 116–17, *117*
medicine chests 75
medicine cupboards 1
medicines 1, 174, 175
    commercial 3, 173
    debate about 145–7
    definition 4
    efficacy 6
    evaluating 23–4
    food as 107–8
    preparation processes 120–1, 121
    professional structure 2–3
melancholy 125, 154–7, **156**
Meldrum, Tim 158
men
    involvement in healthcare 2, 19
    and kitchen physic 104

and medical practitioner advice
18–19
and nursing care 158
plant knowledge 82
Merret, Christopher 75, 120, 145
methodology 5–6
micro-history 5–6
midwives 66
Mildmay, Lady Grace 115
mineral waters 66
mint 95, 96–7
miscarriage 93, 158, 165
mithridate 63
Moore, Philip, *The Hope of Health* 98
More, Henry 16, 28
Mortimer, Ian 3, 4–5, 147
*Most Excellent and Approved
Medicines and Remedies* (Read)
30, 37, 40, 54, 74, 162
Muffet, Thomas 107, 109–10
mustard seeds 61

Nagy, Doreen 2, 145
Natura Exenterata (Talbot) 35, 89, 112,
136
Nature, importance of 162
networks 11
Newcastle 152
Newton, Hannah 27, 135, 139, 142
Norwich 152
nursing care 20–2, 125, 157–9
nutmeg 85, 92, 95, 108

Oldisworth, William 34
opium 154
oranges 59, 61, 64, 92, 107
overeating 111

pain 125, 153–4, 168
paper 115–16, 138
Paracelsus 2
Parkinson, John 82, 89
*Medical Admonitions Addressed to
Families* 148
Theatrum Botanicum 82
Park, Katharine 87
Partridge, John, *The Treasurie of
Commodious Conceits* 34, 95, 112
Pechey, John 18, 96, 97

Pelling, Margaret 154, 157
Penhallow, Elizabeth 51
Pennell, Sarah 48, 118–19
pennyroyal 44–5
Pepys, Samuel 14
Peruvian bark 19, 50, 98, 162
physicians 3, 66, 68–9, 82, 106–7, 113,
125
Pirohakul, Teerapa 72
plantain 95, 96
plants, medicinal 101, 170
for children's ailments 136–7, *137*
costs 86
exotic 79, 90, 97–9
gathering 79, 87–9
knowledge 81–2, 88–9
Mediterranean 90
native 79, 95–7, **96**, 99, 101
preferences *91*
purchases 87–8
recognizing 89–90
source species 80, **81**
plasters 83, 93, 173
Plat, Sir Hugh 118
poison antidotes 63
Pollard, Tanya 80
Pollock, Linda A. 139
poor, the 125, 130–3, 148
poor relief 130–1
poppy 95
poppy water 65–6
pork 110
port books 3
Porter, Dorothy 4
Porter, Roy 4, 13
Port of London 86–7
posset ale 16
posset cup **17**
posset pots 115
possets 16, 31–2, 134
poverty, causes of 5
prayer 21, 23, 27
pregnancy 45, 94, 127, 166
preparation processes 120–1, *121*
preservation methods 117–18
distillation 118, 118–21
preserving rooms 120
Preston, Sir Thomas 8
preventative care 15–16, 26–7, *27*

prices 59–60, 65, 85, 101, 177–87
Primrose, James 146
probate records 3
Protestant individualism 4
providence 14, 23
purges 14, 22, 93–4, 106, 134, 135,
    137, 139, 141–2, 145–6

Queens Closet Opened, The 35, 37, 39,
    40, 112, 130, 135, 138
quicksilver 92
quinces 107
Quincy, John 17, 95–6, 96, 96–7, 107, 120

Ranelagh, Katherine Jones, Lady 35
Ratcliffe, Edward, 6th Earl of Sussex 60
Read, Alexander, *Most Excellent and
    Approved Medicines and Remedies*
    30, 37, 40, 54, 74, 162
Recipes and Expenditure Database 7
recipes and recipe collections 6, 11,
    29–54, 170, 172–3
  ailment categories 35–7, 36
  annotations 2, 37, 39, 40, 48, 53
  'Aqua mirabilis' 40
  attribution 31–2
  Bannister's powder 155–7
  black soap 83
  children's complaints 39, 134–7, 137,
    148
  choice 11
  contributors 11
  'cordial for the rickets' 144
  'cordiall water' 119–20
  dietary advice 49, 108–11
  distilled waters 18
  'Dyet drink for a Scorbutick Dropsy
    and Gout' 51, 52, 53
  efficacy phrases 48
  format 29–30, 49
  gifting 53
  'Green oyntment for Aches Bruises' 43
  humoral perspective 30, 49
  Hungary water 18
  ingredients 11, 30, 40, 42, 43
  ingredient sources 44–5, 46–7, 48
  innovation 49
  inscription 49–50
  magical 80

manuscript collections 30–3, 33
medicinal preparations 116, 116–17,
    117
melancholy 154–7, 156
monetary value 50
oral tradition 32, 33
pain relief 153
polypharmaceutical 43, 44
possets 32
printed sources 31, 33–5, 37, 38, 40
purges 141–2
range of complaints 29
repeated recipes 41–4, 42
salve for an old ulcer 93
selection 29, 35, 37, 39–41, 170–1
sharing 11, 30, 31, 32–3, 40–1, 50,
    50–1, 52, 53–4, 54
simples 43
sources 7, 30–5, 33, 37, 38, 53–4
sweet water 120
syrup of roses 133–4
titles 37
use 48–9
value of 11, 49–50
'A water for after throws' 44–5
'For a woman that cannot be
    delivered' 94
worm treatments 134–5
recipients 125, 127, 128–30, 129, 148,
    174
recovery 22–3
regional variation 7–8
Reinarz, Jonathan 131
religious beliefs 44
remedies, prepared 17–18
resources 55–6, 173
retailing 99
rhubarb 61, 85, 94, 127, 134, 135,
    138–9
rickets 112, 135, 136, 137, 143–5, 174
Robertson, Una 117
Rogers, Timothy 130
rosemary 18, 95
roses 59, 60, 85–6, 92
Rugg, Thomas 14
Russell, Lady Rachel 27

safety 39, 165
saffron 92

sage 43, 95
sal prunella 63
saltpetre 86
sand 115
sarsaparilla 142
Sawyer, Ronald 5
Schwarz, Leonard 131
science and technology, development of
    early modern 2
scurvygrass 59
self-dosing 5
self-help 1, 169, 171–2, 174–5
    boundaries of 147–8
    chronic complaints 151–2, 153–7,
        156, 160–3, 168
    motivation 4–5
    treatment letters 16–18
self-sufficiency 1, 173
senna 63, 134
servants 21–2, 70–1, 126, 128–30,
    157
Shirley, John 2, 35
Short, George 26
simples 43, 55, 63, 79, 82, 99, 101
smallpox 15–16, 142–3
Smith, Helen 49
Smith, Lisa 2, 142
Smith, Richard 154
snakeroot 162
soap 82–3, 86
sorrow, physical effects 15
sources 1, 3, 5–6, 7–8, 9, 11, 29
    recipes 30–5, 33
spas 66
spa water 19
spells 49, 80
Spencer, Margaret 58
spending 66–76, 169–70, 170
    analysis 57–8
    concerns about 73–6
    healthcare 70–2, 76–7
    life cycle changes 71–2
    medical services 3
    on medical services 66–70
    medicinal purchases, early
        seventeenth-century 58–60
    medicinal purchases, later
        seventeenth-century 61–7, 177–83
    named beneficiaries 128

national averages 74
    patterns 55, 68–70, 76–7
    readymade preparations 59
    unexpected costs 73
spices 61, 85, 86, 92, 95, 101, 107–8
spirit of tartar 40
Spirits of Scurvygrass advertisement 99,
    100
Spreat, John 23, 94, 128
Still, Frederic 143
still houses 118, 119
stills 118–19
Stolberg, Michael 167
storage vessels 115
Strachey, Jane 19
strawberries 107
Strode, Anne 9, 86–7
    charitable interests 64–5
    healthcare budget 71
    household accounts 64–6, 68, 68–70,
        77, 128
    household running costs 71
    medical services spending 68, 68–70
    medicinal plant purchases 88
    named beneficiaries 128, 129
    and the poor 131
    stills 119
Strode, Sir John 9
strong water 86
sugar 59, 65, 92, 104, 108
Summers, Anne 20
surgeons 3, 66, 68–9
surgical procedure, dangers of 160–1
sweet water 120
Swinburne, Layinka 144
Sydenham, Thomas 154
syphilis 5
syrup of roses 61, 62, 86, 133–4, 136
syrups 18, 92, 108

Taavitsainen, Irma 49
tacit knowledge 32
Tague, Ingrid 173
Talbot, Alethea, Natura Exenterata 35,
    89, 112, 136
Taunton 8
taxes 86
Tebeaux, Elizabeth 32
teething 138

teeth, loose 19
terminology 3–5
Theophano, Janet 53
Theophrastus 81
therapeutic approaches 125, 126
    children 127, 133–7, *137*
    chronic complaints 152, 159–66,
        168, 171
therapeutic determination 126, 152,
        168
    definition 5
    and medical authority 171–2
Thick, Malcolm 89
Thornton, Alice 27, 144
Thynne, Joan 15
Thynne, John 15
Thynne, Maria 159
Tigner, Amy 98
toothache 153
treacle 63, 92, 136
*Treasurie of Commodious Conceits,
    The* (Partridge) 34, 95, 112
treatments, evaluation 23–4
Trenchard, John 8
Tryon, Thomas 65, 111
tumeric 92
Tunbridge Wells 66
Turner, William 34, 82
turpentine 86

Ugbrooke House, Chudleigh 41
universal medicines 99–101, 146
urine 109

Van Helmont, Francis Mercury 2, 28
Venice treacle 136
Venner, Gustavus (junior) 8
Venner, Gustavus (senior) 8
Venner, Ursula 8, 13, 15, 16–18, 19–23,
        138, 158
verdigris 86
Verney family 14–15
Verney, Dame Margaret 120

Verney, Sir Ralph 21, 105
Vickers powders 132
Vickery, Amanda 173
vipers 73
Virginian snakeroot 99
vomits 14

Walker, Elizabeth 120
Wallis, Patrick 1, 72, 73–4
Wear, Andrew 2, 115
Weisser, Olivia 153
Wentworth, Elizabeth 61
wet nurses 66, 67–8
Whistler, Daniel 143
Whyman, Susan 14–15
Willis, Thomas 35
wine 64
Wolley, Hannah 35, 112
women
    aging 152–3
    alliances 2
    boundaries 54
    brandy drinking 65
    desire for privacy 5
    estate management 21
    hostility towards 145
    housewifely duties 158–9
    ingredient sources and 85
    involvement in healthcare 2
    and kitchen physic 104
    medical books 34–5
    and nursing care 157–9
    plant knowledge 82
    role of 28, 125, 130, 133
Woodall, John 75
Woodforde, Mary 26
wormseed 63, 134
worm treatments 134–5, 137
wormwood 43, 94
worry, avoidance of 15

yellow jaundice 109, 111
Yonge, Sir Walter 8